For the Love of Community Engagement

For the Love of Community Engagement

Insights from a personal expedition to inspire better public participation

Becky Hirst

With a Foreword by Dr Wendy Sarkissian LFPIA

Published by Tablo

Published in 2021 by Tablo Publishing.

Publisher and wholesale enquiries: orders@tablo.io

20 21 22 23 LSC 10 9 8 7 6 5 4 3 2 1

For Mellita, who would have encouraged me to use my stories to inspire others

I acknowledge the traditional owners of the Country on which I sit as I write these stories, the Kaurna people.

I recognise their continuing connection to land, waters, and culture.

I pay my respects to all Indigenous Elders past, present and future.

I give my deepest gratitude for their ongoing lessons on the concept of deep listening.

Always was,
Always will be,
Aboriginal Land.

Table of Contents

Foreword

By Dr Wendy Sarkissian LFPIA

I must confess that when I heard about Becky Hirst, several years ago, I was absolutely terrified. It might sound funny for a person who's got a community engagement award named after her, but I lacked the courage to meet this formidable woman. I was arriving at the unpleasant realisation that I was becoming an old fuddy-duddy.

We first met in 2013, when we were both speakers at a conference in Adelaide. Becky seemed so 'modern' as she enthusiastically presented on what communities can achieve using 21st century technology. I did not want to embrace the online sphere. It did not interest me. And yet, I was running a consulting firm and I knew I had to get with the program. I had to understand what was going on.

Now I know that Becky has an honours degree in contemporary dance. Had I known that all those years ago, I'm not sure how I would have responded. Perhaps even more frightened. This woman knew things I did not know, and I was not sure that I could wrap my mind around them. She represented a vanguard. She was like a Valkyrie, leading people into new territory. And I was a reluctant conscript.

How foolish I was! I think I had been frightened away by the 'corporate' women in the slim black skirts and black high-heeled shoes, who came from associate degrees in communications and marketing and who, I felt, were trashing my profession. I could not believe what was going on. In the large Australian planning and engineering firms, a coterie of these young, bright, apparently competent, young women was ruining community engagement as I knew it. They were 'lost leaders', alright! Becky might be slender in appearance, and might occasionally slip into some heels, but she definitely is *not* one of those women.

I remarked at an Engage 2 Act inaugural event in Melbourne that I was seeking people in sensible shoes to engage with communities. That was my metaphor for real people getting 'down and dirty', being with actual people in their actual places of work and home and attachment. And trying to work out in the muddiness of human life what was actually going on. And what an 'engagement' intervention might look like.

Now I know this brilliant engagement practitioner who frightened me years ago. And, honestly, she is a marvel. And, unlike many people who write Forewords to books, I have actually read this book. I have read every word and every semicolon. I have even negotiated some of those semicolons with the author!

So, what do we have here?

Well, first of all, we have the first book by a skilled community engagement practitioner who is willing to tell us how it is. Not just the pretty side of it but the dark and ugly swamp of despair that sometimes threatens to drown us in this practice.

Becky Hirst is an authentic reflective practitioner: she's consciously reflecting on her actions. She's asking questions about how things could be improved. And, to make matters more challenging, she's running a business and she's successful at it!

When I agreed to help with this book, I had no idea that I had signed up for a voyage of discovery. I thought I was an expert in such matters. Well, I had a lot to learn. This book is jam-packed with vignettes about what really happens in community engagement in Australia and elsewhere. Fortunately, the names have been changed to protect the guilty but there are many despicable people in this book who clearly have no idea what engagement is about.

Further, Becky has put love on the table. Why shouldn't we love our work? Why does love need to be relegated to romance or spiritual enterprises? Can't we love our work, love the people we work with, even love our clients, however difficult they may be at times?

I say that Becky's a reflective practitioner. But what exactly is a reflective practitioner, anyway?

If we turn to Paolo Freire, the liberation theologist, we find that he argues that consciousness alone is not enough. We must have what he calls *meaningful praxis*. And that means that action and reflection must happen together to result in the transformation of the world. We must be engaged so that our whole self is making sense of what is going on.

Maybe it takes an honours degree in contemporary dance to be *embodied* enough to do this work! Because it's about being very, *very* present and constantly questioning what's going on.

When I first began work as an engagement practitioner, I remember thinking that I was like an anthropologist. I didn't really know anything about this alien culture I was entering, this new context, this new engagement project. So I was always asking people, 'What is going on here? What are your perceptions? What are your understandings of life here in this place?'

People were often puzzled that I didn't seem to have any expertise. I think I had some and I think engagement practitioners do have a toolkit of methods and approaches we can bring to a situation. But often we just need to be present. Frequently, we must ask: 'Why is it so bad and how can we make it better?'

Sadly, but redemptively, this book is partly about why things are so bad in community engagement in Australia and how we could make them better. And it's not just about bringing the love to the table, either. Sometimes you need to bring a really sharp, analytical consciousness to figuring out what on Earth is happening here. Like: How did this whole community, this whole town, this whole suburb lose faith in its future?

When people start talking to me about words like *betrayal* and *stigma*, I know that we've slipped over the edge somehow. The situation *is* serious! Something urgent needs to be done.

In the stories in her book, Becky is not only analysing situations, using reflection-in-action; she's also suggesting how things might be improved (reflection-on-action).

Becky is constantly asking: 'How can things be improved here?'

In this respect, she's contributing to our body of professional knowledge by shining the clear light of day on hard truths we can't escape. There are lots of relationships of oppression and domination in the practice of community engagement. So, why don't we just admit what's happening?

We don't need to leave this analytical work to the academic sociologists. I'll give you an example. On the consulting job I thought was probably my finest work, I made promises to residents of a community in south-western Sydney that their voices would be heard in the comprehensive redevelopment of their whole suburb. This was to be a PPP, a public-private partnership: the first of its kind in New South Wales involving the comprehensive redevelopment of a public housing estate. I was the *agent*. And there was a *principal* who finally arrived: a Melbourne building firm that had done similar work that was quite successful.

I ended up tangled in the *Principal-Agent Dilemma* that sociologists talk about. And the neighbourhood ended up being destroyed. Although millions of dollars were spent on probity investigations in selecting the private partner, nobody in government apparently asked what would happen if everything fell apart.

And in 2008, everything fell apart. In a distant Sydney suburb, the flow-on effects of the activities of Goldman Sachs in New York and the Global Financial Crisis destroyed the community renewal project and the builder went bankrupt. Apparently lacking a Plan B, all the New South Wales government could do was to erect barbed wire fencing around the partly constructed houses. And try to figure out what to do next.

The residents were devastated. Two of my beloved friends, both homeowners, who subsequently died, told me the following: 'Wendy, we love you. We think you gave us everything and you tried really hard. We know that. And we learned heaps from you. And you need to know that your work resulted in the deaths of two elderly friends of ours. They died of broken hearts. They died feeling betrayed and hopeless that everything you had promised was destroyed.'

Those two women knew nothing about the GFC. But they knew what betrayal looked like and they lost hope. And they died. And it is well-documented that grieving for a lost home can result in death. We are not exaggerating here. This is the dark side of the *Principal-Agent Dilemma.*

Over the years, I've read insightful articles by academics about 'participating the public' and I thought they were quite smart. But the luxury of being an academic is that you can sit back and reflect on these things and you don't have to worry about where your next consulting job is coming from. Not so with Becky Hirst.

Becky's book is a scream from the depths of the dark swamp of engagement. It's an authentic voice reminding us that all is not well in our profession in Australia. She's celebrating that amazing, wonderful, and transformative processes can occur with community engagement. Individuals and communities can be transformed. The guiding hand of a skilled, reflective practitioner can definitely conjure up community transformation.

However, we must look directly into the eye of one evil aspect of our work. And that is the issue of *influence*. Repeatedly in this book, Becky points out how gatekeepers, the people with clout (often the senior men) squelch innovation and destroy opportunities for community influence over decision-making. If I had a dollar for every one of those gormless people I've encountered in my working life, I can't say what I do with it! But it would be a lot of money!

But let's be clear: this is a book about *love*. It's a book about passion, enthusiasm, and a heartfelt commitment to community empowerment and community building. No question about that!

And it's also a wail of despair and a warning to all of us. Do *not* enter this field if you are gutless. Don't even think about becoming a community engagement practitioner just for the money. If you think it's about communications and marketing, think again.

And if you are willing to be courageous, wear your heart on your sleeve, be blamed for your post-critical naïveté, and vilified for your enthusiasm, *goodonyer*!

Because that's where the love will be. And you will find people loving you back. You will hear people telling you that they trusted you because when they were weeping after that terrible public meeting in that roasting hall a few days before Christmas, you sat beside them and held their hand. You will not even remember doing that because it was just a natural, *loving* thing to do.

You will find your soft heart opening and suffused with the love of community engagement. And you'll be lining up behind the indefatigable Becky Hirst.

And I'll be there to cheer you on. (One way or another.)

But don't even come near it unless you are willing to be courageous.

All love needs courage. There is no love without courage. There is no authentic community engagement without love.

And there is no leadership in our profession without heart.

You will find heart in this book. Buckets of it!

Introduction

Up to this moment, my career has been a self-directed adventure. I've made some good choices and had some great luck. I've also been blessed to work with amazing people, in amazing communities, and in amazing locations. I have a passion for thriving communities. Vibrant conversations, connecting people, working collaboratively and building community pride: these are my reasons for being. After much soul-searching in recent years, I now accept that I'm meant to do this work in my personal and professional life. My work extends far beyond merely being a trade or a business that I've grown. I am passionate about community. I engage with people, groups and communities in decision-making because my heart is thoroughly committed to the belief that the world lacks engagement and needs more of it. I'm incredibly fortunate to create a life dedicated to this work. I've even found a way for my passions to pay the mortgage.

In 2009, I established myself as a consultant to local and state government clients in Australia, helping them involve people, groups and communities in decision making. In Australia, we call this community engagement, but elsewhere this process is labelled as public participation, community participation, civic participation or simply just consultation. Since then, I've not been shy in coming forward about community engagement in a thought-leadership capacity within our sector. Many times, I have heard about my strong reputation for outstanding, high-quality, and authentic community engagement. My clients tell me that I'm a pragmatic, values-driven community engagement practitioner. The people I work with in community settings describe me as authentic, genuine, and 'the real deal'. People say I'm empathic, high on energy, driven and deeply passionate about what I do. My friends tell me I'm a natural community builder, even down to the social gatherings I host. Wendy tells me I'm full of *chutzpah*, oozing confidence and audacity that I use to drive positive change where it's needed.

However, I regularly find myself questioning how or why I came to be these things. What makes my practice stand out as being different? Or special? Did I attend the *University of How to Be a Really Awesome Community Engagement Person*? Do I eat cereal that's high in Authenticity Vitamins for breakfast? Of course, I didn't, and I don't. I'm not certain that anyone can learn the traits or principles that characterise my practice in one training course, even a university course, or on a single project. It's been a rich combination of experiences.

Unknown to me at the time, I embarked on a journey that taught several valuable lessons that shaped me to be the proud community engagement practitioner I am today. I took those lessons on board one by one, popping them in my little skills and expertise backpack so I could pull them out, nurture or reflect on them for future projects. As a highly reflective practitioner, I see writing this book as an opportunity to refine further my principles of high-quality community engagement, based on my skills, knowledge, experience, and stories from the last 22 years. And, of course, to share them with my readers.

I hope that by sharing some of my experiences, lessons, and insights, we can begin a conversation about how to reimagine community engagement.

I hope that students studying community engagement will be encouraged by the contents of this book to think big, understanding that there's way more to this work than learning the kind of consultation processes currently taught in universities. I hope that people already working in community engagement (such as consultants, public servants, in the private sector, or somewhere else) will use my book to reflect on their practice. And that this book will encourage them to think outside their safe and familiar comfort zones. I hope that people already deeply immersed in communities will discover the potential for making an even bigger difference by using their connections with community to inform decision-making at the highest level. I hope that current or aspiring politicians will read my book and reconsider their roles as leaders within our communities. That they will appreciate the importance of genuine listening, authenticity, and empathy, far beyond the once-an-election-cycle presence in communities that many currently have.

As a culture, we have a habit of thinking about community engagement as being touchy-feely, nice-to-have and part of a *soft* skill set. This is completely wrong. To have a thriving society, we need people and communities who are actively involved in civic life. How government and corporations involve people in problem solving and decision making about things that affect or matter to them is *very* serious business. And it requires *hard* skills.

There is no time to waste. I want this book to start conversations with colleagues in the lunchroom; with managers during performance reviews; with politicians when they're door-knocking asking for votes; with children at the dinner table; with lecturers at university; with friends over coffee. With everyone!

To encourage this critical change, at the end of each chapter I pose some *Conversation Starters* to be used as prompts for discussion. The questions are based on the five Ws - who, what, why, when, and where - to provide a range of opportunities for contemplation about people, purpose, places, and the timing of community engagement. They will challenge the bureaucrat to reconnect with their inner citizen and challenge the citizen or local person to consider their connection to the powers that be. These *Conversation Starters* are a combination of different calls to action for the reader to both reflect *and* act.

I dedicate this book to my friend and fellow engagement geek, the late Mellita Froiland, née Kimber, whom I first met and worked with in the Community Engagement Team at the Children, Youth & Women's Health Service in Adelaide back in 2008. In September 2020, she was taken from us, too soon, far too quickly, and way too young. In her final weeks, Mellita and I chatted via SMS about our shared eagerness to make the most out of the short time we have on this Earth. We both admitted that we never really stop unless it's to reflect on how we'd learn from what we just did to make our next venture even better.

Mellita was also described as 'the real deal' by the people she worked with. When her brother made the tragic announcement that she had died, he suggested that we all carry forward Mellita's zest, energy, and passion for a good life by continually asking ourselves, 'What would Mellita do?'

I am certain that Mellita would encourage me to tell my story in this way, to inspire others to be the change we want to see in the world: more high-quality and totally awesome community engagement.

For the love of community engagement.

1. Understand community engagement within the context of society

Change will not come if we wait for some other person or some other time.
We are the ones that we've been waiting for.
We are the change that we seek.

— Barack Obama[1]

It was 1997. I perched on the edge of my single bed in my tiny university bedroom in the north of England. I was curiously opening a package sent by the Labour Party as part of their election campaign for the upcoming national election. The package contained a VHS video tape. How cool to send such a thing to students across the country, I thought to myself! I quickly popped it into my on-trend television with built-in VHS, and music began to pour loudly from the little television. *Things can only get better* by UK nineties pop band D:Ream was the signature campaign tune.[2] I have no idea what else this short film contained, but the memory of this song and its associated political messaging has stayed with me since my 19-year-old-self opened that package.

At the time, I would not have understood why things needed to get better. I was deep in student life, studying for a Bachelor of Arts with Honours in Contemporary Dance, I had little understanding of politics beyond the antics of the Pilates studio where I spent many hours, strengthening my core to prepare to become a professional dancer.

I have few childhood memories of significant happenings at a societal level. Maybe some snippets of miners' riots on the evening news, IRA bombings, the Falklands War, and something to do with Prime Minister Margaret Thatcher having stopped our free milk in schools.

When I think of my high school years, whilst I loved and gained so much from my time at a great girls grammar school in Gloucester, I remember being taught very little about anything current at a societal level. The focus was largely on textbook academia. Even my careers advice was limited, with me knowing exactly how to fudge the little tests they gave us so that the results would tell me that I should be a dance teacher. I feel sad that even a good education for a young girl in as late as the 1990s did not include someone helping me explore different career options – for someone to note my interest in geography, or business studies, or communications – and to encourage me to look at studying topics that I now know I love. I was pigeonholed as a dancer and so dance I would.

And I'm still pleased I was able to study a topic at University that I loved. But oh, how I would have also loved to study international politics or business studies! But it wasn't even on my radar. My older sister, Helene, who had been through the same school nine years ahead of me, had been told that *'girls weren't good at physics'* and was encouraged to consider career choices other than engineering, which she was considering at the time.

Later, I realised that I could not attend University for free. Because of changes in government policy, I needed student loans and my parents' support. Not so for Helene, whose education was fully funded only nine years earlier. Helene graduated with a Double Honours Degree in Mechanical Engineering and Economics by the way, showing that determination really does run deep in us Hirst girls!

Coincidentally with my realisations about the impacts of society on my various life choices, one of my university lecturers introduced me to the concept of community. Dr Chris Lomas was Head of Dance at Bretton Hall College. I remember a rainy afternoon lecture with her about definitions of community. This was not a typical university context. In an Arts degree with a dominant practical focus, we rarely sat in lecture theatres. I remember the pain as I sat on the dance studio floor, my back leaning against the floor-to-ceiling mirror, probably having finished a class in technique, choreography, or something equally exhausting.

Dr Lomas shared an article that examined the concept of 'community' as communities of locality, communities of interest and communities of identities. That single article was a revelation, and it sparked my lifetime interest in community.

Ever since I had a quick play of the game of *Sim City* during my teenage years, I was fascinated by how people live, do business and play in a community of place. Within the game, I loved the concept of starting the building of a city around an industry. So, for example, I'd say, 'let's build a wind farm'. I'd pop a wind farm onto the empty screen, with nothing around it. But then, of course, people would be needed to work at the wind farm, and they'd need to live somewhere, so I'd build some housing. And then I'd need to build ways for people to get from their homes to that wind farm – say, roads or bike paths. And then the people who live in the houses would need to buy food from somewhere. So in would go a supermarket, and then a farm to supply to the supermarket. And I'd need more people to work in the supermarkets.

And, of course, things that couldn't be grown on the farm needed to be brought in from elsewhere, so I'd need to build a freight rail line or an airport, plus warehouses. I'd need train drivers and pilots and warehouse staff. And then, I'd need banks, post offices, pharmacies, and more. And the people in the houses would spend their weekends hiking through the nearby country park or swimming at the local swim centre. Their children would need schools, and playgrounds, dance studios, and sports fields. I'd need teachers, coaches, and people to maintain all the places. Before I knew it, I'd built a little community of place, with all the different people operating within it, all playing integral roles.

I absolutely loved playing this game, perhaps to the point that I should have been encouraged into a career of urban planning. But actually, on reflection, it was the interaction of the people within the community and different communities of interest within it that fascinated me. And even more, I was fascinated by how that community had formed with an initial purpose, and how that purpose was not necessarily of direct interest to the people within that community. That was because other industries had now grown to be their employers. Today, with my clients, I will often describe 'community' as people who live, work and play in an area, based on this exact concept.

There is no community on Earth that I've worked in that illustrates a game of *Sim City* in real life more than when I've worked in the outback town of Roxby Downs in South Australia. I undertook work with the Council and the Community Board during 2013 and I remember looking out of the tiny plane window as we began our descent to the endless flat red desert land. And then to see the tiny town appearing in the distance – just a dot on the horizon. And to recognise its entire reason for being: the Olympic Dam (a copper, uranium, gold and silver mine), next to the town.

This concept of community made me think of a petri dish in a science lab – a contained, defined area where all kinds of cells, cultures, patterns, and growth can be witnessed. In Roxby Down's case, there were unique aspects to life in this town. For example, having a really high birth rate because of the demographic of workers moving to the town to work in the mine. And then being a wealthy community because of readily available, highly paid work. The town had little poverty and most of the town's residents were shift workers. I've loved working there a couple of times now and always enjoy a morning run around the entire circumference of the town – town to the left me, desert on the right.

Even when a community isn't located in the outback, with such a defined border defining exactly where that community ends, every community has these sorts of layers and boundaries, and a reason for being. Whether the community is a high-rise residential tower, a suburban street, a tribe in the deepest, darkest jungle, or a city of 10 million people, in my mind, each of these communities is a petri dish. And that fascinates me.

To illustrate my deep-rooted interest in this concept, one of my favourite films is The Truman Show, where Jim Carrey's entire life is (totally unknown to him) being telecast live around the Earth 24 hours a day, within a totally purpose-built, almost petri-dish-like community. And a song I often sing to my daughters to ease them into sleep is Little Boxes, by Malvina Reynolds. My favourite lines are about the people in the houses who all go to the university and all come out the same! Reynolds wrote this song as a political statement about the uniformity and sameness, of houses along suburban streets with identical floor plans. Perhaps via this bedtime singing I'm subconsciously training my daughters to be community planners!

Back to 1999 and my final year at University. I expanded my interest in dance and the arts in community settings across West Yorkshire. My final assessment reflected my newfound passion: a group of seven high-school non-dancing boys choreographed and performed my final assessment! The image below shows them rehearsing for the piece called *The Road We Travel,* a dance based on patterns and space using their individual journeys to school as a movement stimulus to create patterns of varying dynamic, levels and direction. Apparently, this was yet another indication of my yearning for a career in community planning!

Image 1 - Boys at Crofton High School rehearsing for The Road We Travel, my final assessment at University. Photo by author, 1999.

A couple of years later, I graduated with honours and a new passion: discovering opportunities for making things better. At the tender age of 21, I retired from dance to embrace my love of community.

The beginning of my career coincided with an era immediately following decades of Thatcherism, with a focus on austerity and cuts more than what people needed. Prime Minister Tony Blair's more socially inclusive and progressive ideology was spreading across the nation, reflected in significant investment into public services and a flurry of job openings focusing on community. I applied for and won a National Lottery-funded post in a local, highly deprived and disadvantaged community. My professional life in community engagement then began.

Only now, looking back on my opportunities during those early Blair years of New Labour can I begin to see the impacts of this significant political shift as a catalyst for my journey of passion for conversation, connection, collaboration, and community. My reflection has extended to my childhood years and their effects on my emerging community consciousness. I know that childhood has dramatic and longstanding influences on the values we hold as adults. That gets me thinking about COVID-19 and its effects on the career decisions of children and young people currently living through the pandemic. When I consider the displays of leadership (or lack of leadership) internationally during the pandemic, I wonder about the sorts of leaders these young people might become. Only now, decades after receiving that VHS tape, I realise the significance of the political and societal context in which we operate as community engagement practitioners.

In recent times, I've heard community engagement leader Kylie Cochrane describe a Social Triangle™ theory[3] – a triangle of society, where the three corners represent politics, religion, and community. She discusses the politics and religion corners, reflecting on the recent demise of trust in these two elements of society. Later she emphasises the strong role that community plays in modern society. Kylie argues that, as engagement in religion or politics diminishes as societal connectors, there will be greater emphasis on being a part of our local community – our children's schools, local sporting clubs, service clubs, environmental groups, and more.

I agree with Kylie. In a few decades, I believe that we will recognise the deep significance of low levels of trust in government, business, media, and even not-for-profit organisations. And we will come to understand the impacts on community engagement. We will also acknowledge the effects of the widespread ability of people everywhere to share their opinions through a massive range of online tools. It is a truism that our political leaders, both locally and globally, continue to miss the mark. But there is a huge opportunity nested in this massive failure of leadership. Now, more than ever, we must focus on community-led involvement and activism. We must strive to put people back at the centre of our communities.

In 2013, I caught a glimmer of the potential of a political leader understanding the importance of community engagement when I was appointed to the Premier of South Australia's newly formed Community Engagement Board. How refreshing – a leader of a political party seeking advice on genuine community engagement from specialists! The image overleaf shows me, with His Excellency the Honourable Hieu Van Le AC and Kate Simpson at one of our regular meetings. Sadly, in 2014 the same Premier announced that as part of government reform to improve efficiency, every government board and committee would be abolished unless it could demonstrate that it had an essential purpose that could not be fulfilled in an alternative way. The Community Engagement Board was no more, and instead the Government turned to its own internal resources to engage directly with communities.

Image 2 - Myself, with leaders His Excellency the Honourable Hieu Van Le AC and Kate Simpson at one of our regular Community Engagement Board meetings.
Photo by author, 2013.

For decision-makers (politicians, public servants, corporations, or others) to engage with communities in any positive way, they need to learn new skills. They must abandon stale, top-down approaches of simply broadcasting their messages. They need to embrace two-way dialogue with the people they serve. This is an emergency. We desperately need leaders who listen, empathise, and make considered decisions, based on the contributions of communities of interest and those affected by their actions.

I have an active interest in gender equity, particularly in the political and community leadership space. I strongly believe that feminine principles of leadership are a resource that must be expressed in the 21st century. For hundreds of years, men have taken the lead in the establishment of governance in communities – locally, nationally, and globally. I often wonder what our governments would look like had middle-aged mediocre men had less self-assured confidence and had women been able to lead the development of these systems. In *Authority Magazine,*[4] Akemi Fisher describes the feminine principles of leadership as collaboration, empathy, strategy, long-term planning, and people first. She notes that people are loyal to leaders who are authentic, genuine, and care about their team members.

Just imagine a world where our political leaders demonstrated the feminine principles of leadership while operating within a system designed to support them!

I believe that the world would be a very different place.

Whilst the community engagement movement appears to have excellent representation (if not over-representation) of women and a definite alignment to these principles, I can't help but feel we are attempting to glue-on the concept of listening, connecting, and collaborating with communities to a system that has been designed for the total opposite of this, bar the four-yearly democratic voting process. I also spend much time wondering if our 'softer' feminine driven skill sets are what's holding our community engagement sector back from shouting from the rooftops about our importance.

Further, I firmly believe that community engagement (certainly in Australia during the last two decades) has become stale and boring: a corporatised, bureaucratic process with stagnant top-down, expert-driven, exclusionary approach. Governments regularly miss the mark. As I said before, we are in an emergency. A complete reconceptualisation of community engagement is desperately needed. It must be a process that connects deeply with people, that supports honest and productive collaboration, is driven by communities themselves, and genuinely influences the decisions made and the resulting outcomes in neighbourhoods.

To achieve this radical breakthrough, awareness must be our first principle, just as awareness is the first principle for a dancer. We must unapologetically highlight an awareness of the needs of our broader communities at *every* level. As a matter of urgency, we must exercise our pragmatic muscles in the service of a deep and committed collaboration. Nothing less than this concerted effort is necessary so we can achieve the healthy, thriving communities I care about so passionately, and that our world so desperately needs.

...

Conversation Starters

- **WHO** were the political leaders during your childhood? What impacts did they make on society? How did they affect your outlook on your life or your career?
- **WHAT** does community engagement mean to you? How do you define it?
- **WHY** does community engagement interest you? What sparked that interest?
- **WHEN** we look to the future, what effects do you think the current political and/or societal climate, either locally or globally, is likely to have on children and young people as they embark on their career paths? Will what they are experiencing now affect how they interact with their communities? If yes, how?
- **WHERE** do you see signs of distrust within your own communities, or communities where you work? As a society, how can we work towards building more trust and sustainable trust?

2. Give a voice to the underdog

There is no power for change greater than a community discovering what it cares about.

— Margaret J Wheatley[5]

I grew up in Abbeydale, a modern suburb within the cathedral city of Gloucester, in the south-west of England.

Abbeydale was next door to Matson. Matson was, and still is, a densely populated urban area of relatively high deprivation. The 'new' suburb of Abbeydale was caught in-between the established suburb of Matson and the village of Upton St Leonards, and my parents tell me it felt like a no-man's-land when it was first developed in the late 1970s.

While Abbeydale was on the 'wrong' side of the M5 motorway to be truly part of the upmarket Upton St Leonards community, it was pretty much regarded that Matson was on the 'wrong' side of Painswick Road for Abbeydale folk to relate to.

But that's not to say we didn't connect with Matson. The beautiful little church I attended as a child stood high up on the hill above Matson. I have fond memories of visiting Matson library, and my older brother and sister attended an excellent primary school there. I also remember that Matson had one of the best fish and chip shops around! During my University years, I had a great time working as the Playleader at the Matson Playscheme, a six-week school holiday program for local children.

In 1999, after three years at university in northern England, I was offered a job interview in Matson. That definitely felt like coming home.

My Mum's liberal socialist tendencies taught me to judge no one. From her I learned to be curious about people's stories, regardless of where they lived or what they did for a living. She taught me to embrace the underdog. And Matson was my underdog. Just to be clear about my language here: I see an 'underdog' as a person or group in a competition, usually in sports and creative works, who is generally expected to lose. My Mum used the world of popular culture to make her point. She told me that Cliff Richard was way too 'squeaky clean' as a performer. She found much more joy in the nomadic, waistcoat-wearing David Essex. Mum's popular culture analogy was later reflected in my teenage music choices. I always preferred the hard-edged, East London boys of *East 17* to the more middle-class, pretty boys of *Take That*!

My love of underdogs continued into adulthood. I admire dancers such as Steve Paxton, who in 1970 legitimised ordinary movement as a dance medium,[6] by having forty-two naked redheads walking across the stage, and calling it dance! And Isadora Duncan who was a self-styled revolutionary, becoming known as the *Mother of Dance*.[7] Or stepping away from dance, in 2003, I loved it when magician and illusionist David Blaine spent over six weeks living on just water inside a plexiglass box, hanging thirty feet in the air on the banks of the River Thames. I even made a lone pilgrimage from Gloucester to London for the day to witness him doing just that, thinking to myself how much I admired his determination to do what he wanted, seemingly without worry about what anyone else would say.

In my bedroom I have a photo of Philippe Petit, a French high-wire artist, who famously undertook an unauthorised high-wire walk between the Twin Towers of the World Trade Centre in New York in 1974. His audacity inspires me no end!

Closer to home, and closer to my topic, my good friend Stephen Yarwood, whom I met just as he was announcing his intentions to nominate himself as a candidate for Lord Mayor of Adelaide in the 2010 local government elections, is one of my favourite underdogs. When we first met, he told me enthusiastically about how worn his boots were from walking the streets of Adelaide, door knocking potential voters. He was hearing loud and clear from the people he met that they intended to vote for him and felt quietly confident. Yet I remember watching a televised debate between the candidates when he barely got a look-in, as the media seemed to favour other more well-known candidates. I cheered with delight when Stephen, in my opinion, the underdog, won the election and served as Lord Mayor from 2010-2014, bringing a future thinking and urban planning approach that had rarely been experienced in Adelaide.

When I reflect on my admiration for these people, it's their ability to think for themselves that I admire. They don't try to conform and seemingly push against the tide of convention.

My parents were children of working-class families in the north of England. Mum's relatives were heavily involved in the Jarrow March of 1936, an organised protest against unemployment and poverty in the English town of Jarrow at that time. All their lives, my parents worked incredibly hard, studying, working and in their home life. That gave their children what I'd call a privileged, middle-class upbringing. Nevertheless, their pride in their northern England working-class roots was not lost on us. While we accept that we are privileged, we are grounded and truly grateful.

This underdog affinity also applies to my brother, Richard. He is an assistant headteacher in a secondary school who, from early in his teaching career, had the challenge of teaching gritty, often socially disadvantaged students at government-funded state schools. There were less opportunities to teach the well-behaved, polished jolly-hockey-stick types he'd encounter if he'd taught in a private school. Whilst he admits he'd probably rather this scenario, to this day, his eyes light up when he explains the challenges of teaching disadvantaged students and how he loves helping them complete their education. Like me, he cheers on and supports the underdog, noting that the social disadvantage his career route has exposed him to has been very distant from our upbringing.

Nowadays, I consider many people who I meet through my work with government departments in delivering community engagement as underdogs. Whether it's the truck driver turning up to a community workshop to passionately put forward his concerns about road safety; someone who feels strongly about the environmental impacts of a proposed housing development who's trying to be heard by decision-makers; or a new mother who wants more services delivered to enable women to share post-birth experiences. These are all people who are avidly pushing against a tide of bureaucracy, or the establishment, in their own unique ways, for social things they care about.

I was only 21 and a bit terrified, so I was surprised that my interview for the role of Community Involvement Officer at the Matson Neighbourhood Project went exceptionally well. Already, I could confidently access my passion for the topic and the neighbourhood. I believe that my humble confidence in my ability to do well in the role was a direct result of a childhood spent in the performing arts. And, importantly, a family that offered a strong foundation where we learned about fairness, equity, and kindness.

Andy Jarrett, my soon-to-be-boss, rang to offer me my new job. I tried to play it cool, telling him I'd need time to think about it and I'd call him back. I kept him waiting! My Mum felt the annual salary (£12,500) was not enough for a university graduate. Nevertheless, I had a good feeling. I called Andy back and accepted the post!

...

I still reflect on my projects at the Matson Neighbourhood Project. The Matson Library, located in the neighbourhood's centre, is overlooked by semi-detached and terraced Council housing. One exterior wall, adjoining a large green space, was made of exposed brick that looked drab and attracted graffiti. That became one of my first projects. My new colleague, Sarah Payne and her family had a reputation in Gloucester for being community minded. In our spare time, Sarah and I worked together as Director and Choreographer on productions like *Aladdin* and *Me and My Girl* through both of our voluntary involvement with the Olympus Theatre. Sarah was a straight-talking, strong woman committed to getting things done. Under her wing was a great place for me to be. And to learn.

The agreed plan was to paint a mural on the external wall. I joined Sarah, who was working collaboratively with the two local primary schools. The proposed mural theme was the local environment. The students, aged between 5 and 10, had been exploring the neighbouring country park, Robinswood Hill, which proudly overlooks Matson and the rest of Gloucester. (Adding to its fame is that the hill was the Gloucester Ski Centre, training home for failed-yet-very-famous ski jumper, *Eddie the Eagle*.)

The students drew features of the environment seen on their adventures to Robinswood Hill. A local artist then used the children's individual drawings to create a large mural design that was scaled to the library wall. Then the painting began. The children were not only involved in designing the mural, but they also took turns with painting it! I asked myself, what kind of crazy community involvement workers let the community take full ownership and responsibility? Oh, that's right ... good ones!

Strong visceral memories of that project remain with me. First is the smell of paint, and specifically accompanying Sarah to local paint suppliers to collect donated tins of paint. To honour the children's design decisions, we had conscientiously selected paint colours, not simply picking up a boot-load of multi-coloured paints. I distinctly remember how exhausting that was. And I learned so much! The mural project was a big, early lesson in the importance of the behind-the-scenes effort required for any successful, creative community engagement project or process.

My second distinct memory of the actual painting process was the rain. It absolutely poured and poured with rain. For days! It was a freezing mid-Autumn in the UK. Nevertheless, the scaffolding was up, and a tightly managed roster of children kept coming and coming, painting their designated area, and then leaving. Sarah, I, and the artist would do necessary touch-ups between class visits or at the end of very long days. (You didn't think we'd leave it *totally* in the hands of the community, did you?)

On reflection, this project was a lesson in professionalism. It was not just about having staff. It was about having dedicated staff who gave their all. The community involvement officer had to lead and coordinate, of course! But there was more. So much more! We had to roll up our sleeves, join in, get wet, get cold, and share with children and the wider community the pride of a project well done.

A final memory of this project was about a technical matter that turned out to be crucial to our project's success. Sarah undertook intensive research into the anti-graffiti paint to be applied as a topcoat over the mural. She must have found something that worked because, decades later, the mural still glows. You can bet that the children who designed and painted it now show it to their children. You can see that in the smiling faces of these children in the press cutting below, local people have an extraordinarily strong sense of pride in this project. I suspect that anti-graffiti paint was never actually required.

■ It's a snip. Gloucester MP Tess Kingham cuts the ribbon to mark the completion of the mural painted on Matson Library wall. Photo: Paul Nicholls

Kids' wall unveiled

PUPILS from Matson primary schools turned out to admire their work and to witness the official unveiling of their mural by Gloucester's MP.

Tess Kingham MP cut the ribbon at Matson Community Library to mark the completion of the 10ft high by 20ft long mural, painted by children from Robinswood Primary and Moat Junior school earlier this month.

The mural, which can be seen from Matson Avenue, was partly funded by a £250 British Gas/*The Citizen* Community Project Award.

Sarah Payne, research and development officer at Matson Neighbourhood Project, said: "It is looking fantastic. The children and local youths have worked really hard to achieve something that has made the environment a lot more pleasant."

Sarah also thanked Hobbycraft, Homebase, Crown Paints and Wilkinson who donated materials and Lansford Access who donated scaffolding.

Ms Kingham, said: "I think we could do with some more pieces of community art around the city.

"It's lovely and bright and brightens up a dull and dilapidated building."

Sarah Payne added that she was hoping that work could now begin on the inside of the library itself.

"Now that we've done the mural it's boosted a total renovation of the library interior," she said.

Image 3 - *Local media coverage of the Matson Library Mural project, Gloucester Citizen, 22 October 1999.*

The mural kicked off my time at Matson and my career, with great grassroots gusto. But it wasn't the only project in Matson that fuelled my enthusiasm.

...

Over the years, Matson had received massive amounts of media coverage from local news outlets, usually for the wrong reasons. Stories of unemployment, crime or other bad news dominated press coverage seriously damaging local pride. Increasing the number and quality of positive news stories about the area was an early challenge of mine, as I sought to achieve higher levels of community involvement and an increased sense of community pride. So, I organised a regular column in the local newspaper, the *Gloucester Citizen,* and worked with journalists to produce positive news pieces. Another strategy was to create our own newspaper: *The Matson News*!

I asked myself, how could people get involved in their local community if they didn't feel connected to it, or if they didn't even know what was happening? How could they feel a sense of pride if we didn't share news about the good things that were happening? As eight-year olds, my best friend Laura and I would while away a Saturday afternoon pretending to be magazine publishers, creating our own little photocopied publication called *Format 3* . Little did I know that this creative childhood play would provide the skills to bolster the pride of an entire neighbourhood!

It was relatively easy to get *The Matson News* happening. In the late nineties, we didn't have desktop computers, so I'd sit in the Neighbourhood Project training room where we had a row of newly installed computers and start laying out ideas using Microsoft Publisher or something similar. The training room adjoined the community general store, managed by the Neighbourhood Project, and I'd often be called on to help monitor the children coming in after school to buy their penny sweets. At first, I saw this as a distraction. Later, I saw it as a great way to connect with local children and their parents.

Often, using local noticeboards, I'd send requests for articles, jokes, quizzes, stories, and more. I'd use existing networks to help me reach people who had content to contribute. I'd include upcoming events, useful phone numbers, and maybe even a word search or a crossword. In the early days, I drove the content of *The Matson News*, but after a couple of editions, as word spread, increasingly the local community drove the content.

I approached a couple of local businesses for sponsorship to cover the cost of printing, which wasn't exorbitant for a basic black-and-white, A4, eight-page newsletter. I organised the printing and stapling by another not-for-profit organisation. I remember my excitement at receiving boxes full of something I'd created. But more than that, I was ecstatic to know that so many local people had contributed to the success of the newspaper.

If the planning, design, and production were seamless, the delivery was not so much. We had to deliver *The Matson News* to 10,000 people! Maybe we ran out of money. I forget. But I do remember being with a very small group of volunteers who were hand-delivering *The Matson News* to every Matson household.

Nowadays, as a tired and cranky forty-something, I cannot imagine hand delivering thousands of newsletters to households for a client. But this is now and that was then. And twenty-one-year-old enthusiastic Becky, in her first 'proper' job, was literally skipping through Matson taking in every sight, sound and smell of this densely populated, urban area of high deprivation. What an experience that was! I learned that the best and fastest way to get to know a community you're working in is to hand-deliver something to every single household. It was a steep learning curve, and I embraced all aspects of it, as shown by the media coverage opposite.

A DAY IN THE LIFE OF . . . a community project worker

■ Becky Hirst is hoping to raise the profile of Matson Neighbourhood Project.

I really like my link role

SOMETIMES I get woken up by Steve at 5am as he works shifts as an engineer, but usually I get up at 7.30am and get to the Trinity Centre in Norbury Avenue for 9am.

The first thing I do is find out what's going on around the place and check the mail.

Every Monday we have a team meeting with other members of staff (there are 24 of us in total over three sites) and Andy Jarrett, the project co-ordinator. This morning, we discussed plans for a community garden next to the Trinity Centre and the launch of a Befriender scheme for the old, disabled and housebound.

Then I get on with my own work. I produce the Matson News – I get all the articles together, plan it out on the computer, take it to the printers and distribute about 2,000 copies each month.

Another thing I am spending time on at the moment is Fair Shares. This is a new scheme we have just started where, for every hour someone spends being a good neighbour, they earn one fair share.

They can then spend that on another service that someone offers – anything from washing cars to looking after pets. There is no money involved, so people don't feel pressured if they get into debt.

Basically, it is like a bartering scheme and people are loving it. We have only just launched it and we have already got 10 people involved and are looking for another 10.

We don't really have a lunch break, sometimes I eat my lunch in reception so I can chat to people coming in, as my office is a bit out of the way.

Something else I'm working on at the moment is the Community Resource Fund, which is £5,000 we have to give to local groups in Matson.

Job facts

QUALIFICATIONS: Although Becky has a degree, there are no specific qualifications for the post, although you need to be numerate, literate and have computer skills.

ATTRIBUTES: The ability to get on with people and to encourage and motivate them. Enthusiasm and the ability to sell ideas. You also need to cope with having lots of things on the go at the same time.

SALARY: Becky earns £12,500 a year, plus a pension. Most community work is on fixed term contracts.

BECKY Hirst, 21, is a community involvement worker for the Matson Neighbourhood Project and is a passionate advocate for the district and its people. She was appointed last September after graduating from Leeds University with a degree in dance. Her post is funded by the National Lottery and her role is to raise the profile of the project. She lives at Hardwicke with her fiance.

We have had a few successful applications – for example, St Katherine's Church got £500 for a new amplification system. We have still got money available and I am spending time going through applications, preparing publicity and so on.

Late afternoon, we often get called into the community shop to give a hand, as lots of kids come in.

It's No Smoking Day today so I am giving out stickers and bookmarks. This is the best time to meet people. I usually go home about 4.30pm, although occasionally I have evening meetings.

I'm a member of the Gloucester Operatic and Dramatic Society and at the moment I'm very busy with rehearsals for *Me and My Girl*. I get home from that about 10pm, watch my soaps on video and go to bed. My biggest interest at the moment is getting my garden into shape, although things keep dying on me!

On a Saturday, I teach contemporary dance at the Gloucester Academy of Music and Performing Arts (GAMPA). Although my degree is in dance, I specialised in community dance and when I graduated I wanted to get involved in community work.

I grew up in Gloucester and I used to work on the Matson summer playschemes in my holidays, so it was ideal when this job came up. I'm the link between the people in the community and the project.

The project has been here 10 years now and it offers advice and representation to the people of Matson on issues such as housing, council tax and debt. There are also employment generation workers and we run the Phoenix Club for people with mental health problems and a Carers' Group.

It annoys me that Matson gets such a bad press. There's an awful lot of positive stuff going on here and the people are really friendly.

There are eight community involvement workers in eight neighbourhood projects in Gloucestershire and we meet together every so often.

I really enjoy my job, getting out there and talking to people. My post is funded by the National Lottery until December 2000, so I have got my fingers crossed for more funding. Everyone's got to keep putting their pound on, as that's my wages!

Interview by Alison Fawcett

Image 4 - A day in the life of... a community project worker, Gloucester Citizen, 2000.

At first-hand, I experienced the consequences of high rates of unemployment, teenage pregnancies, low literacy rates, family violence and, of course, local authority high-density housing. It was immersion therapy: stepping over dirty nappies in shared entrance areas to blocks of flats: retching at urine in hallways; dodging used needles on the roadside; and listening to sirens to know which street to avoid. Not all of Matson was shabby and dangerous, of course. For every smelly high-rise apartment block corridor, I'd find a pocket of well-manicured rose gardens reflecting an immense sense of pride. Even the underdog had its underdogs!

...

On my delivery runs, I soon discovered a very cool time-sharing and skill-sharing program called Fair Shares. Fair Shares is still an active initiative in Gloucester. It describes itself as two-way volunteering, whereby its members get rewarded for the time and effort they put into their neighbourhood. And Fair Shares was a great help to me in a community development sense, as I tried to make sense of what I was experiencing. While I was skipping along delivering *The Matson News,* I met a woman with several problems that needed urgent attention. Nellie told me that she was lonely and anxious. Several jobs around her place had fallen into disrepair, and she couldn't afford to hire anyone to help her. Fair Shares came to the rescue for both of us. We did a trade. For every hour Nellie helped me delivering *The Matson News*, she could bank an hour in her time bank to spend on 'buying in' someone to help her.

So, a local man would give an hour of his time to mow her lawn and use the hour he earned to pay for a babysitter for an hour. The babysitter could use the hour they had earned to buy some mentoring from a local maths tutor. The maths tutor could get her lawn mown… and so on. With this simple concept, the economy of time suddenly created a level playing field. And got stuff done!

I am a huge fan of the concept of living in a circular economy – these days hosting guests in a converted shed on our private property via Airbnb; ride sharing with Uber; reducing consumerism from fast fashion through my thrift shopping addiction; and delighting in concepts such as Little Libraries, where my children regularly take and replace books in random roadside locations! A circular economy approach to life strengthens connection and communities.

As these community-led, sharing approaches grow and prosper, I predict that unless there are radical changes, governments will continue to move further away from having genuine connections and relationships with the communities they serve, and those communities will become more *underdog* in their activities. A different approach is needed. One that includes embracing communities through more community immersion, and fewer layers of bureaucracy, which at present simply stifle communities.

...

Conversation Starters

- **WHO** is the underdog in your work or in your life? What's your relationship like with them? How do you react to them, physically and emotionally?
- **WHAT** kind of community engagement could you achieve with a budget of just $50? You don't always need big budgets to engage a community. The next time you find yourself saying, 'There's no budget', consider how you might reframe the situation. What can we do with what we have? What resources can we draw on?
- **WHY** is it so important to genuinely involve people in activities in their neighbourhoods? And why is it so important that we avoid doing everything for them?
- **WHEN** did you last wander around the community in which you live or work, with no purpose other than to become immersed in observing its happenings?
- **WHERE** do you come from? How does this affect your perspective of community engagement?

3. Work from the bottom-up

The ear's hearing something is not as good as the eye's seeing it; the eye's seeing it is not as good as the foot's treading upon it; the foot's treading upon it is not as good as the hands differentiating it.

— Chinese proverb[8]

After an incredibly enriching and motivating 12 months at the Matson Neighbourhood Project, I was looking for my next challenge. Not that opportunities did not continue in Matson (and the funding for my position was secure). It was time for me to move on. The day that I realised that I needed to leave was my first glimmer of my love for moving from project to project… I discovered something about my true nature: I never sit still for long.

And luck was with me. I found a new role within the local health promotion department as their Food & Health Projects Officer. I surprised myself and others, as I won this job over a qualified nutritionist. On paper, they appeared much more suited to preaching the do's and don'ts of dietary requirements to the people of Gloucestershire. However, as with many things in the early 2000s, approaches to health promotion were changing. And fast!

I got the job because of my experiences in Matson. They were looking for someone who knew how to work *together* with people in finding health solutions, as opposed to expert-led solutions. That leads me to a story about soap. Back in the 1930s, if a public health message was that mothers needed to wash their children to prevent all sorts of doom and gloom and spread of various diseases, the health promotion people would simply deliver bars of soap to each household. That might seem like a very practical approach, but it had little educational value.

I imagined that nobody would have thought about whether mothers knew when to use the soap, how to use it properly, why soap was important for the health of their community, or what would happen when soap ran out. I also wondered who was going to pay for the ongoing use of the soap. Could the families even afford the soap? Nobody appeared to have considered the socio-economic circumstances of the family or household receiving the soap, or the effectiveness of these 'paternalistic' behaviour-change campaigns.

I began work in that department while their big yellow health promotion bus was travelling around communities across Gloucestershire providing all kinds of messages about health. There was so much to do. So, they'd progressed from giving out soap. Now health promotion was all about pamphlets and models of digestive tracts. But it was not working: this top-down, information-heavy approach to behaviour change. I found what seemed to be an assumption that if you gave someone the information on how to eat a healthy diet, they would embrace it. As anyone who's ever attempted a healthier lifestyle knows, that isn't necessarily the case!

So, as a young practitioner, I received the most amazing opportunity to apply a different lens to the age-old information-giving approach to health promotion. That approach focussed on the community at the centre of processes and initiatives to improve health.

My hometown of Gloucester is a relatively diverse city, with areas such as Barton Street (where I have many happy childhood memories of performing with my dance school at the local theatre) and Tredworth, said to be home for 45 different ethnic communities, with as many as 50 languages. I became involved in nutrition and health-promotion activities. And one of my projects aimed to improve the nutrition of the South Asian community. Statistics showed significant health inequalities, particularly around mortality and morbidity, compared to the broader population. Research also confirmed a range of likely influences on nutrition, including community and cultural norms, household income, as well as the availability and affordability of food, and more.

Pulling up in Barton Street in our big yellow bus was simply not going to work. Expert information-giving would backfire. So we searched for a more 'bottom-up' approach, flipping previous expert-led models of health promotion on their heads. We needed culturally sensitive interventions that would build on positive food practices and adopt both family-centred and community-centred approaches. My work began with a simple conversation with the right people. Simple as it seems, this time-honoured approach almost always works.

It's important to note here that those 'right people' were not the local Council or the nutritionists. Further, as you can imagine, that conversation most certainly did *not* take place inside the big yellow bus! The conversation occurred when I contacted the Roshni Asian Women's Centre, located in the heart of Barton Street. The Centre, which opened in 1995, was a place for women to meet and interact in a safe environment. Before that, the women met in their own homes.

I knew nobody at the Centre, but I didn't think twice about contacting them, as it seemed the most natural place to start. We needed a way to connect with this specific community about food and nutrition issues. I often laugh that decades later in my community engagement training and workshops, I emphasise the importance of contacting relevant community organisations. It makes such good sense. Participants always nod and take notes, embracing the concept like it's rocket science.

The staff member at the Centre welcomed me warmly and we chatted about the Centre, the women who regularly attended, and the community as a whole. We were comfortable with each other so we discussed the various possibilities before we agreed that she would discuss with the women the potential for food-related programs to be part of the Centre's programs.

Before long, we were running a series of cookery classes, led by a well-known local Asian cookbook author. However, these classes were not simply about teaching women how to cook. They were a forum where participants could share recipe ideas and discuss where they shop, how they budget and so on. We easily introduced a shared, peer-to-peer learning experience in a safe and familiar location. Our targeted approach was a far cry from the top-down 'I'm the expert, listen to me tell you what to do' methodology. Here, again, as can be seen in the news coverage in the image overleaf, I learned about the importance of involving people in decision making and problem solving about issues that affect them at a household level.

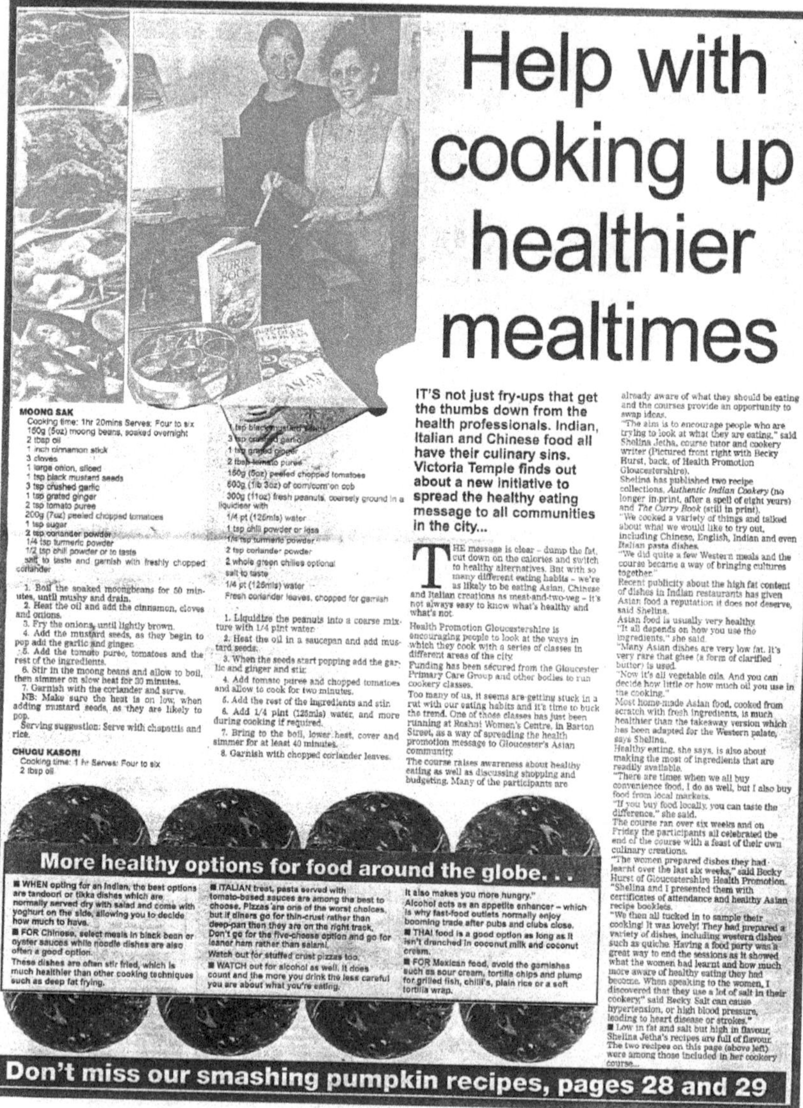

Help with cooking up healthier mealtimes

IT'S not just fry-ups that get the thumbs down from the health professionals. Indian, Italian and Chinese food all have their culinary sins. Victoria Temple finds out about a new initiative to spread the healthy eating message to all communities in the city...

THE message is clear – dump the fat, cut down on the calories and switch to healthy alternatives. But with so many different eating habits – we're as likely to be eating Asian, Chinese and Italian creations as meat-and-two-veg – it's not always easy to know what's healthy and what's not.

Health Promotion Gloucestershire is encouraging people to look at the ways in which they cook with a series of classes in different areas of the city.

Funding has been secured from the Gloucester Primary Care Group and other bodies to run cookery classes.

Too many of us, it seems are getting stuck in a rut with our eating habits and it's time to buck the trend. One of those classes has just been running at Roshni Women's Centre, in Barton Street, as a way of spreading the health promotion message to Gloucester's Asian community.

The course raises awareness about healthy eating as well as discussing shopping and budgeting. Many of the participants are already aware of what they should be eating and the courses provide an opportunity to swap ideas.

"The aim is to encourage people who are trying to look at what they are eating," said Shelina Jetha, course tutor and cookery writer (Pictured front right with Becky Hurst, back, of Health Promotion Gloucestershire).

Shelina has published two recipe collections, *Authentic Indian Cookery* (no longer in print, after a spell of eight years) and *The Curry Book* (still in print).

"We cooked a variety of things and talked about what we would like to try out, including Chinese, English, Indian and even Italian pasta dishes.

"We did quite a few Western meals and the course became a way of bringing cultures together."

Recent publicity about the high fat content of dishes in Indian restaurants has given Asian food a reputation it does not deserve, said Shelina.

Asian food is usually very healthy.

"It all depends on how you use the ingredients," she said.

"Many Asian dishes are very low fat. It's very rare that ghee (a form of clarified butter) is used.

"Now it's all vegetable oils. And you can decide how little or how much oil you use in the cooking."

Most home-made Asian food, cooked from scratch with fresh ingredients, is much healthier than the takeaway version which has been adapted for the Western palate, says Shelina.

Healthy eating, she says, is also about making the most of ingredients that are readily available.

"There are times when we all buy convenience food, I do as well, but I also buy food from local markets.

"If you buy food locally, you can taste the difference," she said.

The course ran over six weeks and on Friday the participants all celebrated the end of the course with a feast of their own culinary creations.

"The women prepared dishes they had learnt over the last six weeks," said Becky Hurst of Gloucestershire Health Promotion.

"Shelina and I presented them with certificates of attendance and healthy Asian recipe booklets.

"We then all tucked in to sample their cooking! It was lovely! They had prepared a variety of dishes, including western dishes such as quiche. Having a food party was a great way to end the sessions as it showed what the women had learnt and how much more aware of healthy eating they had become. When speaking to the women, I discovered that they use a lot of salt in their cookery," said Becky. Salt can cause hypertension, or high blood pressure, leading to heart disease or strokes."

■ Low in fat and salt but high in flavour, Shelina Jetha's recipes are full of flavour. The two recipes on this page (above left) were among those included in her cookery course...

MOONG SAK

Cooking time: 1hr 20mins Serves: Four to six

- 150g (5oz) moong beans, soaked overnight
- 2 tbsp oil
- 1 inch cinnamon stick
- 3 cloves
- 1 large onion, sliced
- 1 tsp black mustard seeds
- 3 tsp crushed garlic
- 1 tsp grated ginger
- 2 tsp tomato puree
- 200g (7oz) peeled chopped tomatoes
- 1 tsp sugar
- 2 tsp coriander powder
- 1/4 tsp turmeric powder
- 1/2 tsp chili powder or to taste
- salt to taste and garnish with freshly chopped coriander

1. Boil the soaked moongbeans for 50 minutes, until mushy and drain.
2. Heat the oil and add the cinnamon, cloves and onions.
3. Fry the onions, until lightly brown.
4. Add the mustard seeds, as they begin to pop add the garlic and ginger.
5. Add the tomato puree, tomatoes and the rest of the ingredients.
6. Stir in the moong beans and allow to boil, then simmer on slow heat for 30 minutes.
7. Garnish with the coriander and serve.

NB: Make sure the heat is on low, when adding mustard seeds, as they are likely to pop.

Serving suggestion: Serve with chapattis and rice.

CHUGU KASORI

Cooking time: 1 hr Serves: Four to six

- 2 tbsp oil
- 1 tsp black mustard seeds
- 3 tsp crushed garlic
- 1 tsp grated ginger
- 2 tbsp tomato puree
- 150g (5oz) peeled chopped tomatoes
- 500g (1lb 3oz) of corn/corn'on cob
- 300g (11oz) fresh peanuts, coarsely ground in a liquidiser with
- 1/4 pt (125mls) water
- 1 tsp chili powder or less
- 1/4 tsp turmeric powder
- 2 tsp coriander powder
- 2 whole green chilies optional
- salt to taste
- 1/4 pt (125mls) water
- Fresh coriander leaves, chopped for garnish

1. Liquidize the peanuts into a coarse mixture with 1/4 pint water.
2. Heat the oil in a saucepan and add mustard seeds.
3. When the seeds start popping add the garlic and ginger and stir.
4. Add tomato puree and chopped tomatoes and allow to cook for two minutes.
5. Add the rest of the ingredients and stir.
6. Add 1/4 pint (125mls) water, and more during cooking if required.
7. Bring to the boil, lower heat, cover and simmer for at least 40 minutes.
8. Garnish with chopped coriander leaves.

More healthy options for food around the globe...

■ WHEN opting for an Indian, the best options are tandoori or tikka dishes which are normally served dry with salad and come with yoghurt on the side, allowing you to decide how much to have.

■ FOR Chinese, select meals in black bean or oyster sauces while noodle dishes are also often a good option.

These dishes are often stir fried, which is much healthier than other cooking techniques such as deep fat frying.

■ ITALIAN treat, pasta served with tomato-based sauces are among the best to choose. Pizzas are one of the worst choices, but if diners go for thin-crust rather than deep-pan then they are on the right track. Don't go for the five-cheese option and go for leaner ham rather than salami.

Watch out for stuffed crust pizzas too.

■ WATCH out for alcohol as well. It does count and the more you drink the less careful you are about what you're eating.

It also makes you more hungry."

Alcohol acts as an appetite enhancer – which is why fast-food outlets normally enjoy booming trade after pubs and clubs close.

■ THAI food is a good option as long as it isn't drenched in coconut milk and coconut cream.

■ FOR Mexican food, avoid the garnishes such as sour cream, tortilla chips and plump for grilled fish, chilli's, plain rice or a soft tortilla wrap.

Don't miss our smashing pumpkin recipes, pages 28 and 29

Image 5 - Media coverage of the work undertaken in partnership with the Roshni Asian Women's Centre, Gloucester Citizen, 25 October 2001.

Of course, there is a role for traditional engagement approaches. And I had my share of them in that job. Sometimes I felt out of my depth, such as when I was delivering nutrition training to a team of NHS Direct call centre nurses.

I was so nervous, young, and unqualified. One man was kind enough to give me feedback that I said 'OK' too many times. What the?! Maybe it was my discomfort showing. Or maybe he was just being a moron.

...

My bosses in the health promotion centre knew I was totally new to health promotion, let alone food and nutrition. They offered to support me through a Graduate Diploma in Health Education Promotion at the University of Gloucestershire. What a wonderful opportunity for a young woman who had been thrown in at the deep end. A day per week from my work life to hang out at the local university and be paid... super indulgent! I made the most of it.

Three significant pieces of learning during that Graduate Diploma year matured my perspectives about community engagement (at the time and ever since). While we had a huge reading list and a diverse range of essays and projects, all three lessons came from the same textbook (that still sits on my desk today: *Health Promotion - Foundations for Practice*[9]).

Lesson One was about models and approaches to health promotion. Beattie's structural analysis of the repertoire of health promotion approaches was the first time I had encountered the various approaches (authoritarian, 'top-down' and expert-led), as opposed to negotiation, 'bottom-up' and valuing individual autonomy. Beattie's model (page 106) explained differences in persuasion interventions aimed at individuals but led by experts, compared to legislative interventions led by experts but intended to protect whole communities. I also learned about personal counselling type interventions (client-led and focused on personal development), with the expert being more of a facilitator. Finally, I learned about the community development approach, which seeks to empower or enhance the skills of a group or local community, helping them to recognise what they have in common and to take action together.

I particularly loved that Beattie's analysis included references to the political ideologies of each of these approaches, from conservatism to reformist, to libertarian, humanist to radical ideology. In my mind, I summarised parts of this model quite simply as the left versus right on a political spectrum, with left equalling collective action and the right being a more individualistic in approach.

I was so open to these concepts at this point in my educational and professional journey. I greatly valued opportunities to explore theoretical concepts of interventions within a health promotion paradigm. I began to connect the dots about my love for community. I remembered that in my early years, New Labour told me that things could only get better. It was all starting to come together and make sense.

Of course, my studies were about approaches of health promotion. However, those approaches equally apply to community engagement.

While I was reading about different political approaches to health promotion, I was aware of my own political leanings. I've always found myself very much in the centre of the political spectrum. Perhaps this is because I spent years being an independent facilitator or advocate. Or perhaps I've always been conscious that my client, the government, could change in an instant at any election and my business always needed to be ready to adapt to suit the policies of the current term. Or perhaps it is that my Dad's parents were traditional working-class conservative 'Tory' supporters, and my Mum's parents were socialist Labour party supporters. Or maybe I just want to be liked by everybody.

Then again, maybe it's that I've always had fairly centralist view of the world. Whatever the reason, I believe it's important to consider that community engagement is not about political persuasion. Left or right doesn't matter as much as whether we are authentic and principled in the work we do.

These days, governments cannot decide whether or not they engage communities. Twenty-first century communities ask to be involved. At times, they demand it. They want governments to be representative of them and their needs and to listen to what they are saying. In recent years working with both left-wing and right-wing governments (and the left, right and central factions within them), I notice that engagement methodologies remain pretty much the same.

In the same Naidoo and Wills book, I discovered Dahlgren and Whitehead's *Determinants of Health* model (1991). That was my second huge revelation. The model explained, layer by layer, the influences on an individual's health. Starting at a very individual level, the authors explained that the first layers of influence are our age, gender, and other hereditary factors. These are closely followed by lifestyle factors, such as levels of support and influence within communities which can sustain or damage health. The next layer is about a person's living and working conditions, as well as their access to facilities and services. And the final layer notes the importance of general socio-economic, cultural, and environmental conditions.

This model referred specifically to layers of influence on a person's health. However, for the young Becky, it opened me to a depth of understanding of the concept of 'community' that I'd never considered. It communicated that a person doesn't simply live in a community. There are so many layers to that person's interactions with that community, whether the layers are of local or global significance.

These days, I use this model to help me consider which layer a particular community project or initiative is addressing. For example, a group of volunteers who meet to plant trees in their neighbourhood once a month may be addressing both the layer regarding their living and working conditions (providing more greenery, better shade). Equally, they may be addressing broader environmental conditions (such as tackling climate change). They are also, of course, individually working on their own lifestyle factors (being active, meeting new people) and building social and community networks.

These layers fascinated me so much that in 2013, I developed my own version of this model. I'd been working intensively across South Australia with several different government clients on a range of different topics. And one of the joys of being a community engagement specialist is that you get to hear a lot of interesting stuff!

What I heard, particularly from people in metropolitan Adelaide, was repetitious. It didn't matter whether my client was the health department asking me to seek contributions for a new policy, or a Council asking me to engage with people to design a new garden as part of the Adelaide parklands, or the Premier's Department working on a new Strategic Plan for the entire State, people were telling me things that were deeply interlinked. Locating the common themes within a model based on the layers within Dahlgren and Whitehead's Determinants of Health provided an ideal platform for my analysis and I put together the 'Healthy Communities' graphic below in Image 6.

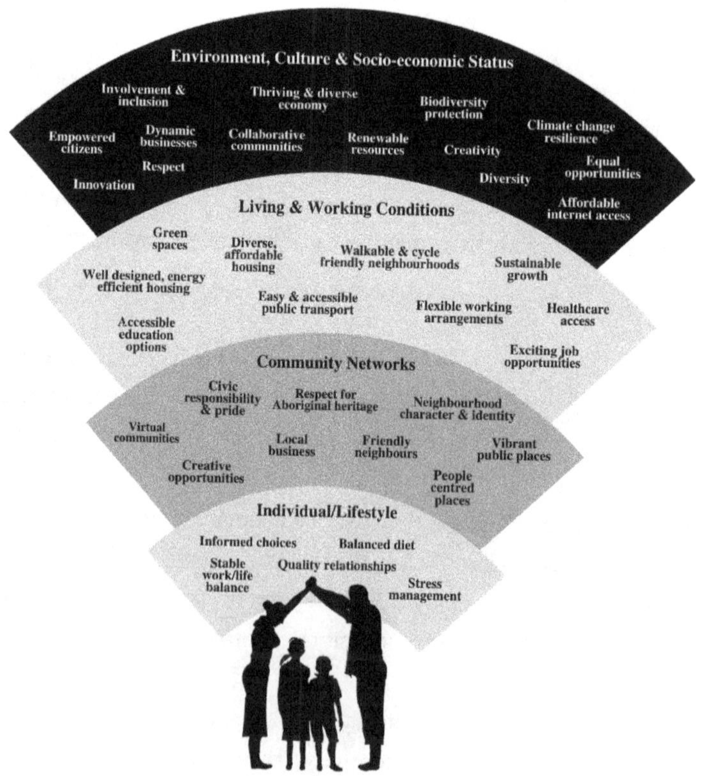

Image 6 – Healthy Communities – A collection of common themes that I was hearing people tell me as their visions for community through my work on a range of initiatives, based on Dahlgren & Whitehead's Determinants of Health model. Hirst, B. 2013.

Now, in 2021, I experience much joy (and equally much frustration) when I consider that these same matters are still being discussed by people in metropolitan Adelaide today. I bet this applies to the whole of the world. We have been talking about these issues for a long time.

The third and final big concept that inspired me during my Graduate Diploma studies was Maslow's famous *Hierarchy of Needs*. When I studied Maslow's model, it had not been the subject of as much scrutiny as it is today. I learned the basics and they really affected how I looked at my work – and my life. Maslow's original *Hierarchy of Needs* built on my understanding and values that a person cannot reach their full potential if their basic needs are not met.

We cannot achieve self-esteem if we lack a feeling of belonging. We cannot feel like we belong without having our safety needs met. And before we have our safety needs meet, we need our basic physiological needs met. I've since learned that Maslow's Hierarchy has been critiqued over the decades. And with good cause. I have a close friend who lost his livelihood and home in the last few years. Yet he still holds the ability to seek out deep learning, understanding, and self-awareness; often regularly helping others by way of a higher state of transcendence. This experience reminds me that the hierarchy is not necessarily as straightforward (or constraining) as it seems.

The model has also evolved over time to include cognitive, aesthetic, and transcendent needs, as shown in image 7.[10] Not only did Maslow's model further enrich my deep understanding, as did other models, providing a much deeper understanding of individuals and community, but it also reminded me of another of my passions in the world of community engagement... the basic need of a sense of belonging.

As with my fascination with a real-life game of *Sim City* and the relationships among everyone living in communities of place, in her book *Belonging*,[11] Toko-pa Turner notes that, as humans, we are remembering how to be an ecosystem. She suggests that we must look after each other, reconstituting the world through many small contributions, collaborations, and general sense of togetherness.

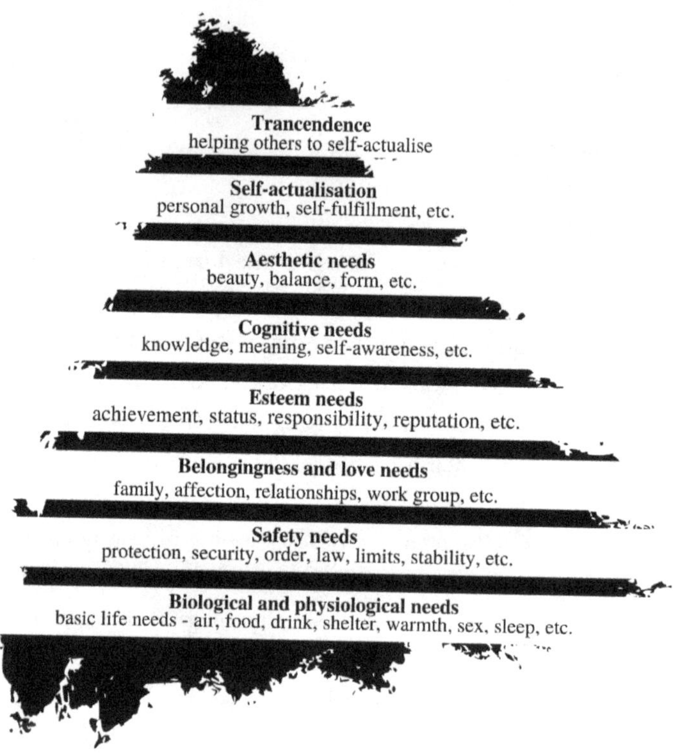

Image 7 - Maslow's Extended Hierarchy of Needs further inspired by understanding of people and community, triggering my interest in a sense of belonging being a basic human need. McLeod, S. 2020.

I believe that good community engagement not only contributes to considered decision-making (that in turn leads to thriving communities), but also when community engagement is done well, it can build a strong sense of belonging. Maslow's model confirms as it was for me that feeling like you belong somewhere isn't just a 'nice-to-have' feeling, but a critical need for our overall well-being as individuals.

...

Health promotion was good for me and I was good for it. I loved the food and health-related community projects. Working across the county of Gloucestershire meant traveling between meetings in the depths of the Forest of Dean with school principals to support establishment of breakfast clubs, to visiting the urban suburbs of Gloucester to work with Neighbourhood Projects setting up food cooperatives so local people could bulk buy staple food items. I loved my work establishing the Gloucestershire Food in Schools group, a multi-disciplinary collective of professionals who met regularly to work on healthy eating initiatives in schools. Membership ranged from school nurses to principals, to qualified nutritionists and local GPs. There I learned about the importance of people meeting regularly together to tackle a community issue.

I also participated in a fantastic multi-disciplinary team of health promotion specialists, learning about initiatives to reduce high teenage pregnancy rates, to programs about reducing sexually transmitted diseases. I was grateful to witness the exciting smoking cessation movement of fully trained Stop Smoking Advisors at the time being available to the public at no cost.

This era also provided an anchor for me in a rapidly changing world. By 2001, we had computers on our desks and had joined the twenty-first century! I revelled in being allowed to choose the colour of my office walls. I felt like a very modern professional. The joy of having my very own computer in my brightly painted office was tragically eclipsed by witnessing via my newly installed Internet, the collapse of the Twin Towers at the World Trade Centre in New York, on 11 September 2001.

That was the first I'd heard of Al-Qaeda. Sadly, it would not be the last. For our global community, that was a defining moment for me, as a young professional. Together, the global community witnessed an outpouring of love, support and camaraderie for America and beyond.

...

Conversation Starters

- **WHO** could you be having a conversation with about something important: a person you haven't yet had a conversation with?
- **WHAT** fascinates you about communities? Is it the people? The infrastructure? The environment? Health needs? Housing? Or the whole ecosystem?
- **WHY** is it important to put communities at the centre of everything we do? How can we do this better?
- **WHEN** have you witnessed a community or communities demanding to be heard?
- **WHERE** do you sit on the political spectrum? How does this affect your perception of communities and/or community engagement?

4. Form powerful partnerships

If you want to go fast, go alone. If you want to go far, go together.

— African Proverb, source unknown

The Gloucester Leisure Centre was where I learned to swim as a child. I hated swimming lessons and have nothing but terrible memories of clinging onto the side for dear life, whilst my best friend Laura clung on for her dear life right alongside me.

That's not to say my memories of the place are bad, however. The vending machines in the cafeteria stocked delicious little rainbow popcorn snacks. As a teenager, I took the pilgrimage to the Centre to have my ears pierced in the beauty salon, as well as countless visits to the now-illegal-in-many-countries tanning beds. The local nightclub, Fifth Avenue, was located under the same roof. I have some dubious memories of it. And in earlier years when the club was called Cinderella's, I remember going along to watch my Mum and her friends doing their 1980s-style, lycra-clad, daytime aerobics in there.

In 1992, I spent a week at the Gloucester Leisure Centre doing my work experience for school, splitting my time hanging out with the lifeguards, on reception, and with the maintenance team. I was fascinated by the concept of a place that offered so many different leisure functions for community. By far my favourite job during that week was sitting in the key exchange booth by the swimming pool, swapping locker keys for rubber wristbands to be worn by swimmers. I enjoyed witnessing firsthand a building as a community of place, providing facilities for communities of interest, ranging from swimmers, to gymnasts, and everyone in-between.

During my time in the health promotion department, I'd heard murmurs that as part of the rebuilding of this city-based Leisure Centre during 2001, there would be a new exciting partnership between the owners of the Centre, the Gloucester City Council, my current employers, the West Gloucestershire Primary Care Trust and the University of Gloucestershire. And that the initiative, to be called the Living and Learning Centre, would need a manager.

The timeline for applying for the Living and Learning Centre Manager's role wasn't ideal. The advertisement went live in mid-December 2001, and I was in the midst of getting ready for my fast-approaching New Year's Eve wedding. But I was so excited and intrigued by the potential of this role that I managed to get my application in by the end of January and won the job. Funny though, some of the criticism hurled at me by my now ex-husband during our marriage breakdown a couple of years later was that I'd spent time during our honeymoon (lying on a sun lounger in Phuket), writing my application for this job. Hey, a girl's got to do what a girl's got to do. Right? And I'm not the type to kick back with a copy of *Hello* magazine, whatever the occasion!

Despite the awkward timing of the application process, the timing of my recruitment was impeccable, as I was on board and ready to roll from before the Leisure Centre opened. The partners were keen to have me as an integral part of the Leisure Centre management team. Each week, we would visit the building-site Centre, wearing plastic coverings over our shoes to protect the immaculate flooring, to follow the progress on the build. I felt so proud and excited for Gloucester. It was a 15-million-pound investment in physical infrastructure, but it was also an investment in our health and leisure.

This place was a state-of-the-art Centre, with stunning features, such as a national short course 8-lane 25-metre competition pool (with an incredible moveable floor to alter its depth for different events); a separate 25-metre training pool, learner pool and children's water play area; indoor bowls, a fully fitted out gymnastics training hall; a martial arts hall, a three-storey health and fitness centre; badminton courts; a major, eight-court sports hall with a capacity to be a 1,600 seater entertainment venue, plus a beauty salon, a bar, and a café. It was the 'bee's knees' of leisure centres! I treasured the opportunity to work alongside the other managers, learning all about the operations of a huge Leisure Centre.

The Living and Learning Centre was on the ground floor, close to the main reception, opposite the café, and at the entrance to the Horizons health club area, where people would come for the gym, exercise classes, or to have a sauna. The Living and Learning Centre was a small space, probably no bigger than fifty square metres, and in those early days, I had great fun planning the furniture, with my tiny budget. I ended up creating zones within the small space so that, in the true spirit of the partnership, the Living and Learning Centre could be used for a multitude of offerings.

Cathy Daley was the overall manager of the Leisure Centre, now called GL1. She was my day-to-day line manager. I had a lot of respect for her because of her straight-talking ability to make things happen. Early on, I remember hearing her explain that, whilst this all-singing-all-dancing, state of the art Leisure Centre was in inner city Gloucester, surrounded by a low socioeconomic demographic of residents who probably most needed a healthier lifestyle, the majority of users of the Centre would be the more affluent residents of Gloucester (who would drive in from the outer suburbs of town to use our facilities). Whilst Cathy didn't mind this from a business perspective, from a social perspective this didn't sit well with her, particularly given this was a public leisure centre and not a private health club. She explained that her priority was to connect with the immediate local community.

From the perspective of the University, based in the neighbouring and much more upper-class town of Cheltenham, this was an opportunity to connect with the people of Gloucester. Using this unique setting, Jane, my manager from the University, was keen to promote a message of lifelong learning and to demystify some of the pomp and ceremony associated with University. Having recently studied there myself, and having spent plenty of my childhood attending lectures with my Mum as a mature-aged student, I had a strong connection with the organisation and was excited by the challenge.

The third partner, the West Gloucestershire Primary Care Trust, saw this as an opportunity to promote healthy living messages to the users of GL1. And, as with Cathy, my health promotion manager, Sue specifically focussed on immediate neighbours living in the lower socioeconomic areas surrounding the Centre.

I could soon see that the coming together of Cathy, Jane, and Sue in this form of strategic partnership was going to be significant. And even more significant *for me* was that they were willing to trust me to guide the evolvement of the Living and Learning Centre as I saw fit. Whilst each of them had investment, both financially and in interest (an annual £15,000 per organisation to cover my salary and a small operating budget). They trusted me with the briefs they gave me and allowed me to run with it.

As a consultant nowadays, it's rare that I get an open-ended brief, although I encourage my clients to let me guide them through a process without a specific end in mind. These occasions are often the ones that result in the most creative, innovative, and high-performing solutions. In community engagement, this approach is critical: we must trust in communities to evolve during an engagement process, on their terms, using their skills and knowledge.

GL1 opened to the public on the 12 August 2002, and the Centre's adventure began! Summarised as a centre to promote health, leisure and learning to local residents, it acted as both a drop-in venue but also a base for which a range of outreach programs occurred: always in partnership with others.

We partnered with the health service to run support groups for pregnant women wanting to stop smoking. We partnered with local career advisor to run a *Live the Life You Want* workshop. For Stroke Awareness Week, we welcomed 26 older people to drop-in for blood pressure checks. And, as part of the Strolling in Gloucestershire Festival and Adult Learners Week, we hosted a guided walk about the historic city. Working collaboratively with Black and Minority Ethnic community groups, we undertook tours of GL1, focusing on the women-only swim sessions. We established strong, ongoing partnerships with organisations such as the Education Achievement Zone, Sure Start, ACET (Adult Continuing Education and Training), the Information, Advice and Guidance Partnership, local surgeries and the Library Service.

One of the big success stories of those early months was the Family Learning Weekend, called *Live It Up*, which involved a range of organisations working together with the Centre to offer a range of activities for local families. I have a vague recollection of the event involving free swim sessions, career advice, and 'have-a-go-at-kickboxing' sessions.

One memory stands out: the incredibly popular 'Meet a Rugby Player' session. We worked together with Gloucester Rugby Club to host a brilliant event with two of their popular players, shown in image 8. The event won a national award from the Campaign for Learning, noting its innovation in combining health, education and leisure promotion and connection to community. The following year, we ran another event as part of Family Learning Week that we called *Step Back in Time*, and installed Victorian-styled classrooms for local children to experience, with an actor playing a very strict Victorian-era teacher.

Image 8 - Living it Up at GL1's Family Learning Weekend with Chris Catlin and Thinus Delport, who played for the Gloucester Rugby Club at the time. Photo by author, 2002.

One of my favourite, fun and creative memories of the work of the Centre was planning and implementing a Valentine's Day initiative. Love poetry was displayed on all the public café tables for the week to promote reading. The local Library Service's Reader in Residence attended to recite poetry to people between the ages of 14 and 25, aiming to promote reading specifically to this age group.

Art was a big feature of my time at the Centre. With the Primary Care Trust, we worked with graphic design and multimedia students from Gloucestershire College of Arts & Technology to deliver an exhibition for No Smoking Day in 2004. That year's theme was 'for smokers who want out'. The students created artwork to illustrate why two thirds of adult smokers wanted to quit smoking. The artwork had a powerful impact and its placement in a Leisure Centre reached a different demographic than would normally attend an art exhibition (or potentially a more traditional health service). Another initiative saw us working with Leo Saunders, a local 'fusion' artist, who mixed media such as photography, paint and screenpaint, to install a stunning exhibition of his work in the main GL1 reception area. The exhibition gained plenty of media coverage, as well as raised eyebrows, attracting some not-your-usual-suspects into the Centre.

The somewhat hedonistic lifestyle of working in the *leisure and pleasure industry,* as it was aptly nicknamed by colleagues (recognising the long out-of-office-hours working in a venue where the majority of people spent their spare time), gave me the escape I needed from my already failing marriage. It provided the essential support I needed when my marriage ended. I built some great friendships during my time at GL1. There I learned the true meaning of having a 'work family'.

It also convinced me of the potential of partnerships – both at a strategic level and operational level. The Living and Learning Centre would have been nothing without those partnerships.

...

Conversation Starters

- **WHO** would you like to see proactively working together in your workplace or communities?
- **WHAT** partnerships have you been involved with? This can be personal or professional! What did you learn from the experience? How can you use

what you learned during this experience to form strong partnerships in the future?

- **WHY** collaborate? What benefits might collaboration bring?
- **WHEN** have you witnessed great things being achieved by people, groups or organisations working together?
- **WHERE** have you seen significant financial investment in infrastructure happen in your communities? Were you interested or involved in it? If yes, did you have much influence over the process? If no, what stopped you being interested or getting involved?

5. Use creative and innovative processes

Creativity is the necessary work of evolving community engagement practice using methods that honour people's individual and collective knowledge about their lives and their environments.

— Wendy Sarkissian[12]

My year in my mid-twenties traveling to Australia on a working holiday visa is worthy of a book of its own. However, to summarise, in early 2004, circumstances in my personal life led me to quit my job, sell my house, and set sail for the other side of the world. Perhaps saying I 'set sail' is a bit overdramatic, but you get the gist. The bright blue skies and glistening waters of Sydney were the tonic I needed at an exceedingly difficult time in my personal life. Although I was nursing a battered heart, I settled comfortably into a footloose and fancy-free lifestyle in Sydney. For this reason, amongst others, Sydney will always hold a special place in my heart.

Work-wise, the working holiday visa limitations meant I could only work for periods of 3 months or less. So I was having a blast, taking on typical backpacker jobs (jobs nobody else was prepared to do!) I remember feeling out of place attending a briefing to be a 'promo chick' for a well-known pharmaceutical company. I flinched at hearing I'd need to wear a pink bow in my hair, whilst sporting a short spiky, bleached-blonde look. That job was definitely not going to work out. One job involved being up before dawn to greet commuters in North Sydney with promotions for a newly opened gym. My assignment was to help the guy dressed up as a big muscle man not to trip over. I've since worked with clients and colleagues in North Sydney and always give a cheeky smile to, and take a pamphlet from, any person I see on the street. Who knows what their journey is?

I worked for a day in a call centre, making cold calls inviting farmers to attend a conference about something, somewhere. I can't remember the details, other than by the end of the day I knew I couldn't face it, so I quit on the spot! I covered a lunchtime shift in one of Australia's leading telecommunications company's headquarters inbound call centre, thankfully for only a few hours. I spent a couple of weeks working for a leading Australian insurer, as… wait for it… a *Demetaliser*! I made up my title to make the job of removing staples from endless documents to be digitised sound a bit more high-tech. I remember the great elation I felt when I was promoted to scanning from staple removal!

One job I'll never forget played an incredibly significant role in my life. It's another reason Sydney is so special. The infamous *Route 69* pub crawl had been advertising for 'reps' and I thought it sounded like fun. It sounded like a guarantee for the good, slightly wild, social life I sought. I'll let non-Australian readers do your own online research into the Aussie slang involved in this business name. I was poor at the hard sell of getting backpackers to buy tickets to join our bus to visit Sydney's coolest pubs and clubs. But I did meet Dan, a fellow UK backpacker, also living his best quarter-life crisis under the bright lights of Sydney. Dan quickly became my best friend, my partner, and in recent years, the father of my children!

One beloved job was a temporary role as a receptionist at Tourism Australia. I'm not good at reception skills. I had a bad habit of hanging up on people while trying to transfer their calls, but I remember applying my creative skills to developing up an *A-Z of Reception FAQs* during the quieter times. And, of course, being an engager at heart, my welcome was always warm. Having dabbled in tourism recently in the McLaren Vale region, I wish I could return to that role just to eavesdrop on the conversations in the corridors. Maybe my path crossed with Australian Prime Minister Scott Morrison, who was one of the Managing Directors there at the time. Maybe I even hung up on him!

One sunny Saturday morning, in between backpacker jobs, I was sitting on the balcony of my shared Pyrmont apartment flicking through the newspaper. Curiosity about the job market beyond the backpacker scene had me glancing at the employment section. One advertisement caught my eye. Parramatta City Council was looking for an Arts & Cultural Development Officer to join their Community Development Team on a three-month contract. I couldn't believe it. Here was a job I could do. I had the qualifications that perfectly suited the demanding visa restrictions. Of course, I applied, I attended the interview with a confident spring in my step and was offered the job. And so, my wild backpacking days transformed into a daily commute on the train from Central Station to Parramatta. And I loved every minute of it!

Sydney was the first big city I'd ever lived in. My hometown of Gloucester is a city because it has a cathedral. But it's not a 'city' city. Sydney was the first place I'd lived that had a Central Business District, where people rushed about *en masse* , in suits. It was the first place I'd lived where the buildings were taller than four or five storeys. While I've never been a suit-wearer (my absolute favourite thing about community engagement is the unspoken right to wear denim to work). But I absolutely loved the rush of passing through Town Hall Station at 8 am on a weekday, followed by the dash along the platform at Central Station to board one of the double-decker trains to Parramatta. Here I was being lucky again. I had an opportunity to immerse myself in a community. And how exciting to be on the other side of the world, exploring and learning about a community in a totally different country.

...

As part of the Greater Granville Regeneration Plan, the Council was eager to undertake community engagement regarding perceptions of safety within this diverse suburb, known for its high proportion of older residents, single-person households, and large families with remarkably diverse backgrounds. Of course, there are limits to what you can achieve on a three-month contract. And I was in a totally unfamiliar environment. But I had enthusiasm and passion (and dare I say, the energy of a woman in her mid-twenties) on my side. My boss gave me leadership of the 'Perceptions of Safety' project, and I embraced it. An interesting plot twist helped me succeed. The funding was to be used for arts and cultural development. So my brief was to add creativity to the engagement process. Hmmm.... here was my opportunity to do something really cool!

Community engagement was already underway for the overall Regeneration Plan by planners Hassell, with Sarkissian Associates Planners taking the lead.

Wendy and her team were already using a comprehensive suite of creative engagement tools to generate discussion and draw out community contributions, including a key stakeholders' workshop, a SpeakOut, and 'A Week with a Camera' exercise where local children contributed their assessments with the help of teachers at two local primary schools. My job was to undertake additional engagement, specifically regarding people's perception of safety in Granville, targeting young people and older people.

As with any new project, in any community, from my experiences hand delivering *The Matson News*, my first task was to immerse myself in the neighbourhood to gain an overview of where I was, what the neighbourhood was like, and to generate ideas or inspiration for making a start on delivering this project. A few weeks earlier, I'd been manually removing staples from documents in a backpacker sweatshop. Suddenly, here I am, cruising around western Sydney's sunny suburbs in a close-to-brand-new Toyota Camry from the Council's carpool.

This was the first time I'd driven in Australia. I felt overwhelmed, yet excited, by the street grid, wide roads, huge volumes of traffic, and the bright (yet low) winter sun, requiring constant use of the visor. These were pre-GPS-satellite-navigation days, so I needed the Sydney & Suburbs street directory as I explored my new territory. I had to pull over regularly to check where I was and to stay on course.

This was also the first time I'd explored a community in Australia with any kind of diversity or disadvantage. My exploration had been limited to the Sydney CBD, the leafy suburb of Pyrmont where I lived, and day trips to the Hunter Valley and the Blue Mountains. I'd also briefly travelled along the East Coast, including the tourist hotspots of Byron Bay and Surfers Paradise. But there my exploration was limited to bars, beaches, and burger joints!

I was immediately fascinated by the difference in housing stock. A comparable UK suburb would have very dense, high-rise Council housing. But here in Australia were pockets of high levels of deprivation in estates of detached government housing -some with gardens on quarter-acre blocks! As I drove around, I soon noticed visible signs of unemployment, crime, poverty, and more.

I learned that that deprivation could exist even in the presence of ample space and glorious sunshine.

Taking detailed notes, I found community centres, churches, schools, cafes, shopping centres, parks, and childcare centres. I observed bus stops, bus routes, and train stations. I noted areas where I saw graffiti, abandoned shopping trolleys. I searched for street furniture with shade or drinking water fountains. I studied community noticeboards, which are always guaranteed to provide glimpses into community life, wherever in the world they are.

I now call this my 'community immersion process' and I undertake it on any project with a new community. It's my critical exercise in learning about the people who live there and understanding how they live. Of course, most of my observations are assumptions initially and they may not influence the final project plan. Nevertheless, it's critical for an engagement practitioner to try to understand what makes a community tick. I see this process as our obligation to that community. And we need to do that even if it makes us feel uncomfortable.

My fascination with how a community looks and feels, and how the people interact or move around it helped me, no end. My immersive exploration led me to a community hall that offered social programs for older people, luckily, as my objective was to engage older people about their perceptions of safety. And, as my Gloucester community health promotion days taught me, working with organisations to reach a target group makes a lot of sense. My initial conversations revealed that the organisation was totally open to changes in their activity program. So I immediately had fifteen older people eager for conversations about safety. Tick!

But how could I make this project 'creative', as per my brief? I was also involved with other arts and culture groups and networks within the Parramatta area and I'd heard about a woman who was a creative writer… and she ran workshops… and my mind went into solution-focused overdrive. So, we organised for the creative writing specialist and me to run a creative writing workshop in the community hall with older people. I remember explaining who I was and what we were doing and seeing so many eyes watching with anticipation. I sensed both their wisdom and experience, as well as their fragility and vulnerability.

Working in pairs, the creative writer suggested we brainstorm participants' meaning of neighbourhood safety. After more workshopping, we began to turn ideas into stories, which the participants then shared.

I was still in my early twenties, so I didn't have many benchmarks. But the richness of the response astonished me. Our highly effective approach was exceptional for gaining high-quality contributions to the overall neighbourhood regeneration process. And our participants were some of the community's most vulnerable members. For example, there was Ynette. I'd expected that Ynette, the woman I was paired with, to say things about police presence, better lighting, or fewer young people hanging around in large numbers. At least, I thought that these were typical responses that we might elicit using conventional engagement tools. Ynette had different ideas altogether. Feeling safe came down to something as simple as the emergency call button she wore around her neck at home. She told a story about falling and being unable to get up. And how the little button had saved the day. And possibly saved her life.

Another participant spoke about being able to easily use the disabled parking spaces outside the shops. No hard-hitting crime worries here, simply the ability to go about his day comfortably and easily, doing what he needed to do. There was a richness to the texture of the stories we heard. Nobody wanted to leave. So we stayed for tea and cake and a demonstration of their indoor bowls prowess.

I had also found an opportunity to engage creatively with young people on this project. Working with Council's youth workers, nine local young people, representing a diverse mix of cultural backgrounds, attended a song-writing workshop facilitated by a professional musician. The workshop began with a general brainstorming regarding participants' impressions of safety in Granville. Then they turned their ideas into music and lyrics. Suddenly the project had a theme tune written by local young people!

Again, the contributions and insights we gathered by taking creative approaches provided a richness that amazed me. I could not imagine gaining such insights via surveys or public meetings.

We went from strength to strength. For the reporting-back stage, I hired a local filmmaker to capture both the processes and the outcomes in a short film. That way, Council decision makers heard first-hand local people's perceptions of safety. And in those days, it was not nearly as easy as it is today to report back via video. Creative community engagement can benefit from smartphones and apps for video editing, yet creative reporting back is still relatively rare. We must never underestimate the creative art of storytelling, whatever the medium: through written word or song, or whatever. It is an incredibly valuable tool for gathering community insights.

I have always imagined that, as a left-hander, creativity comes naturally to me. Apparently, it's something to do with the hemispheres of the brain. My creative side is certainly linked up. As a bonus, I'm ambidextrous: I write (and iron!) with my left hand but do everything else with my stronger, dominant right hand. My theory is that this gives me the creative attributes of a left-hander, combined with the logical, straightforward thinking of a right-hander.

This morning, for example, a colleague who's planning to attend my training session tomorrow sent an SMS saying how excited she was about my pre-workshop email which featured the analogy of boarding a flight to present the information for joining the online session. I've found the simpler the creativity, the better. In these times, there's so much dry content around that people jump up and down with excitement at even the simplest play on words. And all the white noise in the world means that communicating as simply and creatively as you can is a bonus.

...

Conversation Starters

- **WHO** is the most creative person in your team or your community? How could they be involved to enhance your community engagement practice?
- **WHAT** could you do to make reporting processes more creative?
- **WHY** don't we apply creativity and innovation to all of our community engagement practice? What stops us?
- **WHEN** have you worked creatively? Or witnessed creativity in your own community?
- **WHERE** have you been that is *on* the beaten track, and where have you been that is *off* the beaten track? What did you see that is different between places that are seen, and places that aren't seen?

6. Facilitate the telling of stories for rich conversation

Narrative imagining - story - is the fundamental instrument of thought. Rational capacities depend upon it. It is our chief means of looking into the future, or predicting, of planning, and of explaining.

— Mark Turner[13]

Jumping forward a decade from my Parramatta days of song and creative writing, I now use creative and innovative tools or techniques to engage people as standard practice. No matter how conventional the topic, I always provide people with at least a glimmer of opportunity to tell their story. It's in our nature to tell stories. Rich insights and ideas dwell in stories. While I may not seek to elicit a person's entire life story, I am seeking a story that connects them to the topic being discussed.

During 2020, I was undertaking a strategic planning exercise in a small, yet geographically vast, regional municipality in South Australia. This planning process offered an opportunity for specific engagement about a future vision for a foreshore area. We used a range of engagement processes, including township workshops, panel Q&A events on topics ranging from the environment to farming, arts and culture, to jobs and tourism, an online discussion forum, engagement with children from the three schools, and a district-wide household survey. In addition, we decided to use a SpeakOut to focus on foreshore planning.

A SpeakOut is a staffed exhibition that aims to provide an informal and interactive meeting environment where a wide range of people have a chance to participate. It is designed to facilitate structured drop-in participation. The SpeakOut was devised by Wendy Sarkissian and Andrea Cook in 1990 as antidote to the Open House model that seemed to dominate much of participatory planning, especially in Vancouver.[21]

For our foreshore visioning exercise, we held a SpeakOut during the summer school holidays in the middle of the foreshore, on a lush area of lawn next to a popular beach. Our choice of timing aimed to reach people participating in foreshore activities. We were eager to listen to two groups: people who lived in the area and visitors. Thus, we felt that the drop-in format would work well, as it was in the area under discussion and would run in the daytime and into the early evening.

One thing I vividly remember about our SpeakOut was how hot it was: a roasting 40 degrees Celsius, in the shade. We knew this weather was coming and weighed up our options. We had booked a marquee for overhead shade, but could we open up the sides? A difficult decision, to be sure. That would allow for a cooling sea breeze. But what about the impacts on the six issue stalls, each with interactive displays? What if they blew over, or, worse still, injured a small child, or a pet dog. Or something equally harrowing? We could imagine the headlines. However, with the help of the Council's outdoor maintenance team, we decided the risks of cancelling the event far outweighed the risks of going ahead.

We made a bold decision to proceed. Despite the thermometer reaching 37 degrees by midday, people queued to enter the marquee thirty minutes before the start, followed by a steady stream of locals and beachgoers throughout the day. In the end, over 400 people engaged in detailed discussions about their future visions for their foreshore.

The Council's CEO encouraged us to use creative engagement approaches throughout the entire strategic planning process, especially on this particular topic. He had heard mixed messages from the communities about this site. Some locals said they wanted more car parking options. Others wanted more green space. He challenged us to tackle this dilemma at the SpeakOut. Maybe something visual could trigger valuable conversations?

Remembering my days in Matson loading paint into my car boot, I visited hardware stores in search of ideas and resources, emailing photos of Perspex tubes and garden ornaments to the Council team. In the end, the activity consisted of a large piece of plywood from my shed, painted white and marked with two hundred car parking spaces, a basket full of Matchbox cars (purchased second-hand from a ten-year-old boy on Facebook Marketplace), next to a pile of synthetic turf cut up by the Council's Community Outreach team at Council into two hundred small pieces. This interactive activity was a resounding success, as it was a visual voting tool that elicited conversations and allowed for probing by SpeakOut staff. Oh, and as image 9 below shows, green space won the competition by a landslide. The pile of Matchbox cars was barely touched.

Image 9 - More car parking or more green space? That was the question we posed at a SpeakOut, held in a popular beachside destination. Photo by author, 2020.

Wendy and Andrea regularly confide that magic often happens at SpeakOuts. And that's what happened in this project. Amidst the buzz of the SpeakOut interactive issue stalls, with hundreds of people passing through, I was lucky to witness a magical moment. The length of the jetty had always been a contentious issue. I have heard it's not about what you've got, but how you use it. In all seriousness, this jetty is truly short. Many damaging storms have left it, well, a little bit stubby. There is no local agreement about whether it should be longer or stay the same. Some think that extending it would be a waste of taxpayers' money.

Several SpeakOut issue stalls provided opportunities to comment on the jetty length. 'Yes, please give us a longer jetty!' or 'Don't waste money on the jetty!' were typical comments, followed by participants' reasons.

Towards the end of a long, hot and sticky day, the owner of a local holiday home and a well-known leader in wellbeing and resilience in South Australia, wandered into the marquee in her swimwear. She had her beach towel in one hand and her takeaway fish and chips in the other. Her husband hung about, keeping an eye on their grandchild, who was colouring at the kids' table. So, this woman struck up a conversation with one of the Elected Members, who'd just arrived for the final shift staffing one of the issue stalls.

Inevitably, the topic of the length of the jetty came up. The Elected Member explained that he'd never really understood why anyone wanted a longer jetty: 'I mean, you can go fishing off your boat, or elsewhere, and we've installed a pontoon out in the water for the kids to swim out to and jump off. What's the point of having a longer jetty?' In response, the woman launched into an eloquent monologue about the significance of a jetty. She told a story of balmy summer evenings, in other locations, where people would stroll to the foreshore and wander out along the jetty, perhaps with their loved ones, perhaps alone. She spoke of the feeling of calm that you get as you wander outwards along a long jetty, overlooking the calmness of the sea or the waves rolling into the shoreline. She described the distant horizon you stroll towards, yet it never gets closer, and always holds your imagination. And then she described the moment where you reach the end of these long jetties and the sense of separation that you feel from the land you have left, filling you with calmness and more perspective. And how you then turn to look back at the land you came from and feel a calm sense of a different viewpoint, even just for a moment.

To say this was awesome is an understatement.

The Elected Member was speechless. Even I was lost for words. Time stood still while this woman shared her beautiful, detailed story. The Elected Member replied, 'Wow! I really hadn't thought of it like that before. That's such an amazing perspective. Next time this topic comes up in the Council chamber, I'll certainly remember this conversation'.

Wendy and Andrea have repeatedly emphasised that the SpeakOut is designed for this exact sort of occurrence. And I saw it with my own eyes. THIS is community engagement. Here was an elected official stepping out of the comfort zone of the Council chamber and engaging in a rich and diverse conversation about an important local topic. It wasn't a forced conversation, seeking definitive answers, or a survey tallying up random uninformed opinions to create a set of numeric results. It seemed almost accidental, yet the SpeakOut model is designed for these precise interactions: an opportune moment within a highly creative engagement activity. The SpeakOut model fosters these kinds of rich conversations based on sharing stories. These occasions are the absolute pinnacle of authentic community engagement.

That Elected Member would never have 'got' it by reading the results of a survey questionnaire completed by that woman. Her story would never have had the same impact had she made a presentation to a Council meeting on a cold winter's evening. That magical moment happened because two people with a common interest came together informally for a conversation, on location, with sand under their toes, to talk about what was important.

As recent as last week, I was working with a Chief Executive of a state government agency, helping to engage with a regional Australian community in some important conversations to guide the work of his department. The Chief Executive was clearly out of his comfort zone as he arrived in the hot, stuffy community hall (in Australia do the richest processes happen on the hottest days or is it just coincidence?!). But he embraced the situation. After spending a couple of hours in deep dialogue with the six community members present, after the meeting he reflected with me that the process had been absolutely worth the time away from the office, the five-hour round trip drive and overnight stay away from home. Even though six people do not represent an entire community, and in a survey-situation would be thrown out for being an inadequate 'sample' size, the Chief Executive heard a range of different stories and perspectives that opened his mind and inspired his thinking. It's not always about big numbers and bums-on-seats. More often than not, it's about being open to a process of deep listening to hear the stories that people are telling you.

With the same goal of storytelling and idea sharing in mind, in August 2013, I worked with the Office for Design and Architecture in Adelaide to undertake some community engagement as part of a state government decision-making process about the relocation of the Royal Adelaide Hospital. This piece of engagement didn't focus on the new hospital, but instead examined potential uses for the existing, significant central-Adelaide site that would soon be empty when the new hospital opened.

Using the SpeakOut model as a basis, I developed an event called the Open Ideas Marketplace, whereby a series of stations were set up based on the key objectives to be considered. For example, we didn't want people just turning up, giving their ideas, and walking away again. We wanted to take them on a journey of thinking about their idea in relation to the neighbouring parklands; or the use of sustainable design; or the economically viability of their idea; and so each station reflected these themes. In addition to the stations, we set up a video diary room, where an interviewer extracted ideas and stories from members of the public onto film.

My favourite part of the Open Ideas Marketplace, however, was our Speakers Corner. Based on the concept of the famous Speakers Corner in Hyde Park, London (where co-incidentally my maternal grandfather, Jack, would attend during the 1930s as a member of the Church Army, to preach his beliefs to the world), the space, set up in the large atrium entrance of the State Library of South Australia, provided the opportunity for people to hear from a range of speakers who would each share their stories, perspectives, and ideas.

I enjoyed hearing the South Australian Premier at the time, Jay Weatherill, speak at the Corner, but I found even more delight in witnessing him stand amongst the crowd listening to the other speakers, as shown in image 10. Storytelling that enables others to deeply listen and reflect, including key decision makers. This floats my boat. A lot.

Image 10 – An audience gathered at the Speakers Corner, as part of an Open Ideas Marketplace to consider the future land use of the former Royal Adelaide Hospital. The then Premier of South Australia Jay Weatherill can be seen amongst the crowd, standing on the back row, actively listening to people share their stories and ideas . Photo by author, 2013.

And then there is business-as-usual. As usual.

My Council recently invited me to participate in an online survey about a proposed new bike path. The dedicated bike path would be a shared-use path for walkers, runners, and bike users and no doubt for my young family, scooters and baby doll strollers and whatever else we end up dragging from the house. It would join two country townships. I fully supported the proposal and was more than happy to complete the questionnaire. In fact, I was so excited by the proposal I thought I'd use this opportunity to tell them that their initiative had motivated me to get back into running. The idea of being able to jog down the hill from my property, join a dedicated path that meanders through the vines to take me from one country township to the next, inspired me greatly. Even though the bike path is probably years away, I'm starting my training now to be able to make the most of it when it does arrive!

I wanted to let them know my opinions and my passion and to explain that this path has importance well beyond simply connecting A and B. It's about lots more than safely separating bike users and joggers from traffic on busy country roads. It excites me, and it's inspiring the health and wellbeing of their residents! I felt that, in the long term, this inspired initiative would lead to a happier, healthier, and stronger community. I was hot to explain my passion and the knock-on benefits I'd identified.

The online survey did not really accommodate my passion and enthusiasm, but a section at the end offered a spot to make comments. I tapped my enthusiasm into the little text box. My enthusiasm was, of course, met by absolute silence. No energy. Nobody at home. Nobody receiving my passionate explanation. Nobody to nod in agreement, to raise their eyebrows in amazement that I was so enthusiastic about this bike path. Nobody to say, 'Wow, I hadn't thought of it like that'. Or even to thank me for joining the conversation.

When I hit the 'submit' button, all my enthusiasm fell into what I call a 'black hole of bureaucracy'. To be clear: I'm not dismissing the use of online tools. I am dismissing a one-way conversation: conversation that wasn't really a conversation but simply an opportunity for me to 'have my say'. To give my Council some credit, richer conversations had occurred about this bike path with a group of passionate locals who had proposed the idea in the first place. Nevertheless, this widespread and broad-brush 'have-your-say' mentality, has in my opinion, ruined community engagement practice. We've lost the art of conversation.

Have.
Your.
Say.

This catchphrase is the epitome of top-down, organisation-centric, we-are-more-important-than-you-are community engagement. To me, it says *we*, the mighty-powerful-big-boys-and-girls are making the decision and *you*, the little-lesser-important-people, are welcome to have your say on it. Whether we listen or not is for us to decide. Ugh. Whether it's the patronising tone, or simply its overuse in Australia, the expression repulses me.

Wendy comments that often her clients choose this exact catchphrase because they find 'SpeakOut' to be much too 'radical' a term. She says she's explained repeatedly that speaking out in communities is hardly a radical act, but many clients change the name of the process to 'Have Your Say Day', even though they are having SpeakOuts, plain and simple.

Googling 'Have Your Say Day' yields 2,960,000,000 hits!

Jacinta Cubis acknowledges 'Have your say' websites that have no real place to have a *real* say as part of her *Non-engagement Spectrum,*[14] under the heading of 'non-sultation' that was a term coined by Max Hardy and Nicole Endacott.

This is a Have Your Say global pandemic!

So, what's the answer? As a response to the horrid catchphrase, I encourage my clients to use more inclusive terminology such as 'Join the Conversation', if there must be a three-word call to action. But of course, this is a highly complex issue. There is no one simple way to achieve better, deeper, more conversation-based engagement, and it certainly doesn't happen through having the right tag line. Nevertheless, we need to strive to be more creative. And simple conversations are a vehicle that we should embrace as often as we possibly can. As practitioners, we can use innovative and creative methodologies so people can share their stories and contribute to decision-making processes.

There are also larger structural issues related to community engagement that can't be addressed solely by creative, story inspired approaches. A large Council like mine, acting on behalf of 172,000 people, with only 12 people elected to represent us, plus one Mayor, makes deep connection with our various communities quite challenging. One answer is smaller, more intimate, local Councils, where your elected representatives are known within the communities that they serve. This would be a full-circle return to the way they used to be.

However, if we are determined to have large Councils, another approach could be more decentralised decision-making processes, making use of formal residents or business associations feeding into a hub-and-spoke type model.

Regardless of the governance, I would like to see local Councils, and governments in general, being more 'local', and, in turn, more connected to the heartbeats of the communities they serve, providing opportunities for stories to be shared, connections to be made, and communities to thrive. I'd like to see the return of high-quality conversations, where the sharing of stories and active listening are the norm.

Back to the jetty story. Not surprisingly, the final report did not contain an exact record of the conversation between the woman and the Elected Member. I felt it wasn't necessary. The story had such an impact on the Elected Member that he carried it forward in his capacity as a decision maker. I heard that he shared it as *his* story about what he'd heard. He is, after all, the politician and a decision maker. I saw that as a good outcome. And I feel that our SpeakOut allowed the original conversation to take place.

...

Conversation Starters

- **WHO** represents you in your communities? When did you last have the opportunity to tell your story to them? When did you last feel heard by them?
- **WHAT** do you think about small, local government versus bigger, centralised government? What are the pros and cons of each in relation to building thriving communities?
- **WHY** is conversation important? Think about this in relation to your personal relationships, at work, in your communities, as well as with governments.
- **WHEN** did you last have a rich conversation with someone about something important in your local community?

- **WHERE** could you provide opportunity for people to share their stories? At the dinner table? In your next team meeting? At the local market?

7. Use and nurture the Third Sector

The important work of moving the world forward
does not wait to be done by perfect men.

— George Eliot[15]

In the middle of 2005, Dan and I had both returned to the UK from our twelve-month working holiday escapades in Australia. We'd spent a leisurely month exploring Thailand on the way home. Now, 15 years later, juggling life, businesses, and a young family, we look back with absolute disbelief that we managed to spend so much time lying in hammocks, taking long train journeys, hiking through mountains, hanging out in bars, eating amazing food, and having so many massages! Our visas had expired, and it was time to return to the motherland. Our families were excited to have us home, particularly as we'd both set off as single people twelve months before and returned together as a couple. My parents had visited Sydney while we were there and had met Dan, but I hadn't met his parents. Arriving back at Heathrow was a pretty cool 'Love Actually' way of meeting the in-laws.

In those exciting days, we knew we were entering the next chapter, but had no idea what it was. We spent the first few weeks moving between our parents' places (mine in Gloucester and his in Surrey). Life was pretty leisurely, as we explored many options, even possibility running a pub! (I have no recollection of how we funded ourselves during this time.)

Eventually, something like common sense kicked in and we gravitated to London. And I, of course, gravitated towards community. I'd spent time in Sydney and a short spell in Perth, but I had never experienced anything like living in London. London had been a favourite place of mine to visit with my parents, so I had many happy childhood memories of day trips to see shows in the West End, as well as all the usual sights. When I'd attend ballet exams in Richmond, we'd use that as an excuse to spend a few days in our caravan on the outskirts of

London, catching the tube in each day to visit places like Madam Tussauds and the Tower of London. Gloucester is just a two-hour drive west of London, so day trips to the West End were also possible.

We would always start with the bus dropping us off at the Marble Arch end of Oxford Street, where my Mum would delight in the wonders of the huge Marks and Spencers there. My Dad has always been a keen family historian. I remember him using the opportunities of the Big Smoke to visit national records offices on fact-finding missions. At high school and college, we'd have London excursions where all sorts of mischief were made. And in later years, I have great memories of weekends in London with my Gloucester friends, or Laura and I revisiting our Sydney backpacking days by randomly spending nights in hostels near the bright night lights of Leicester Square. However, as with my early days in Australia, I'd generally stick to the tourist hotspots, never really experiencing true city or community life in London.

This chapter of my London journey began early one afternoon, in the grittiest of places for this country bumpkin... underneath the Westway. I made my journey into London from Dan's parents place in Surrey, via the once-a-day village bus, on the overland train at Dorking, and then on the tube from Victoria to Ladbroke Grove. (For those not familiar with London, the Westway is a 2.5-mile elevated dual carriage way section of the extremely busy A40 trunk road, which runs from Paddington to North Kensington.) My job interview took place in an office directly underneath it. Not next to it; directly under it.

A few weeks earlier, I'd been in the calming and cool temples of Chiang Mai and the relaxed beachside bars of Koh Phangan. I can still recall the shock of the intensely repetitive, intense sound clamour of the traffic directly as I walked from the tube station towards the office. It was noisy in the extreme. Vehicles barrelling along above me, with a monotonous *duf-duf* as they went over a bump. Put simply, the huge road was oppressive.

Once inside the building, however, life was quite the opposite. On the interview panel, my soon-to-be colleague and now life-long friend, Aneesa Chaudhry, provided warm, comforting smiles and nods during my interview. One of my favourite memories of working with Aneesa (there are so many) was at a later date when someone dropped into the office unannounced, and they were experiencing deafness. Aneesa rose to the occasion, surprising us all with her fluent sign language. Skilled, responsive, and adaptable – that's the sign of a good engager!

I was interviewed for the position of Development Officer – Health at the Kensington & Chelsea Social Council. You might imagine that this organisation is a social club for Chelsea footballers' wives or rich Kensington toffs. Far from it. It's actually a Council for Voluntary Services: an organisation dedicated to strengthening local voluntary and community organisations.

I had a fairly good idea already that the voluntary sector was pretty big in its own right in the UK. It's often called the *Third Sector* or the not-for-profit sector. The situation is different from that in Australia, where I've noticed that this sector has far less presence or influence. Australians talk a lot about the government or public sector, and the private sector. But organisations with social impact, rather than the provision of public services or generation of profit, tend to fade into the background. Australia places more emphasis on the role of government and business and often ignores the hard work in the incredibly significant third sector. Maybe the difference reflects grassroots activism across the UK during the seventies, whereas here in Australia, with a few uprisings, it's been a relatively smooth journey for many Australians.

I believe that Australia has ignored this sector at its peril. There's a huge gap, particularly in helping government decision-makers reach people with active interests and involvement in particular realms. And what about the role that these organisations' employees could play in advocating for or representing the needs of their diverse communities of interest? In Australia, I've become a broken record when it comes to trying to encourage government clients to engage peak bodies or leaders of community organisations. It doesn't matter what the scale is (a particular project or a broader, ongoing scenario). We never quite hit the mark. At least, not like we used to in my London days.

After I got the job, much of my work focussed on this exact opportunity. I worked regularly with both the Royal Borough of Kensington & Chelsea and the Kensington & Chelsea Primary Care Trust to help them connect with the local voluntary organisations who worked in the health space. I remember many brilliant meetings with the Chairman and Chief Executive of the local Primary Care Trust, usually over cups of tea at the local Café Rouge, with them taking such an active and collaborative interest in how the sectors could work better together. I remember the distinct feeling of them truly valuing the voluntary sector and being willing to work together.

This relationship became even stronger when the commissioning agenda swept across the UK, with a huge move towards the public service commissioning voluntary sector organisations to deliver services on its behalf. While I believe that the UK has now moved further beyond this model, I still occasionally suggest the idea of community organisations being commissioned to deliver services on behalf of the public sector here in Australia. My suggestions are often received with a blank look. I feel like I've just reported that life has been found on Jupiter and we should go there immediately to engage with them.

Kensington was the home of Princess Diana, as well as Sir Richard Branson, Rowan Atkinson, and Robbie Williams. I believe that the neighbourhood of Chelsea was also littered with the rich and famous, including Kylie Minogue, Eric Clapton and in previous years, Freddie Mercury. We had the wealthy shopping streets of Kensington High Street in the middle of the borough, with the famous shopping precinct of Kings Road to the south. Towards the northern end of the borough was the world-famous Portobello Road market, made even more famous being the location for the film *Notting Hill* with Hugh Grant and Julia Roberts. The borough was neighbour to Knightsbridge, meaning a quick pop to Harrods during my lunch break was totally possible. My credit card had quite a workout during those years.

On face value, from a health perspective, you might assume that the London Borough of Kensington & Chelsea is thriving. Yet the borough's champagne lifestyle reputation often over-shadowed the realities of life for many 'real' people living here. The lifestyles of the rich and famous, the shops, the palaces: that's the image. Step off that beaten track of glitz and glamour and expensive houses, and you hear a very a different story. Never had I heard such huge differences in the average age of life expectancy within one borough. In 2006, life expectancy was said to differ by up to 18 years from one postcode to another, within the same relatively small borough.

In Chelsea, just off the famous Kings Road, was World's End. With a history of slums back in the Victorian era, now seven huge red-brick brutalist tower blocks housed over 750 Council homes. Their location on the edge of the River Thames is enviable and they overlook neighbouring homes worth millions of pounds. However, the dense living conditions, crime, gangs and poverty is far from life in the rest of Chelsea – or Chelsea's image. At the opposite end of the borough is the Dalgarno estate, a 1930s dense, red brick social housing estate that also faces 'ghetto' status, with high poverty and crime rates, particularly among its younger residents.

Being a long, thin borough, squeezed into the Greater London landscape, we would continually have to monitor that our work involved working together with organisations from both the north and the south. Image 11 shows former Chair of the Social Council, Robin Tuck, arriving at an event and being asked to place a sticky dot on the postcode area in which he lived. I'm not sure why I had a palm tree at the top of our borough – I suspect it was my humour alluding to us being an island in the sea! Who knows!

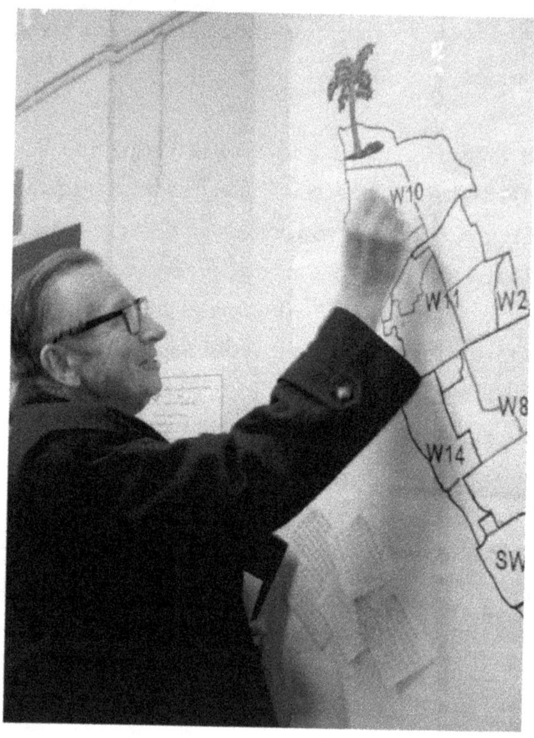

Image 11 – Former Chair of the Kensington and Chelsea Social Council, Robin Tuck, participating in one of the arrival activities to keep tabs on postcode participation in the borough. Photo by author, 2006.

One building that always fascinated me was the Trellick Tower in the Cheltenham Estate, shown on the cover of this book. I loved its tall, thin, dominance over the neighbourhood, as well as its quirky brutalist architecture with a separate lift and service tower. Overlooking the Westway, this tower block of high-rise apartments, while still maintaining a high proportion of social housing, had become a desirable place to live (with high demand for private flats). I would walk below it, straining my neck looking up, absorbed in daydreaming about all of the balconies, each telling a different story about the people who lived there. With my fascination of communities of place, I wondered whether the people who lived there interacted much as a community or whether being surrounded by so many people provided the opposite effect of a sense of belonging.

Why did they choose to live in such a tower? Did they choose to live there, or was it the only option? What were the demographics of the residents? Did parents worry about their children climbing on the balconies? Did older residents feel isolated, or appreciate the perspective that the view gave them? Did the people below know the people above? Did the residents leave notes for each other in the lifts? My busy mind, always fascinated.

Also within the borough was the ill-fated Grenfell Tower, which was destroyed in June 2017 by a fire that ravaged the building at great speed, leading to the tragic deaths of 72 people. In response to this terrifying fire, the Social Council committed to focussing on grass-roots community development to enable them to work more closely with residents alongside their voluntary sector colleagues.

When I arrived in 2005, it was clear that there was a lot of work to be done in Kensington & Chelsea to address the health inequalities I've described. My work focussed primarily on strengthening and supporting the voluntary organisations working across the borough. A standout memory of my work in the borough of Kensington & Chelsea, which turned into a powerful lesson, was about the strengths that you can achieve by working together – across all sectors for the common good.

The team at the Kensington & Chelsea Social Council worked tirelessly to support a brilliant governance model that consisted of several Voluntary Organisations Forums (VOF). These forums were open to all voluntary and community organisations that worked in or served the borough. They ensured that a diverse collective of people could discuss the key issues affecting the community. It was a busy time and the VOFs provided grist to the mill. A day didn't go by where a colleague wasn't dashing off to their allocated 'VOF' to provide critical support in facilitating conversations, addressing current local issues, or coordinating the planning of future work.

My allocated 'VOF' was on the topic of older people, not surprisingly, because of its close connection to community health. I remember the diversity of the membership – ranging from the Council and the Primary Care Trust as the public sector, through to Age Concern and the Citizen's Advice Bureau as larger voluntary organisations, with numerous other smaller organisations (migrant resource groups, or residents' groups) that worked directly with older people. These VOFs were open to any organisation who felt they would benefit from attending. I valued the open, transparent way of connecting likeminded organisations to be strategic in providing the best possible solutions for the borough's older people. I approved that decisions were in the hands of the people and not in the hands of us, the Council, or the Primary Care Trust. I loved that members set the monthly agendas. I loved that the forums operated under an ongoing model of engagement, rather than on a project-by-project basis. I just loved this work and valued the model that supported it.

I had experienced community-centric collaborative approaches before, not just through partnerships such as the Gloucestershire Food in Schools Group, but also through the Matson Forum, where there would be a monthly meeting between representatives of the Neighbourhood Project, Housing Association, Council, Police and more, all working together on an ongoing basis for the betterment of the support provided to that community. During those early days of my career, this kind of collaborative working was the norm.

Everything included in the meetings was an eye-opener to me. They would include discussions on current issues affecting service users or organisations, news and updates of local happenings, expert contributions via presentations, and opportunities to influence decision making. Sometimes the meetings would be massive – 20 or 30 people attending – but they would always be physically set up at one large table, ensuring that everyone had an equal voice.

Another part of my work involved being an active member of the Black & Minority Ethnic (BME) Forum, a well-established partnership between voluntary and community organisations, healthcare providers, commissioners, and local authorities. The work of this collective aimed to improve the quality of health and social care services specifically for people from deprived backgrounds living in West London. Again, with a huge and massively engaged membership, this forum met four times a year to promote ongoing, two-way communication between the National Health Service and the BME community sector. This structure meant that the forum could easily disseminate information about services, events, funding, or changes in policy, and facilitate involvement in decision-making as required.

In 2019, I caught up with members of the team I was a part of at the Kensington & Chelsea Social Council during a visit to London. We reflected on our pride in the advocacy and support role we collectively provided to the voluntary organisations who worked tirelessly across the borough. Each of us, in this incredible group of young professionals, contributed our unique skill set and personality, but shared common values of equity, giving people a voice, and bringing people together to achieve good outcomes. All these people became my friends, and all have moved on to different roles for different organisations, in different parts of the world. And we shared something remarkable: having been open to the opportunities that the late-nineties UK social inclusion agenda in those powerful years at the turn of the new century.

These days, when you hear me talking about 'having the right people at the table', I'm fantasising about the days of my involvement in the voluntary sector of Kensington & Chelsea. It wasn't a fantasy then. It was real. We did it tirelessly, every day. It worked. And we always knew without a shadow of doubt that, that the right people were at the table.

I would love to see more emphasis being placed on communities leading their own agendas, through the creation and nurturing of voluntary organisations, and less call for the government sector to do everything for us.

The world needs more of this kind of ongoing, collaboration across all sectors – driven from the bottom, up. Project-by-project community engagement isn't sustainable. And in our modern world we need that even more than we did in our heady days in Kensington & Chelsea.

...

Conversation Starters

- **WHO** is missing from your decision-making table? Who would add value, insight and perspective that isn't currently there?

- **WHAT** is your experience of the 'third sector'? What role does it play in your work or community life?
- **WHY** is community engagement so often delivered on a project-by-project basis and not seen as a more ongoing philosophy?
- **WHEN** did you last bring together a group of people who share different perspectives to work towards one common goal?
- **WHERE** fascinates you? Why?

8. Go where the people are

For a community to be whole and healthy,
it must be based on people's love and concern for each other.

— Millard Fuller[16]

I'd dabbled with smoking throughout my teenage years, and for some reason (possibly rebellion), took it up again during my backpacking days in Australia, thankfully quitting before I became addicted. I'd also dabbled in smoking cessation during my early career, establishing the Living & Learning Centre in Gloucester, working in partnership with Stop Smoking Advisors from the West Gloucestershire Primary Care Trust. I guess I'm your typical dual-sided Gemini – happy to egg you on to have a quick cigarette together, but equally happy to help you stop.

Now I had to choose sides. It was my turn to help people break the habit. And I was excited to embrace this new challenge. The Camden Primary Care Trust wanted to try something different from the standard smoking cessation service. To begin with, commuting to Camden from our tiny flat in Chiswick was full-on. Camden is such a fabulously edgy place, hugely different from the leafy suburbs of Kensington & Chelsea. I caught the most horrendous flu during my first week commuting on the tube to Camden. My first couple of weeks of my new job I spent bedridden on sick leave. What had I done?! The Northern Line had hardcore germs!

Camden Primary Care Trust worked out that some significant minority populations in the Borough were heavy smokers. Like *really* heavy smokers. And lots of them. My new nine-month contract was to apply my community know-how to address inequalities in access to smoking cessation services. The Bangladeshi community, a significant proportion of Camden's population, had a shockingly high percentage of its male population as smokers, compared to the national average. And further, within the Borough was a large Irish population that also scored very high on the smoking spectrum (for both men and women).

The support services were there, as they had been for years, in their predictable, 'mainstream' way. These were the days where smoking cessation services were well funded, with call centres, access to Stop Smoking Advisors, and all the trimmings. But these services were offered in conventional settings that required a visit to a mainstream healthcare setting, such as a GP surgery, a local hospital, or a healthcare centre. For a variety of cultural, social and other reasons, the people we were targeting were not lining up for these services.

We needed a more targeted and tailored approach. Immersion was the answer for me in the short term. Again! I needed to immerse myself in the community to observe, learn, and make connections. I was excited about this challenge because, I was setting off on an expedition: a fact-finding mission about specific groups of people living within a particular place. A place I knew nothing about.

The area of Kilburn, in north west London, became a hub for the Irish community from the mid-twentieth century onwards. Irish migrants coming to London for work were seeking a home away from home. I worked out that when groups of migrants or people with a particular connection or common interest live together, we see a very real example of people needing a sense of belonging. Communities of commonality seek (and achieve) belonging by seeking each other out and coexisting within a community of place.

Here in South Australia, we have suburbs with huge Italian and Greek communities, as well as areas with a high concentration of Vietnamese people. Here, in regional areas we now see even more diversity. People are moving to country towns for employment opportunities, often at large food-processing plants or other large-scale employers. Mass migrations of English-born folk moved to places like the suburb of Elizabeth in the north of Adelaide (in response to South Australian government migration policies in the UK) and to Hallett Cove in the south.

Being English-born, I often laugh that a visit to the Foodland supermarket in Hallett Cove is like being in Yorkshire. Oh, those familiar accents! Interestingly, as English migrants, we chose to live an hour south of Adelaide in McLaren Vale. We were seeking 'Australia': the quintessential Australian lifestyle of food, wine, and beaches. I think we consciously avoided those 'pom' hotspots. When we migrated, we wanted the full Australian experience. We wanted to move beyond our comfort zones.

Surprisingly, we ended up living in a township experiencing a massive influx of people just like us. So, my example isn't so much about seeking that sense of belonging as about communities that form out of similar interests, opportunity seeking, choices, or perhaps even coincidence. As I'd heard about the Irish hotspot of Kilburn, I decided to see what I could learn about it, and critically, how I might connect to provide stop-smoking support services.

We didn't need a car in London, as public transport was accessible and affordable. We were young and spritely, so we loved exploring the city on foot. On my way to Kilburn on the bus, I'd remind myself that my first activity should be simply to wander around, looking out for any connections to the Irish community. On reflection, that was like suggesting a drive through the McLaren Vale wine region looking for grapevines. Kilburn did not disappoint. I was delighted to discover that I had entered Little Ireland.

And the Kilburn High Road quickly revealed that Kilburn was home to much more than the Irish community. This was place with multicultural people and multicultural businesses. It was easy for me to work out how to connect with the people I was looking for: places where Irish people (specifically, Irish smokers) regularly hung out. My first stop was the Sacred Heart Church. It felt like an episode of *Father Ted*. To find where Irish people go, en masse? It's the local Catholic Church! Now, clearly not all Irish people repent their sins in church. But for me, young and enthusiastic, working out this basic principle of life in Kilburn was like striking gold. I had found a door into this community.

Inside the church, I saw quiet worshippers coming and going, but no sign of the priest. Maybe it was best to send a short email introducing myself. He might think me weird if I approached him at the altar, whispering my question about whether many of his parishioners smoked. I was delighted to receive a prompt reply from Father Ray. Yes, not surprisingly, many parishioners did smoke. Some had already shown an interest in trying to stop. He loved the idea of working together to devise a solution.

In 2006, my project was part of a huge national push to reduce smoking in the UK. A nationwide smoking ban on 1 July 2007 would make it illegal to smoke in all enclosed workplaces. This meant that smoking, or more fittingly, *not* smoking, was on people's minds, particularly in communities with significantly high smoking rates. Father Ray and I met over a cup of tea in the church office. The luck of the Irish must have been in full flow as he was so incredibly supportive. We decided that I would establish a Stop Smoking support group in a small room at the back of the church, on a Thursday morning after the Morning Prayer service. Even better, he'd promote it during his sermon.

Astonishingly, our plan worked well, of course it did, because we were going to where the people already were, offering a support service they wanted, with the full backing of their leader, the priest. I began my weekly sessions with the group of parishioners and before long they were fully knowledgeable about the preparation required to quit, had received prescriptions for Nicotine Replacement Therapy, and were ready to support each other moving forward.

It's important to note here that I'm not a churchgoer. But in working with communities, I've learned that it is important that my work isn't about *me*. Instead, it is about the people I am working with. It is about going to where *they* are at, whether I agree with their beliefs or not.

During my walk about Kilburn, I'd also noticed the bingo hall. And now that I was in weekly contact with local parishioners, I was also learning about the area's vices. For any readers not familiar with bingo, it involves players marking off numbers on their cards as they're drawn at random by a caller, with the winner of the cash prize being the first person to mark off all their numbers. Once an incredibly popular game in the UK, particularly amongst older people, these often-old-fashioned venues declined rapidly in popularity and many have now closed. The bingo hall on Kilburn High Road is no exception.

The pending smoking ban was a great concern to both the management and patrons of the bingo hall. On my initial visit, I could see that smoking was a large part of the culture. The large high-ceilinged auditorium of this former cinema building was filled with smoke, pluming up from the cigarettes of eager bingo enthusiasts. Patrons would often spend full days there, addicted to the promise of winning, either in the bingo in the main hall, or from the fruit machines (known as pokies in Australia) in the lobby. Because of their high nicotine content, smoking cigarettes is highly addictive. I had a problem on my hands. Even I could see that it wasn't going to be a simple case of allowing smoking the one day and banning it the next.

Learning from my successes with the priest, I met with the bingo hall manager and we discussed options. As luck would again have it, he had already chatted with some of his regular patrons and they felt that offering a Stop Smoking support group would be a great idea. So we followed exactly the same format that has worked with the church. The Bingo Caller would announce the support group during his equivalent of the sermon, and the congregation would make their way to the side room after their game had finished to participate in the group 'Quit & Win' session, facilitated by me.

Returning to the bingo hall week after week was an introduction to a whole new world. I had to leave my 'expert' self at home. This was not an environment for a prompt-starting expert to preach messaging around how you're more than likely to die of a horrid, slow and painful smoking related disease, unless you quit right away. Not in a million years. I needed to bring another self. And I did. This work needed relaxed, non-judgemental Becky. This work needed me to be their friend, not their health professional. It needed me to understand that the woman joining the group after sitting at the fruit machine for hours, emptying her purse of her entire week's budget, would not attend until that machine paid out (assuming it would pay out).

Now I must watch, listen, and learn, witnessing first-hand the real-life struggle in the journey to quit smoking. The week before, the group would have reached their quit date and shared their last cigarette. Yet, the next week I'd see them playing their game before our support session, casually smoking as they crossed off the numbers. I learned that it was more than simply a case of replacing the addictive nicotine that their bodies craved. It was also deeply rooted habit and culture of smoking. Hard to be part of and hard to leave at the same time.

While this book is not about addiction or therapy, my Kilburn experience offered some dramatic lessons in listening and not judging. It taught me the importance of taking time to witness, to respect people's individual circumstances and viewpoints, and to try to understand. For the NHS to succeed in reducing smoking in any population, a tailored, empathic approach would be needed. This insight applies to community engagement, regardless of the topic.

I was getting on with my work in Kilburn and had a nodding acquaintance with many folks in the Catholic Church and the bingo hall. I was almost a fully-fledged local. Soon, another location that caught my eye: Conway House, a hostel facility providing shelter and support services specifically for Irish men facing homelessness. Again, Father Ray (my gatekeeper) conducted the appropriate introductions and before I knew it, we'd set up one-to-one support services at the hostel. While I'm a firm believer that quitting smoking is probably the last thing on your mind when you are facing homelessness (connecting back to what I'd previously learned about Maslow and his theory of needs being a complex layered system), I was surprised at the popularity of the inhouse service and as shown in the image opposite, the initiative attracted the attention of the national Irish media.

I learned lots of lessons from my time working with the Irish community of Kilburn and surrounds. Distilled into one lesson, it was definitely about the power of going to where people already are.

Irish community gets help to quit smoking

BY **NIAMH HENNESSY**

IRISH smokers in London are kicking the habit — with one quitter even saving for a holiday with the money she's saving.

The quitters are members of support groups which have been established in Kilburn, West Hampstead and Fortune Green to help Irish people who want to stop.

The groups have been established at a significant time considering a smoking ban like the one in place in Ireland will be implemented in Britain next year.

The NHS-run Camden Primary Care Trust is running two support groups in Kilburn to help smokers quit. Support is offered in group and one-to-one sessions. One of the groups will be held at the Sacred Heart of Jesus Church on Quex Road.

Community Stop Smoking Advisor Becky Hirst said: "This group hopes to attract the congregation and also parents who have children at the neighbouring schools. Fr Raymond Warren will be promoting the support groups through his sermons and community connections."

Becky has been recruited to work as part of a smoke-free team in Kilburn for the next seven months and hopes that after this she can continue her work in other areas.

She said: "I am very excited to be running these two new local support groups. Stopping smoking can be very hard to do but by attending our group sessions smokers' chances of quitting will be four times more likely than trying to quit on their own."

One quitter who wished to remain anonymous said: "I wasn't sure whether the group would be right for me but once I came along and met the other people I felt much happier.

"Having the support of everyone here along with the patches and gum made it much easier to quit."

Another added: "The best thing has been meeting the other group members and finding out how they have been getting on. I also loved having my carbon monoxide reading taken each week — it really motivated me to stop!

"It has really helped having the patches. It was especially good that they were on prescription so I got them free. I'm saving the money I would have spent on smoking and have £100 after just three weeks."

■ **KICKING THE HABIT:** Fr Raymond Warren, Becky Hirst and John Gleason of Conway Hous in Kilburn.

According to research over one in three Irish people smoke compared with just over one in four of the general population.

Over 2,000 people live in the Kilburn, West Hampstead and Fortune Green areas which according to the NHS means very high numbers of smokers.

The specialised groups run for an hour a week for seven weeks. The first two weeks focus on helping members prepare to stop smoking and everyone stops together in the third week. The following sessions help them to stay stopped and the groups are open to all smokers who wish to quit.

■ **For more information smokers should contact the Stop Smoking Service on freephone 0800 10 70 401.**

Image 12 - Working together with the local priest to support Irish smokers in the community, The Irish Post. 16 December 2006.

...

Conversation Starters

- **WHO** are you specifically trying to work with in the community? Be specific.
- **WHAT** steps can you take to find out more about the people within a particular community?
- **WHY** is empathy so important in community engagement?
- **WHEN** have you put your own beliefs aside to work neutrally with a group of people on something that is important to them?
- **WHERE** do the people you are trying to work with already go? Where do they feel safe?

9. Work together with key influencers and community leaders

How we behave matters because within human society everything is contagious — sadness and anger, yes, but also patience and generosity. Which means we all have more influence than we realize. No matter who you are, or where you are, or how mundane or tough your situation may seem, I believe you can illuminate your world.

— Elizabeth Gilbert[17]

Having grown up in the rugby town of Gloucester, I can spot a rugby club a mile off. As I was taking London's Irish population by storm with my quit-smoking support initiatives, I noticed that they had their very own rugby team. Reaching a target demographic had never felt easier. I guess when I'm on a roll… with the church onboard… and the bingo hall… and the men's hostel… I might as well get the rugby club involved. I kinda left no stone unturned.

London Irish Rugby Football Club warmly welcomed me. I soon learned that clubs generally have a commitment to Corporate Social Responsibility (CSR). Further, they loved the positive health messaging of the local community's support to stop smoking initiative. On National No Smoking Day, the second Wednesday in March, as shown in image 13 overleaf, I hung out with a few London Irish Rugby players on Kilburn High Road to promote local support services. You can imagine the popularity of this initiative with local rugby-loving Irish and passers-by in general. We had a huge amount of fun, resulting in great awareness raising. In that banner year (2007), I learned about the power of working with key influencers to reach a target demographic. But my lessons didn't stop with the Irish. Not by a long shot.

Image 13 - National No Smoking Day, working with members of the London Irish Rugby team on Kilburn High Road. Photo by author, 2007.

As I mentioned, the Bangladeshi community makes up a significant proportion of Camden's population. And it had a shockingly high percentage of its male population as smokers, compared to the national average. My brief extended to this community targeting stop smoking support services. Like Irish people in Kilburn, members of the Bangladeshi community were scattered across London, but were highly concentrated in specific neighbourhoods. I remember my boss, Katherine, a brilliant Australian public health specialist who was enjoying life in London, turning to me in the office and saying (in her beautiful Aussie accent): 'Becky, we should really go to Drummond Street for lunch to start our research about this particular community…' And lunch we did.

Drummond Street is lined with Indian and Bangladeshi restaurants and shops. So an all-you-can-eat Bengali buffet lunch went without saying. All in the name of research!

This lunch performed two essential tasks in my young life. First, it led to my sensational discovery of the use of paneer cheese in curry. That was a gastronomic milestone, to be sure. But even more important, it marked the start of one of my favourite projects. During lunch, Katherine and I were introduced to some restaurant owners by a member of the Primary Care Trust's health promotion team, who was, rather conveniently a member of the Bengali community. As you can imagine, introductions within this tight-knit community were critical to the success of any engagement venture.

With all the restaurants located so close to each other, a strong network of owners and waiting staff could easily be accessed for our mission. As the upcoming smoking ban would directly affect their restaurants (indoor smoking would be prohibited), owners and managers were eager to find solutions that would help both their staff and patrons adapt to the new world. A fairly quick solution emerged: a group of male Bengali waiters volunteered to be trained as stop smoking advisors. It was a dream come true. Imagine informed and up-to-date waiters offering their colleagues and customers reliable information about stopping smoking. As is often the case, however, the Bengali smoking campaign was being fought on a gendered landscape. There were massive power imbalances between men and women within that community. It was clear to me from the start that the restaurant owners and staff were all men. Further research revealed, of course, the massive inequities in terms of women's education and employment. In addition, there was a strict system of religious personal laws that restricted women's decision-making freedom in the public realm.

I had to leave my opinions on gender inequity at home and get on with this job. It was to work out how we could most effectively target the stop smoking support services to the highest smokers in this community. The Bangladeshi women had issues of their own in relation to tobacco, with many addicted to chewing it. However, in this instance, my job was to respect the demographics and tackle the male smokers. My Kilburn triumphs with the church and the bingo hall just wouldn't cut it here. I was a white, western woman. No question about that. I could not visit a mosque, much less run a stop smoking session there. I knew as a white woman, I must tread carefully. How do I even broach the subject of our work with this community?

However, we had made a good start with the introductions at our first lunch on Drummond Street. So I suggested establishing a working group to include local community leaders from within the Bangladeshi community. Let me rephrase that: I had the idea, and then it was put forward to the leaders via the *male* Bangladeshi health promotion team member, who had made the initial introductions, being careful not to overstep my place in this game of power imbalance. I had to manage both myself and the situation very carefully and give regard to the cultural and social norms of this community. I didn't have the experience, the time or the opportunity to challenge those cultural norms. But trust me, I had the inclination!

Amazingly, the community welcomed my suggestions to work together. We formed a working group, and I was invited to attend. Before I knew it, the community leaders' group was coming up with all manner of ideas for helping their fellow Bengali men quit smoking. And they had specific advice for government which I had to pass on. If the NHS was genuinely sincere about helping their community members stop smoking, they needed to provide culturally appropriate services. That meant, for a start, translation of stop smoking resources. However, the men were quick to point out that many older men were unlikely to read Bengali. Support services should include a male Bengali-speaking advisor. Katherine leapt at that precise recommendation (she was a true doer – a great boss). She allocated some spare funds, and presto, only a month or two later, I was working with a working group of male Bangladeshi community leaders *and* a paid male Bengali-speaking stop smoking advisor.

The working group then began exploring how to encourage Bangladeshi men to engage with the available support. On the one hand, the men knew that smoking was bad for them and soon it was going to be harder to smoke in many of their favourite places. Nevertheless, my advisors felt that many would not be motivated to attend the local health centre and meet with the advisor. It was a dilemma. Even a 'wicked problem'.

As we mulled over our dilemma, I remember one of the men suddenly blurting out, 'Well, we like badminton!' and we all stared at him, puzzled. He went on: 'How about we get the men along for a badminton tournament and when they're there, they could get help in giving up smoking?' Genius! All heads nodded. I was given the task of making it happen. This hot tip was inside knowledge I would never have known. It emerged after a long chain of events, including being introduced to leaders from this community and providing space and time to brainstorm. I'd found the equivalent of bingo for the Bangladeshi community.

I immediately set to work, feeling that such a brilliant idea needed immediate implementation. And also, time was of the essence. I contacted the local community centre that housed a badminton court and booked it every Wednesday morning for a seven-week period. That was long enough to run a group stop smoking program alongside a badminton tournament. In typical Becky style, I mulled over some plays on words. The working group loved my title for the initiative: *Quit & Get Fit.*

To promote the sessions, community leaders in the working group helped spread the word, and (as we had done with the Catholic Church in Kilburn), leaders also ensured the promotional assistance of the mosques. The leaders also led me to Channel S, apparently the most popular Bengali channel outside of Bangladesh, broadcasting across the UK and Europe. I wasn't sure what to expect when I arrived at their studios in Walthamstow, but I was warmly welcomed. The Channel S staff embraced with excitement my fresh broadcasting content, shown in image 14. My Bengali TV debut had me talking about the project. Some of the men who attended the Quit & Get fit sessions said they'd seen me on TV. That made my day!

Image 14 - Making my debut on Channel S, reaching out to London's Bangladeshi community. Photo owned by author, 2007.

It had been a wild ride. My contract came to an end at the Camden Primary Care Trust, and I had only a couple of months before Dan I would emigrate to Australia.

...

Conversation Starters

- **WHO** has significant influence in your communities? Who is well networked? Who holds critical knowledge that you could tap into? Who can introduce you to the right people?
- **WHAT** is different about the community or communities you work with to the community you live in?
- **WHY** do we so often assume that leaders in our communities are simply the people who have been voted to make decisions via the political system?
- **WHEN** have you been a leader in your own community?
- **WHERE** do the people in your communities get their news and information from? Is there a specific website, local newsletter, social media or TV channel that they tune into?

10. Use engagement to strengthen communities

Do not judge me by my success, judge me by how many times I fell down and got back up again.

— Nelson Mandela[18]

Our two years spent living and working in the metropolis of London were quite a journey. We became accustomed to having everything on our doorstep, including incredible shopping, being able to get around so easily without owning a car, discovering hidden gems, rich diversity, and more. However, I struggled with the fast-paced city life. It was not so much the speed of life but the anonymity of people bustling around me. I remembered our first few weeks living in London, catching the tube from Gunnersbury station to Kensington High Street station on workdays, flabbergasted that hundreds of passengers were onboard at any moment, yet not one person would make eye contact. Everyone had their heads buried in their newspapers (now it would be mobile phones). I craved connection with another human being, but this was a rarity on the underground. When I think of communities, and the way all facets interact with each other, as in a game of *Sim City*, living in a large city like London revealed some shocking insights. People within that community of place go about their days in an almost robot-like fashion, programmed to get to where they need to be, as directly as possible and with as little human interaction as possible.

I felt that way until one of the strangest mornings of my life, specifically Thursday 7 July 2005. My brother Richard had stayed with us overnight, visiting London from Yorkshire to attend a teaching conference at Russell Square. We'd somewhat overindulged in red wine the night before and all three of us were nursing sore heads. Dan was working from home that day and he kindly packed bacon sandwiches for my brother and me as we set off for our working days in the City. We wandered along to Gunnersbury tube station to catch the District

Line, and after a short journey with standing room only, I said goodbye to Richard as he changed onto the Piccadilly line towards Russell Square.

After a short while, my underground train came to a standstill. This was a pretty normal occurrence, but on this occasion after about ten minutes, the train hadn't moved from the tunnel. I was starting to feel hot and slightly claustrophobic with the aroma of the bacon sandwich wafting up from my bag at my feet. I slipped my jacket off and held it under one arm. My other arm waited patiently for the train to start moving again when I would grab the rail above my head to keep my balance. But it didn't start up again, not for at least another ten minutes or so. Meanwhile, the robotic commuters kept their heads buried in their newspapers, seemingly avoiding the awful awkward silence throughout the carriage, as we all wondered what was going on.

Eventually the driver made an announcement over the loudspeaker, explaining that we would be moving shortly. Before long, I was disembarking at my stop. As I walked through Kensington High Street station, slightly puzzled by such a delay, I saw a handwritten Transport for London whiteboard explaining that there had been a network-wide power cut and there were delays across all lines. I'd never heard of such a thing before. But I walked to my office. As I arrived at work, none of my team had arrived, as all of them would have experienced delays. I tried to call my brother but couldn't get through.

Then my phone rang. It was Dan calling from home. 'Have you seen the news?' he asked hastily. 'There's been a bomb. On the tube. You should check your brother is OK'.

I hung up immediately and tried Richard again. Still nothing, so I switched on my computer and looked up the news. Just before 8.50 am, three bombs had gone off on trains that had departed Kings Cross station, one on the Piccadilly Line between Kings Cross and Russell Square. As I stood alone in the office, my heart sunk. This explained the delays, and now Richard was somewhere out there on the tube network. I gasped for breath. I didn't know where and I couldn't get hold of him. I remember having trouble dialling as I was shaking so much. I called my parents in Gloucester. I told them that the last I had seen of Richard was as he was heading in the direction of where one of the bombs had exploded.

By about 9.50 am, all mobile phone networks were now down. Trying to do something useful, I studied the tube map and comforted myself that Richard was unlikely to be on one of the bombed trains. I was happy with my hopeful imagination that he'd been evacuated from his tube and was safely above ground at Russell Square. Then my phone rang, and it was Dan again. 'There's been another bomb. They've blown up a double-decker bus now. It was at Tavistock Square which is close to Russell Square station'.

I spent several more hours alone at the office, unable to reach by brother. The live newsfeed via my computer showed unimaginable damage. Already there were reports of many lives lost and hundreds of people injured. I waited in agony until I heard the good news. Richard finally managed to call his wife at work in Yorkshire from a payphone in Kings Cross. He was safe. I was overwhelmed by relief and also shattered by the horror that had occurred.

By afternoon, we were assured it was safe to go outside. But even though buses were running again, many Londoners walked home that afternoon. As I began my four-mile journey by foot, Richard boarded his National Rail service home to Yorkshire. We later discovered that Germaine Lindsay, the 24-year-old man who detonated the bomb on the tube line Richard was on, killing 26 people, was a pupil of Richard's at Rawthorpe High School, a few years earlier.

I share this story because of what I saw in the ensuing hours and weeks. I saw a community change. People who had been going about their daily commute in an almost computerised fashion seemed like different people, exchanging glances, smiles and even hugs. During the days and weeks that followed, I saw a warmer, more compassionate side of London life. Crowds gathered at key locations for memorial services and commuters, in particular, appeared to be more alive, less robotic, and appeared to be much more aware of their surroundings.

Two weeks later, another four men attempted to set off homemade bombs across the London transport network. Thankfully, none detonated properly, and no one was injured. Two men were arrested in a flat in Dalgarno Gardens, north of the Borough of Kensington and Chelsea where I was currently working. That event shocked that community. Sadly, the new 'human' community did not last long.

But equally while I observed a shaken and seemingly more human community, the London community bounced back. Travelling on the underground today is probably as impersonal as ever. During this time in London my passion for community resilience evolved.

Community resilience is about a community having the ability to respond to, withstand, and recover from adverse situations. Adverse situations might include things like bushfires, earthquakes, hurricanes, terrorist attacks, health pandemics, or societal or economic collapse. For a community to be able to respond to and recover from such disasters, certain fundamental things must be in place, such as a capacity for self-organising, social connectedness, empowerment, the understanding of risks and uncertainty, effective communication, and more.

I'm a huge fan of Facebook, and more so Facebook groups in local communities. On a day-to-day basis, they provide a forum for sharing local gossip or lost dog sightings. However, in the event of an adverse situation, they are a pre-existing communication tool that many communities have already self-organised. I established my local community Facebook group for this exact reason. On an average day, posts are relatively mundane, but in the event of a local bushfire, it's an instant way to communicate to those residents of that community of place. Not only does it provide an instant way to reach a number of local people, but also over the years it's been building relationships within the community. The names are familiar. We recognise the local Country Fire Service volunteers who post in the group, we know the owners of the such-and-such vineyard down the road. We are connected before disaster strikes and can therefore respond to and recover from disaster. Of course, not everyone uses Facebook. But this is a simple example of a basic community connection tool that is a valuable one in the disaster toolkit.

Recently my family participated in *Clean Up Australia* day in our local area. After a morning of picking up copious amounts of litter with tongs, building an impressive list of randomly discarded items found in the roadside verges, an environmentally conscious friend pointed out to me that for her, every day is about picking up litter. Not just one day of the year. Of course, I agreed. But for me these kinds of initiatives are about *way* more than the litter. They are even more than the collective impact that can be made by working together. Our local event had been organised by a family who'd recently moved to the area, knew nobody and wanted to meet other likeminded souls. It was about connectivity.

My brother lives on a very connected street in West Yorkshire. They use a What's App group to connect. Admittedly, their group formed as a response to the adverse situation of the Covid-19 global health pandemic, with them planning socially distanced street activities during lockdown. Now they have a platform on which to easily connect, if necessary, in the future. The simple concept of knowing your neighbours is a powerful resource and a rich commodity.

With my passion for connectivity as a tool for resilience in mind, I've been mindful that when governments are working with communities to seek their contributions in decision making, an opportunity to build resilience always presents itself. Recently, I was conducting a series of Township Forums for a regional Council across their district. We were gathering contributions for their strategic plan. My favourite moments of the whole process weren't actually gathering ideas for the future, but in seeing the ways that people connect. In one particular township, a resident described her desire for a community garden. Another participant put up his hand from across the room and announced he had some land he would like to use for a community garden. And they connected. And started the ball rolling about how they could work together to make both of their community garden dreams come true.

The same thing happened during a meeting I was facilitating for a Council in the northern suburbs of Adelaide. Again, it seemed like synchronicity. One participant said she was struggling to access support around a particular health need. Then another spoke up saying he could help her, as he had some knowledge in that area. They swapped numbers and made the connection. Fostering these outcomes was not our specific intention for the engagement activity. They were unintended outcomes. They showed us something about people's desires to cooperate. And they offered significant potential for strengthening that community into the future.

As community engagement practitioners, we have a duty to do more than simply descend on a community to extract their 'input'. Or to dig out what we want or need for a decision to be made by our client, our employer, or the project team. Instead, as lovers of community, we have a lot more to do and our work has a greater potential than we may ever realise. We have a bigger responsibility in using engagement as an opportunity to strengthen and build community capacity. We may never know exactly what the results are or where that work eventually leads. But when we are present and principled in our practice, I believe that our work inevitably leads to better futures for communities.

...

Conversation Starters

- **WHOSE** responsibility is it to build strong, connected communities?
- **WHAT** can you add to your community engagement practice to enhance community connectivity that could build resilience?
- **WHY** is it important for communities to be resilient?
- **WHEN** have you experienced a community working together in the face of difficulty or disaster? What was already in place to help them work together?
- **WHERE** do you turn for information in your communities when something bad happens?

11. Give engagement the leadership kudos it deserves

It takes courage and strength to be empathetic, and I'm very proudly an empathetic and compassionate leader. I am trying to chart a different path, and that will attract criticism, but I can only be true to myself and the form of leadership I believe in.

— Jacinda Ardern[19]

The moment I permanently touched down on Australia's red dirt in 2007, my career transformed into its second phase. I walked into a professional world that was alien to me. I felt as though I had come from another planet. Another galaxy. Little did I know that the 'community engagement' jobs I was applying for would be *very* different from what I assumed. So much for assumptions, migrant-Becky! Before we migrated to Australia in 2007, my partner Dan and I spent a couple of years preparing. Our application for permanent residency succeeded because of my skills as a Community Worker (on the 'occupations in demand' list for South Australia). Dan has many talents but his occupation as Marketing Manager was not in demand in South Australia. So he migrated as my *de facto*. I was amused by Dan being my 'plus-one'!

Applying for jobs was a big part of migrating, particularly in the months leading up to our one-way flight. I'd seen an advertisement for a Community Engagement Officer at a metropolitan Adelaide Council, so I had submitted my application with confidence. I'd had a telephone interview with the recruitment agency and passed with flying colours. The face-to-face interview was lined up for the day after we landed. So, in a jet leg haze, in an unfamiliar city, I attended the interview.

I felt I was doing well, was in full flow of conversation with the interviewers, sharing my experiences of working with various communities on different and exciting projects. Things were going well until one of the women interrupted me and said, 'Becky, please can you just clarify something for me. All these examples sound a lot like community *development*. The position you've applied for is community *engagement*. What experience do you have in community *engagement*?'.

If I hadn't been in full 'impress-them-in-the-interview-because-I-desperately-need-a-job' mode, this question would have left me speechless. I didn't know what on earth she meant! I answered the question, babbling my way through the terminology possibly meaning different things in different countries, and ended up stripping it back to basics regarding my experience being all about people, groups and communities working together to improve social outcomes, and so on.

It seemed to work because I got the job. But it was a warning. (Sort of.)

...

My road ahead was not that easy. I had a lot to learn.

During my first week, the woman who'd challenged me in the interview called me into her office. This time it was to offer me some help: 'Becky, there's an organisation that's doing a lot of work in the public participation space. They're rapidly growing across Australia and you ought to check them out. Actually… they've got some training coming up and we can book you a place if you like?'

After my early confusion with the role, I eagerly attended the five-day community engagement training being held at the Adelaide Oval. The last time I'd been to the Oval was as backpacker on a 38-degree day, watching an Australia versus New Zealand test match!

My trainers were renowned community engagement specialists, both highly respected and well-regarded. Their style of presenting held my interest for the entire week in the training rooms underneath the grandstand. And my questions about community *engagement* began to be answered.

The teachings of the training I was attending and the principles of the approach I was learning, didn't sit well with me. I quickly realised that the concept of community engagement I was being taught was not where I'd come from. I understood that, whilst the model enabled a process of collaboration, or even empowerment of communities in decision-making, the process of determining what level of involvement, and in turn influence, communities might have in any decision-making process, sat very firmly with a sponsor organisation, generally the government or a corporation.

As much as my trainers and the experience of the training were excellent, to me, the approach I was learning felt very top-heavy. On the one hand, it preached an inclusive process, but it felt incredibly paternalistic. It was very much *we*, the powerful organisation, are going to make a decision and *we* are going to be deciding the level *you* be engaged in it. And *we* have decided that it's a little, a small amount, or a lot. *We* might even let you make the whole decision if you're really lucky! (But probably not!) *We* will decide how much influence *you*, the little people, are going to have in *our* decision-making processes.

Admittedly, the approach I was being taught did come with some disclaimers that good engagement involves the people being engaged in determining when and how they will be involved in the decision-making process (though I note I have rarely witnessed this happening). And, admittedly, I'm overdramatising the *we's* and the *you's* for the purpose of making my point. However, in a nutshell, the approach to community engagement that I had suddenly found myself employed in, ten thousand miles away from my comfort zone of home, was not what I thought I'd signed up for.

Don't get me wrong. I think the approach I learned at the 5-day training was well-intentioned and does provide a good basis on which we can deliver *some* community engagement activity. But by no means should we be delivering *all* community engagement in this top-down manner, as so many government entities and corporations have been doing in recent years. And all over the Western world, at that!

I returned to the office the following Monday morning, switched on my computer, checked my inbox and began catching up on the week that I'd spent out of the office. What I'd learned at the training was on my mind and I was determined to at least try to put into practice some of the newfound community *engagement* theory I had learned.

One of my first challenges was to develop a *Community Engagement Model* for the Council. Other than the legislatively required Public Consultation Policy (which all Councils are required to have, under the Local Government Act 1999, here in South Australia) to my knowledge, the organisation had never placed any emphasis on any frameworks or procedures beyond this bare minimum policy.

Whilst I knew that I would, and should, include the model that I'd been taught at the training, I knew that how I was going to go about developing the model was totally different from anything this Council had ever done before.

A quick search of the Council's online records management system gave me names and numbers of the community members they most often heard from. A quick chat with the Chief Executive Officer and General Managers confirmed these names and gave me insights into the kinds of reasons these community members contacted Council. A quick chat with Elected Members before their meetings in the Council Chamber gave me a sense of personalities, key topics of interest or contention in the community, and confirmed the key players.

And then I went wild. I contacted the most active community members known to Council, whose names alone made even the strongest bureaucrats shudder with anxiety. I introduced myself as Council's new Community Engagement Officer and I organised to meet. I didn't invite these community members to the Council office. No. I purposely made the effort to meet them in their environments, on their turf, at their convenience. I met with individuals in coffee shops; I met with residents' groups in lounge rooms; I even enjoyed a delicious glass of Margaret River Chardonnay and some exceptionally fine conversation at the dining table of one of the most active antagonists (for good reason, in my humble opinion) known to Council.

Some might have considered this activity naïve. My managers within Council would have warned me against engaging with these well-known community members, whose constant queries or challenge of Council's motives absorbed so much staff time and energy. But I did it anyway. And I did it with a precise strategy in mind.

My strategy was about building relationships with the people who had the most interest in Council activity. The ones with the loudest voices. Because if I could impress these people by truly listening to them, it was possible that they would become champions for the work I was doing. And listen I did. I spent a lot of time asking questions about their experiences with Council, what frustrated them, and how they would like to see Council engaging with their community in the future.

My research was also a form of community immersion. For this work, my immersion wasn't simply about seeking out people to work with at the grassroots level. Instead, I was finding out what the people with the loudest voices had to say about their Council because even though they had loud voices, nobody was listening. These people welcomed me with open arms. They couldn't believe that someone from Council was sitting with them in their lounge room, taking notes on the frustrations they'd had with Council for years, sometimes decades. I remained realistic, never promising that I could change things. Nevertheless, the simple fact I was there, listening, impressed them.

During these conversations, I explained how I was planning to prepare a Community Engagement Model, which would outline commitments to improving how the organisation engaged with its communities, particularly when making decisions or solving problems. My commitment impressed them, and when I asked if they'd be willing to help me with it, they jumped at the chance.

Engaging with any community on the topic of how they would like to be engaged is always a challenge. Community engagement is a bizarre enough concept in itself, let alone trying to engage about engagement! (Try explaining what you do for a living to your friends – I'm generally met with puzzled expressions.)

But with these community members and groups, I took the simple approach of sharing my draft ideas and firming them up together. I remember sitting with members of one particularly active resident's association, in a home office above one of their member's garage, going through the Community Engagement Model word-for-word, taking on board and discussing their wording suggestions. This was very much a 'word-smithing' process, and something I generally avoid, as it can get very time-consuming. In this case, however, it was another critical part of the trust-building and listening exercise.

I also ran a public workshop. By now, I had built strong relationships with key community members, so I drew a crowd easily, helped by their word of-mouth communication.

In an extraordinary move to build even further trust and transparency, I ran the entire workshop 'in the round'. Anyone who's ever been involved in the performing arts will know that performing in the round (where you stand in the middle of a large circle of inward-facing chairs) is incredibly intimidating. All eyes are on you. There is literally nowhere to hide. And for some strange, yet 'genius', reason, I chose to make myself totally open and vulnerable.

I tried everything in this project's early days! I used a Samoan Conversation Circle process, with four chairs in their own mini circle, inside the larger group circle. I set an overarching, broad-themed question along the lines of *how people would like their Council to be engaging with them*. Participants joined the smaller circle when they wanted to speak. There were only four chairs in the conversation circle so if people wanted to say something, they had to stand behind one of the people in the chairs and wait for them to move back to the outer circle.

I remember these community members, so used to shaking their fists at Council, literally sitting on the edges of their seats in amazement at the process unfolding in front of them. They had never seen anything like it, and certainly not from their Council. I felt I was winning.

This ability to appear like a graceful swan above the surface, whilst paddling like crazy below water works both in my favour, and against it. Sometimes I feel frustrated with my bubbly personality and confidence to 'perform', as it can quite easily mask decades of experience managing complex groups and situations. To be totally honest, one of my intentions with writing this book is to present myself as more than 'just the facilitator' which I am so often labelled.

A couple of years ago my local Member of Parliament attended a meeting I was facilitating. I had 65 local people laughing together, working proactively on a plan for their future. The meeting was ridiculously positive, and we achieved so much. His follow up Facebook post said, *'Well done Becky Hirst for moderating and making it fun'*. This response did not sit well with me at all. It was nice to get a mention alongside some great photos. But fun? FUN?! Did he realise the amount of preparation that went into that meeting? Did he realise the complex strategy that underpinned every single aspect of it? Did he consider my breadth and depth of experience in that pulled off such a positive process in a local government setting? Every *single* thing that happened at that meeting was strategised, even down to my English banter – all instigated as strategy to put participants at ease, build rapport, and set a positive atmosphere. Successful community engagement is so much more than simply turning up, putting on your best smile, and doing something fun. It's a *hard* skill.

...

The process I've just described back at the Council in 2007 was a relatively authoritarian, top-down, preparing-a-Council-document style of engagement. Clearly, *I* was deciding how, when and where the communities were to be engaged. However, my approach was to do it in a way that built relationships by working closely with key community members.

The Model was developed, and the community loved it. It just needed to be adopted officially in the Council chamber.

Now for another big challenge! Whilst I'd engaged with some of the Elected Members during the process, many of them simply did not 'get' the concept of community engagement. This young English woman appeared to be 'siding' with community people who usually cause the most headaches for Council. They simply didn't understand it. To make matters worse, the conceptual model being proposed (really just the approach I'd learned at the recent 5-day training) was far too radical.

The Mayor was the most aggrieved. He was an older man, who had been involved in politics for over twenty years and had some pretty strong opinions on how things should be run. Put frankly, he didn't believe in community engagement. He firmly believed he, and his fellow Councillors, were elected to represent their communities by their communities. Thus, no further engagement was required.

On the evening the Community Engagement Model went to the Council meeting for adoption, I watched anxiously from the public gallery. In this, my first experience of attending a formal Council meeting, I was overwhelmed by the formalities. But I was also excited. I was proud of the connections I'd formed with the community and confident that the document provided a direction for high-quality community engagement to occur.

Call me a lamb to slaughter: a naïve, now pale-faced, lamb. From his seat overlooking the chamber, the Mayor switched on his little microphone and began to berate me. Not just the document, but me. Personally. He made a full speech declaring his disgust at the engagement process that the 'said officer' had undertaken. I was shocked and disgusted that he couldn't even bring himself to say my name. I had to sit, silently, in the public gallery and listen to this ferocious attack on my work, and more specifically my approach to community engagement. It was one of the worst experiences of my professional life.

Of course, the Model was not endorsed. Trying to save face, the Chief Executive Officer made some promises that the contents of the document would be revisited. I immediately left the Council chamber and drove home in floods of tears.

I didn't last much longer at that Council. After six months, I decided that they weren't ready for me. I wasn't sure if *Australia* was ready for me. To be fair, I was still relatively young, new to Australia, and new to this top-down approach of community engagement. What I did know was that I didn't have the energy or the desire to challenge the blockages I was encountering.

The pushback from the Mayor was a significant roadblock, but I was also frustrated with my lack of visibility within the organisation as a community expert. As a Community Engagement Officer, I reported to the Marketing and Communications Manager. She reported to the Manager of Community Services. She reported to the General Manager for *Something Above That*. And she reported to the Chief Executive Officer. And he answered to the Mayor and the Elected Members. I must surmount at least three layers of middle-management bureaucracy even to speak to the Chief Executive.

Let me be perfectly clear. Community engagement in a Council setting is highly important. It's the bread and butter of local government, in my opinion. Councillors are elected to represent the needs of their communities. Therefore, they must know and understand those needs, on an ongoing basis. And those needs will inevitably change! They answer to the communities. The communities vote them in, and the communities vote them out. The communities pay rates to fund the operations of the Council. The communities are, or at least should be, at the absolute centre of local government. End of story!

Therefore, I believe community engagement positions or teams should report directly to the Chief Executive Officer. They should operate at a strategic level, across the whole organisation, with the ability to have direct access to the ear of the most senior leaders within that organisation.

And there is more. I am perpetually disappointed that local Councils employ management teams that are comprised of bureaucrats who lack fundamental 'people' skills. I worked recently with a Council in which the majority of the senior management team refused to attend community engagement workshops because they didn't see it in their role to do so. When they were made to attend, they came with sulkier faces than my four-year old daughter conjures up when she isn't allowed ice cream for breakfast.

Wendy tells a story of her experience as a local government manager in the 1980s. Of course, she was the Community Services Manager, being a woman. At that time, she was the highest paid woman in local government in Australia (and she still did not have equal pay). Anyway, one of her staff planned a future visioning workshop for the senior managers. The Manager of Planning and Engineering wrote back to say that he had consulted his job description and 'the future 'was not included. So he would not be attending.

We need leaders of these organisations to be visible in communities, actively demonstrating our Council rates at work. Of course, I appreciate that local government managers have office work to do, but their visibility in, and connection to, the communities they serve are equally important. These skills should be clearly identified in their recruitment processes.

The same goes for state government. All too often, community engagement roles are hidden away in marketing and communication teams. I need to be clear here: authentic community engagement is not marketing and communications. Far from it! I dream of community engagement specialists working directly alongside the most senior leaders, if not directly with government Ministers. I dream of the day where I meet with a Ministerial Advisor who understands the power and benefits of truly listening to, being guided by, or working in authentic partnership with communities. Instead, these days, I meet young men (and occasionally women) who are in it for the political game playing. I want to see more grassroots approaches to community engagement. And I want to see the grassroots reflected at the top.

Recently in South Australia, our Minister for Child Protection was in the news. The topic was abuse of teenagers in state care, or as we call it here in South Australia, 'under the Guardianship of the Minister'. These young women were sexually abused by male staff members, resulting in pregnancy. As it turned out, the Minister in question hadn't been briefed. I was a shocked community member to witness this dereliction of duty. And I began to think, why or how can Ministers become so detached from what's happening on the ground – in the care homes where these children and young people live. I accept that a Minister can't be across every single event, but, honestly, as a bare minimum, I'd expect some regular, ongoing connection with the children and young people living in state care.

And I'm not talking Ministerial visits here – always planned to the enth degree. I mean the Minister popping in on a Saturday evening, in her jeans and t-shirt, to make some pizzas with the young people, whilst having a chat about how things are going. Again, you might call me naïve or unrealistic to suggest such a level of connection. But it does happen in other places (and Wendy tells me that once upon a time, it happened here in South Australia during the halcyon 'Dunstan years') and this is what the world is lacking. And it's not that hard to fix this problem.

This is where Jacinda Ardern, the current Prime Minister of New Zealand is excelling. She is a real person! And New Zealand is doing exceptionally well under her leadership. She is also a prime minister who can compassionately hug people from the Muslim community shaken by a horrific shooting in their place of worship in Christchurch in March 2019. Jacinda is my model of a Prime Minister, who demonstrates a refreshing and genuine connection with people.

Back to local Councils. Nowadays I laugh in the face of Elected Members who challenge the concept of community engagement. My confidence has grown tenfold since those early days. I rise to the challenge of transforming doubt in politicians by taking them on a journey. Recently an Elected Member of another Council client said that a proposed community engagement approach of taking a blank page to the community to involve them in shaping the organisations strategic plan was 'perverse'. Perverse! Let's define *perverse,* for a moment: 'in a way that shows a deliberate and obstinate desire to behave in an unreasonable or unacceptable manner; in a manner contrary to what is expected or accepted'. Yep, it's *perverse*, all right!

Again, watching from the public gallery, I could not respond. But compared to the younger me – thirteen years ago, leaving the Council Chamber in tears, I shrug it off with a chuckle at *their* naïveté. I promise myself that by the end of the process, I'll have that person raving about community engagement.

I need to sound a warning here. To be taken seriously as a sector, we must get better at proving our worth. We can see it: we have witnessed numerous well-considered decisions that involved the right people, at the right time. We have seen the positive impacts of this approach of working together. It makes total sense to us. But we must get better at evaluating our work so that we have reams and reams of evidence that we can draw on, for those who need convincing. We'll need to extend our reach to include cost-benefit analysis type scenarios, or social return on investment, whereby we put numbers against our success.

I don't believe we should have to become 'statistical' and turn our work into one big risk mitigation strategy, but to convince those whose priority might be economics, or who need hard evidence, then we must strengthen our portfolio, written in their language. Evidence-based research is what we need. And lots of it.

I always imagine meeting a man named Frank Discussion. When I left the Council back in 2007, the Chief Executive and I had a frank discussion about the concerns I've discussed in this chapter. We got on well during my short time there and he remains one of my absolute favourite Council executives in Australia. We discussed an increase in pay and moving the role up the hierarchy by a couple of notches. But my mind was made up. After the experience with the Mayor that night in the Council chamber, I was done. As a result of my leaving, the position *did* get a significant upgrade and I like to think that the ripples I made caused the tide to change for that Council. And about time, too!

Eventually, the much-despised Community Engagement Model was approved, with minimal changes. The Chief Executive (who had lots of experience in working with elected officials) knew the strings he needed to pull.

...

Conversation Starters

- **WHO** stands between you and relevant decision-makers in your communities? How many layers of people or processes are there?
- **WHAT** can we do to raise the profile of the much-needed skills, knowledge, and expertise that community engagement practitioners have?
- **WHY** is community engagement not a skill required to be understood by all leaders within the public service?
- **WHEN** have you been challenged on your beliefs regarding community engagement? How did this make you feel?
- **WHERE** does the expertise of community engagement sit within your local Council? Where do you think it should sit?

12. Position engagement to be seen and heard

It is not the critic who counts; not the man who points out how the strong man stumbles, or where the doer of deeds could have done them better. The credit belongs to the man who is actually in the arena, whose face is marred by dust and sweat and blood; who strives valiantly; who at best knows in the end the triumph of high achievement, and who at worst, if he fails, at least fails while daring greatly.

— Theodore Roosevelt[20]

I'd been resident in Australia for only six months, but I knew things weren't going to work out the way that I wanted at the Council. To bring about any change in the foreseeable future required a dramatic walk-out by the newly arrived, enthusiastic English woman, who'd already created a stir with her new-fangled ways of connecting with the local community. Here I was, on the lookout for my next opportunity, hoping I could find a job where I could apply my genuine love of involving people in decision making and problem solving.

I'd spent six months wrestling with the difference between community engagement and community development, and I was tired of semantics. My next adventure was a significant jaunt back into the world of health, where I took up a role as a Community Participation Facilitator for South Australia's Children, Youth & Women's Health Service. Whoever made that title up had had a bad night! How I love my job titles! They highlight the breadth of language we can apply to the concept of involving people in things that matter.

The moment I began my new job, based at the Women's and Children's Hospital in North Adelaide, I felt at home (despite being 10,000 miles from home). I was back in a familiar healthcare setting, like where I began my health promotion journey at the Gloucestershire Royal Hospital (where I was born). I found it grounding to working there, with regular sightings of patients and visitors constantly reminding me why health promotion, prevention, and care are so important. For me, nothing was more grounding than being based in a hospital that specialised in treating women and children. My role was to facilitate involvement of patients, carers and the broader community in decision-making for both the hospital and the broader health service.

I stepped away from my quick, and slightly abusive, affair with local government, and, fortunately, my engagement no longer involved fence heights and updating suburban masterplans. Now I heard children receiving cancer treatment explain how to improve their experience. Or listened to parents who'd spent months with babies in the Neonatal Intensive Care Unit contributing to the redesign of that ward. This work pulled at my heartstrings! This was real life, it was raw, and we could not mess with engagement here. It had to be authentic. *I* had to be authentic. I could not play with emotions – mine or anyone else's. Our engagement had to be the real deal. I quickly worked out that this was going to be a test of character.

One of my jobs required me to engage with staff of the health service to develop a Cultural Diversity Framework. a brand-new concept for the organisation. The hope was that it would be warmly welcomed, particularly for supporting diversity and demonstrating the organisation's strong intolerance of discrimination. With management's full support, I convened a meeting of a wide range of staff to discuss cultural diversity.

On reflection, I was very much in 'performance' mode during those early days in Adelaide. I responded positively to comments like 'that was so refreshing' from people who attended my meetings or workshops. I tried to prove my worth (as a migrant) and drew on every ounce of creativity to 'shock and awe' people into imagining different ways of operating. I was using my enthusiasm to motivate, inspire, and energise people to have good conversations about things that mattered.

You might say I was trying to shake Adelaide up a little. In the dusty, beige-coloured meeting room shown in images 15 and 16, in what felt like the basement of the Women's and Children's Hospital, with tiny windows facing the trades entrance, I pinned up huge colourful world maps, sticky walls, flip-chart paper with handwritten objectives. I arranged the room with small tables and chairs, encouraging high-quality small group conversations. I turned my back on the norm of rows of chairs with a projector and screen at the front. In my view, that approach stifles any decent conversation among participants.

Image 15 - Facilitating dynamic group conversations about things that matter - at the Cultural Diversity Forum of the Children, Youth & Women's Health Service. Photo owned by author, 2008.

Image 16 - Staff from the Children, Youth & Women's Health Service developing a Cultural Diversity Framework, getting 'hands on' by sharing their place of birth with others to highlight the diversity in the room. Photo by author, 2008

In that same dusty room, I first encountered the Consumer & Community Advisory Group. This group comprised people with a lived experience of the Children, Youth & Women's Health Service, or members of the broader community with interest in the service. This group had a common interest of providing advice to the health service and were very diverse in their individual skills, knowledge and experiences. Diversity was their middle name: a new parent who'd recently experienced the post-natal support services, mother of a young boy with severe, multiple, disabilities and complex chronic health needs, and many in between. These amazing people were very real to me. Their situations were compelling. Many faced severe difficulties or situations that life's journey had thrown at them. And, amazingly, these people wanted to make a difference by volunteering their time to help their health service be the best it could be.

What a contrast to the world of local government I'd recently escaped. In their view, the 'community' comprised retired white men looking for something to fill their time. By contrast, these people were so busy with their lives. And yet they were volunteering to help us. Any parent will tell you there is nothing more time or energy-consuming than caring for a sick child or a newborn baby. This group of committed individuals believed so much in continuous improvement that they managed to squeeze in a three-hour monthly meeting, as well as the communication we had with them in-between meetings.

I was the Advisory Group's Executive Officer. And it involved much more than organising agendas and taking minutes. I was their arms and legs, trying to make things happen between meetings. I thoroughly respected their cause and enjoyed compiling pretty weighty agendas, with the items reflecting conversations I had with members between meetings. We would meet, discuss the topics and after each meeting I would be armed with a list of items to find out more about, seek answers to, or to just make things happen. I felt empowered. And I believe they did, too.

A couple of weeks ago I was at the hospital for a health check-up with one of my daughters and I smiled as my smartphone asked me if I'd like to join the WiFi network. I remember the exact moment, now over a decade ago, when a passionate member of the Advisory Group had made the suggestion that the hospital should have free WiFi for all of the parents spending extraordinary amounts of time there. It's hard to believe that at the time this was quite an out-of-left-field idea. But with her determination, and my activism on the ground, we made it happen!

From the start, I felt uncomfortable with our meeting space: a dingy room hidden away in the hospital's darkest corner. It felt like our meetings happened in secret, occasionally 'discovered' by a staff member who presented to the group. It felt 'hidden'. And the group's enthusiasm, passion, and work for the betterment of healthcare services was not being seen or acknowledged. This felt wrong. A group of such committed consumers and community members donating their time each month! At least we owed them a nice meeting room with daylight. I knew the perfect location for the monthly meeting. I had to grovel to the keeper of the room diary. Nice meeting rooms are hard to come by. I moved our meetings to a beautiful day-lit, spacious, non-dusty room. I learned a lot from that experience. The conditions of success include comfort. The topics were already so painful and demanding. At least we could work in comfort!

I had a hidden agenda for the room change. I wanted to give these wonderful people the daylight they deserved. But more than that, it was about visibility. I wanted their work (*our* work) to be more visible across the organisation. Of course, other options were open to me, like sharing their agendas and meeting summaries at every opportunity and having members profiled in the monthly staff newsletter. Or something similar. Or, as I did, I could raise their profile significantly by booking the boardroom in the Executive Team office suite for their monthly meetings. Don't get me wrong here, I employed all the other activities to raise their profile across the organisation using 'traditional' means. But the room change was a complete game changer. I don't think I've ever engineered such a calculated, strategic, and successful move as that room change.

Consumer & Community Advisory Group meetings would begin in the late afternoon to accommodate members' school pick-up and work schedules. Mostly, we'd work into the evenings. So, each month, members would arrive as the Executive Team was finishing up their day, often physically crossing paths in the lift lobby. Even better, Executive Team members would be locking the office and realise someone was still in the meeting room. They would ask, 'What's happening in there?'

And I would be there, all smiles, advising, 'Oh, that's the Consumer & Community Advisory Group having their monthly meeting.'

Best.
Profile-raising.
Ever.

Before long, I could book our meetings not just in the room-booking diary, but in the Chief Executive Officer's diary. As the room adjoined her office, how convenient for her to attend each month! Yes, we were doing great work that was worthy of her interest and attendance. But the room change made all the difference. Something about proximity? Being close to the action?

The room change taught me a lesson I'll never forget. Space matters. Place matters. Symbolism matters. Establishing the physical conditions for success matters. I learned a big lesson from the room change, which is why I place such emphasis on venue selection in my professional work. Always!

You want your training course to be taken seriously? Hire a room on the local University campus to hold it in, so that you've got an academic-sounding address when you promote it. Want to be seen as an active consultant in the government sector? Have all your coffee meetings in the café directly below the State Administration Building. Want to hold an engagement event in a regional Australian town? Book the sports club, the lawn bowls club, or the function room at the pub. Your venue choice speaks a thousand words and can save you a million hours in profile raising!

And the same goes with the set-up of a room. How can we show participants of any community engagement process that we are serious about creating a space in which we intend to work together with them, if we're inviting them to meet in a room that's dark, dusty or appears to be the storage room for old furniture that the rest of the organisation no longer needs? One of the first things I'll do if presented with a furniture graveyard for my meeting or workshop is tidy up.

It's the least we can do to create a welcoming, productive environment. I'll even go so far as to play welcoming music or use a diffuser to fill the room with a fragrance other than the aroma of stale carpet.

Wendy Sarkissian agrees with this, noting that *location is everything* and conveniently provides some handy checklists for consideration in *SpeakOut: The Step-by-Step Guide to SpeakOuts and Community Workshops*,[21] which I highly recommend.

A couple of years ago, I was working closely with a group of Elected Members in a Council. I was setting up for a workshop with them on the topic of community engagement – something I enjoy doing where I explore what it means to them, how they feel they are faring, and so on. The only room available was their official Council Chamber and I was told quite sternly by the person who took the room booking that under no circumstances could their u-shaped furniture arrangement be changed because of the location of the microphone cables. I had caused tidal waves of distress by opening the blinds to let daylight in!

So, instead of moving the tables, I decided to move the chairs in front of the u-shape tables. The chairs formed a little circle. The members' jaws literally dropped as they walked in. I am amazed that such a small shift in furniture can create such a stir, but it can also create such a fresh space in which to think, plan, and do things differently.

Back to the Consumer and Community Advisory Group meetings. The Chief Executive's regular attendance was invaluable. Witnessing 'real-life' consumers conversing directly with a key decision maker warmed my heart and made my job a lot easier. She clearly valued their conversations as she attended more and more meetings. I acknowledged her involvement in, and respect for, the Consumer and Community Advisory Group when she asked for my support for the group's smooth transition into a new governance structure following introduction of the Health Care Act 2008. The Act placed greater emphasis on consumer participation and given our group's strength, it was placed right in the heart of the organisational structure, providing direct advice and guidance to the Executive Team. This development was truly monumental, both for me as an engagement professional but more so for the consumers and confirmed that listening to the voices of consumers and community can play a significant role in healthcare governance.

•••

Conversation Starters

- **WHO** would benefit from witnessing your community engagement processes in action?
- **WHAT** could you do to make your community engagement activity more visible to those who need to witness it?
- **WHY** is it important for community engagement to be visible?
- **WHEN** have you felt uninspired by an inappropriate or uncomfortable venue?
- **WHERE** has your community engagement typically taken place? Where else could it take place?

13. Listen deeply without always needing to find an answer

The time has now come for the nation to turn a new page in Australia's history by righting the wrongs of the past and so moving forward with confidence to the future. We apologise for the laws and policies of successive parliaments and governments that have inflicted profound grief, suffering and loss on these our fellow Australians...

— Kevin Rudd, Sorry Speech, 12 February 2008[22]

I am sorry to say that when I was growing up in the UK, I learned little about Aboriginal Australia. Our history lessons, from primary school through high school, focussed largely on Great Britain, usually relating to the pomp and ceremony of Kings and Queens through the centuries, or the two world wars. When I recall any learning in relation to invasion, it was always about the people who invaded us. We spent a lot of time learning about the how the Romans invaded us back in 43AD, all because we'd sided with Julius Caesar or something. And, while it was fascinating to grow up in a town where Roman ruins still exist, I look back and wonder what I *should* have been learning about.

I wish I'd learned more about, or at least known about, OUR invasion of other countries, particularly Australia: the impacts that *we*, England, had on the rest of the world over the years. Funnily enough, that wasn't mentioned much either. I have searched to the depths of my mind to recall at least some mention of colonisation in Australia during my childhood or early adulthood. I can't locate a single memory. Not a single thing. When I try to think more in depth about our high school history lessons, I can remember only a few lessons on the Tudor times. Maybe we touched on the Stone Age. Australia was a faraway, distant country. I am ashamed to admit that all I knew about it was that it was a continent where Kylie Minogue and Jason Donovan hailed from.

I first came to Australia because my best friend Laura was backpacking here. I was on a soul-searching mission after my relationship breakdown. I knew little about the country when I arrived in Sydney on a hot summer morning in late 2003. Being a backpacker in Sydney opened my eyes to a glimpse of history. But I lacked depth. Aboriginal digeridoo players and dancers would draw a large crowd at Circular Quay, tourist shops would sell (probably fake) Aboriginal artwork, and Captain Cook Cruises would spend their days showing tourists around the harbour. I thought I was getting a taste of Australia but, really, I was not.

Even three months working in Parramatta, the land of the Burramattagal people, working in an arts and culture community role, I still didn't grasp the severity of the effects of colonisation on Aboriginal people. I began to learn more about Aboriginal culture, and would hear stories of struggle and inequity from my colleague and now friend Boe Rambaldini, a proud Bundjalung man, who I had the good fortune to work with for that short time. However, it took several years, in my role at the Children, Youth & Women's Health Service, on the Kaurna people's land, that I finally began to connect the dots. There was a lot of connecting to do!

On the morning of 13 February 2008, I stood in Adelaide's Tarntanya Wama, also known as Elder Park, invited along by colleagues to witness our new Prime Minister, Kevin Rudd, say sorry.

Sorry? Sorry for what? Saying sorry to who? What's happened? Why's he saying sorry? What's he done? Why are the government sorry? What did they do? You mean this country isn't just all about happy days in the sunshine?

I'm embarrassed to admit that Kevin Rudd's apology, a few months before my 30th birthday, was the first I'd heard of what had been happening since that First Fleet arrived. I'd somehow remained sheltered from the harsh realities of the cruelty, dispossession, and inhumane treatment of Aboriginal people. Sadly, my ignorance and naïveté are representative of mainstream populations worldwide.

There is no way my book can respectfully explain the horrors experienced by the Stolen Generations and their families and communities. It would be foolish to attempt to summarise that painful chapter in Australia's past. The pain and suffering endured because of the forced removal of Indigenous children from their families is unforgivable. We white fellas cannot even begin to comprehend the devastation and destruction our ancestor's actions caused and the effects on Aboriginal people and their communities.

I will never forget Kevin Rudd's apology. As bright Adelaide sunshine illuminated thousands watching the live broadcast on a huge screen, I turned to look around. What I saw astonished me. Emotional outpouring was everywhere, as though a dam had broken. People held hands, hugged, sobbed, and cheered. Aboriginal and non-Aboriginal people had waited for this moment for so, *so* long. That moment changed me at a visceral level. I had witnessed something gigantic. Now, my efforts must, at some level, match the enormity of what I had witnessed. I could no longer be a bystander in my own life.

That day transformed my perspective on Aboriginal affairs in Australia. As a recent arrival, I needed to commit to learning about the Stolen Generations and the consequences of the mistreatment Aboriginal people had experienced (and continue to experience). Life then took charge of my education, providing exactly what I needed to learn. Word came through that Rudd's apology had touched our Chief Executive. She was eager to follow suit at a more local level. Being a government service, the Hospital had almost certainly been involved in removal of children. Rudd's apology precipitated my new project.

'The past, the present and the future' project was the brainchild of Karen Glover, a Mein:tnk and Wotjobaluk woman, and Director of Aboriginal Health within the organisation. I remember visiting Karen in her South Terrace office to discuss Aboriginal engagement within the health service. I remember her calm voice as she explained her ideas for the project. I remember her standing at her whiteboard as we discussed the likely historical context in South Australia and the urgent need for conversations with Aboriginal communities to draw a line in the sand and plan to move forward with regard to health matters.

Karen had clearly been thinking about this topic for a long time. She argued that, as a matter of urgency, we must create a space for people to share their stories. We must acknowledge where we are now. And we must look to the future to help shape our shared vision. As we began planning the engagement process, Karen was adamant that all our meetings required trained counsellors. This was serious business, this Sorry Business, and we needed to be prepared to support people as strong emotions surfaced. Participants would almost certainly share harrowing stories of how they had been affected by our health service. We would likely meet people who had seen children removed from their families, and possibly even those who were themselves taken away as young children. This was not the sort of engagement where you could waltz into a room, deliver a PowerPoint presentation, open up for a quick Q&A, and scurry away again with your notepad under your arm full of notes to type into a smart little report. This was deep and incredibly sensitive engagement that needed to be handled extraordinarily carefully.

I was surprised that our community meetings, held in culturally appropriate places such as the Tauondi Aboriginal College in Port Adelaide and the Kaurna Plains School in Elizabeth, were so well attended. Twenty to thirty people would attend each meeting, with ages ranging from children and young people through to Elders. I was initially impressed at the level of trust from participants that I saw reflected in their acceptance of our invitation to attend. Soon, however, I realised that there was understandably zero trust in government. These people were attending because Karen and her Aboriginal colleagues were involved, or because this could only be a step in the right direction after the last couple of hundreds of years of violence.

At the meetings, we provided an open floor. We invited participants to share their stories. Karen was a fantastic leader, opening each session in a calm and compassionate manner, respecting the sensitivity required. I purposely played no active role, other than to support Karen and to listen. On this kind of topic, where an entire generation (or generations) of children were forcibly removed from their families, it seemed impossible to know how to begin. Karen knew how. She simply invited people to share the stories that they felt needed sharing. After an awkward silence, one by one the stories came out. Tears flowed and hearts pounded. We didn't fight our tears or try to facilitate our way out of the situation. We just listened. It hurt. And this painful experience of speaking about, and listening to, what had happened was critical in enabling any kind of reconciliation.

The storytelling process was a symbolic and cathartic experience that cleared the way for discussions about the present situation in healthcare in South Australia for Aboriginal women and children. Karen asked participants to reflect on their current day experiences with the Women's and Children's Hospital. Many issues of concern were raised, including everything from the environment of the hospital feeling big and unfriendly, through to difficulties of getting appointments and there being not enough Aboriginal people working within the organisation or involved in decision making business.

Once these present-day concerns had been discussed, Karen guided the group to the next stage: looking to the future. She had a beautiful way of recapping on how we'd shared stories of the past, reflected on the present day, but that now she wanted us to draw a line in the sand and work together to create the future that we all wanted. From the visions discussed during these meetings, Karen and her team compiled an extensive Action Plan[23] for moving forward, including a summary of what we'd heard and how we'd be responding as the State government's health department for children, young people and women.

This incredibly rich process taught me so much, both personally and professionally. I learned what privilege meant, and, more specifically, white privilege. I learned of the horrific things that those who'd arrived before me had done to the Indigenous people. I felt disgusted, embarrassed, and ashamed to be British. I witnessed genuine sensitivity and skill on the part of a facilitator managing a difficult and highly sensitive topic. I've since experienced discussions about other highly sensitive topics, where it was important to acknowledge that working together with people with lived experience can impede their personal survival. I also learned that this process had nothing to do with me or my needs. Yes, it hurt to hear the stories, but it didn't hurt half as much as it did for the people who had experienced the stories.

During this intensive process of deep listening, a partnership was formed with the staff and community from the Tauondi Aboriginal Community College. We explored the idea of how to share visually with others the process that had occurred. The result was in three paintings that represented the past, the present and the future. They took shape during a series of events where the artists, staff and community members contributed by placing their mark on the artwork. I vividly remember how special it felt to be invited, as a non-Aboriginal person, to contribute to 'the future' dot painting. The one tiny white dot I added to that painting served as an ongoing reminder of my important role in the journey of reconciliation, moving forward.

This was my first exposure to issues of this kind in Australia. It was a heart-opening and mind-blowing experience. I've since worked with other clients on reconciliation issues, including significant and exciting processes aimed at the decolonisation of some government services. This opportunity to work with Karen, early in my time in Australia, taught me some critical things that I must always consider. None more so important as the criticality of listening. Deeply. With no intention other than to hear what is being said.

I should add that whilst I refer to *my* or *our* ancestors, I am speaking broadly as white fellas. I hear many non-Indigenous Australians say, *Oh, well it wasn't actually my great, great grandfather who came and did those awful things, so why should I feel bad for what happened?* However, I believe that it's important that we, as non-Indigenous Australians, *all* acknowledge the brutality that happened and that if we are anything other than Indigenous to the land on which we now live, we must hear and acknowledge the pain and suffering that has gone before us.

Interestingly, about this time as I was on this journey of discovery, my Dad's family history research discovered that Harris Hirst, a younger brother of my great-great grandfather, arrived in Melbourne in 1878 on the SS Great Britain. That discovery promptly dissolved my theory that I was the first Hirst to have migrated to Australia! Whilst Harris wouldn't have been one of the first settlers in Australia, my Dad also discovered that John Morton, one of my distant relatives on my paternal grandmother's side of the family, was one of *The Three Greenhorns*, who were the first white settlers in Vancouver, Canada, on the land that later became the City of Vancouver. Of course, this was a distant family connection. As John Morton and I are something like tenth cousins, five times removed, this was a timely reminder that *my* ancestors did directly play a part in colonisation and that I therefore feel a direct responsibility regarding reconciliation moving forward.

...

The Children, Youth & Women's Health Service was a multi-faceted organisation, with many different services within it. During my time there, I worked on everything from a state-wide consultation reviewing the 'Blue Book' health record that every South Australian baby received over the last several decades, to writing and delivering *Ready, Steady, Engage* training that I'd deliver to staff across the organisation. I worked hand-in-hand with Mellita Kimber, the young, lively, and super switched-on Youth Participation Officer. She taught me a lot about engaging with children and young people to inform decision-making through sessions that we'd facilitate together at the Second Story Youth Health Service in Adelaide.

I'd get all kinds of emails from across the organisation about a variety topics. One day, an email popped up on my screen advertising a secondment opportunity at Women's Health Statewide, a centre providing clinical and emotional health and wellbeing services for women, including a range of health promotion initiatives. The opportunity interested me greatly for a number of reasons, including: a team leader role; a focus on health promotion; and being four days per week. I had been thinking about going part-time so I could start my own business.

When I took the secondment to Women's Health Statewide in 2009, the centre was located on Pennington Terrace in North Adelaide in a large Gothic inspired building built in the mid-1800s, with a long history of being home to various Adelaide gentry. I have no memories of ghost stories, surprisingly, because if ever there was a building that would give you the shivers, it is this one! Despite the building's spooky façade, I found a workplace that was warm, nurturing, and supportive. And it felt ironic that in that colonial and gentrified building, I experienced my first full exposure to feminism, the concept of women supporting women, and advocacy for women's rights.

This was also my first exposure to managing people. I had responsibility for a few teams, including the Aboriginal Health team. Having learned so much during *The Past, The Present and The Future* project with Karen Glover, I had a spring in my step, feeling well equipped with my new knowledge of the injustices faced by Aboriginal women and my strong desire to play my part in reconciliation. In true Becky style, I committed to the role with great gusto.

I still had so much to learn.

Little did I know that my journey was about to get a whole lot deeper.

My teams based in the main building, such as the Administration and Reception team, were ticking along nicely with our regular fortnightly meetings. I had various personnel issues to deal with, which I enjoyed. And I had great results forming positive connections with staff members who needed a compassionate yet focused team leader. However, my plans with the Aboriginal Health team weren't going quite as I'd hoped.

First, I knew that the dynamic was weird. A non-Aboriginal woman being 'in charge' of an Aboriginal Health team. I knew this and did my best to not be too 'top-heavy' in my management style. As this isn't my approach anyway, it wasn't tricky to do.

However, I remember a particular team meeting where four or five of us sat in a small circle. I can't remember what we were talking about, but I can remember feeling an unspoken tension between myself and Ingrid O'Loughlin, a Narungga woman, who was employed by Women's Health Statewide as the Aboriginal Project Officer. I felt the tension reach a point where I remember Ingrid taking a deep breath and gesturing at me with her hands that she needed to speak. And she needed me to listen. In her beautiful, soft, calm voice, she spoke some words that changed my perspective on everything:

'Becky. You need to listen to me now. Are you listening?'

She paused, before continuing.'You need to slow down. You need to stop and listen. You are always looking for an answer or a solution. You must stop this. Sometimes we just need a conversation. A good yarn. We don't always need to find the answers. You need to listen. Deeply. You need to learn. And most of all, you need to put down that notepad.'

Those words stopped me in my tracks. I knew from what I'd learned with Karen that Ingrid was right. My cultural way of doing things was not the right way of doing things, especially in this context.

I've since learned that the Aboriginal word 'Dadirri' means inner deep listening. Deep listening describes the processes of deep and respectful listeningto build community—a way of encouraging people to explore and learn from the ancient heritage of Aboriginal culture, knowledge and understanding.[24]

I use Ingrid's words of wisdom to this day. In countless workshops or meetings that I have facilitated, across a wealth of settings, I use World Café processes of small group conversations purposely to encourage deep conversation and listening, without necessarily finding solutions. I ask participants to simply talk and listen to each other. I remind them that, as white fellas, we are obsessed with taking notes on reams and reams of paper. We are obsessed with capturing everything we say and endlessly analysing it to attempt to solve our problems.

I ask them to consider how this predisposition influences our conversation style and effectiveness. I ask them to take the opportunity to have deep and meaningful conversations with each other, because it's not often that we do that - at home, at work, or in our communities — and it's actually what the world needs. And every single time I do it, I think of Ingrid. I hope that she knows how seriously I took her words and how much I've learned and changed as a result, and how dutifully I've passed them on to others.

From that moment on, everything changed with Ingrid. I was no longer her team leader. Instead, I was her colleague, and she was my Elder. I listened intently to what she said and worked hard at not always trying to find solutions.

Together, we did some incredibly meaningful work. I was enriching *my* journey of deep listening and together we were making the path of *our* journey of reconciliation. We organised a staff excursion to the Colebrook Reconciliation Park, a memorial to the children and families who experienced harsh regimes as a result of being removed from their families. Our group sat around an open fire where we chatted, listened, and deeply reflected. On another occasion, we organised a staff movie afternoon, where we watched *Rabbit Proof Fence*, loosely based on the story of three Aboriginal girls forcibly removed from their families in 1931. Together we sobbed, and I felt ashamed to have the same British accent as Kenneth Branagh, who played the part of the horrid and cruel 'Chief Protector of Aborigines'.

Image 17 shows me and Ingrid co-facilitating a panel event called *Reconciliation: Let's See It Through*, as part of Reconciliation Week in 2010. It was an honour to stand side-by-side, an Aboriginal woman and a non-Aboriginal woman, together on a journey of reconciliation.

Image 17 - Working together, side-by-side, towards reconciliation. Ingrid and I co-facilitated the Reconciliation: Let's See it Through event at Women's Health Statewide as part of Reconciliation Week. Photo owned by author, 2010.

...

Conversation Starters

- **WHO** has inspired you to listen deeply to others? Who do you know who is a really good listener?
- **WHAT** is your knowledge and understanding of the traditional owners of the land on which you live? How could you learn more?
- **WHY** is the Western culture so obsessed with taking notes? When did we lose the art of conversation? Did we ever actually have it?! How can we create more invitations to authentic conversations?
- **WHEN** did you last listen deeply to what was being said, without feeling the need to respond or find a solution?
- **WHERE** do your favourite conversations take place? How could you apply the essence of these conversations to your community engagement practice?

14. Understand community engagement in the context of your own motives

Being good is good business.

— Dame Anita Roddick[25]

It was a hot Sunday morning in January 2009. We sat in the sunny courtyard of our Semaphore beachside townhouse. Semaphore is the seaside suburb to the north-west of Adelaide we'd chosen on our arrival in Australia as permanent residents a couple of years earlier. These heavenly years of pet-free, child-free living were filled with leisurely late-morning brunches at local cafés, afternoon naps on the beach, and late evenings socialising with friends, or attending functions in the City. We were living the dream in our new life Down Under.

Having recently turned thirty, I had been putting a great deal of thought (as one generally does at the turn of any decade) into my life goals. Turning thirty felt significant, and I'm not one to enjoy wasting any of my precious time on this Earth. Therefore, having already made the significant decision to migrate to Australia with Dan, I had decided I had wanted to achieve four key goals in the coming decade:

1. To own our own home.
2. To become citizens of Australia.
3. To have two children.
4. To be self-employed and happy with our work.

These felt like huge goals at the time, but owning our own home was already imminent, as we had begun building a house on a block of land we'd purchased in the McLaren Vale wine region, an hour south of Adelaide. Our goal of becoming Australian citizens was also on track. It was just a matter of living in the country for two years as permanent residents, then the paperwork and booking the citizenship test. With regard to having children, I knew this was something we both wanted. My biological clock was going to start ticking louder as we moved deeper into the coming decade. But we knew we weren't quite ready for no-lie-ins just yet. We were happy to wait until the timing was absolutely right to make this particular dream come true.

And so that left the job of becoming self-employed and happy with our work. And this topic was very much front of mind that morning. Ever since I was a child, where I'd design my own caravan parks or publish magazines with Laura, I wanted my own business. I'd been inspired by my sister's first husband. He had been in my life since I was five and had an amazing business. My first job was typing invoices for him. I loved coming up with an idea, selling it, and making money from it. And I loved the idea of being in control.

As Dan and I sat under the shade of the umbrella in our little courtyard, flitting between reading the newspapers and pouring more coffee, I reached for my laptop and applied for an Australian Business Number for Becky Hirst Consulting. For ten years of my career to that point, I'd enjoyed every step but noticed that I especially enjoyed moving from project to project. I was not someone who stayed in one job for a long time. Rather, I was someone who'd hit a project with great gusto with a general aim to motivate, inspire, shake things up or just simply deliver what needed delivering. I'd get bored or frustrated if I stayed for too long so I'd look out for new opportunities. This attribute generally worked in my favour, given that most of the roles I'd undertaken were on a temporary contract basis. I realised it would most definitely work in my favour to become a consultant.

At the time, I'd been feeling a sense of frustration about disliking being talked at, talked down to, or told what to do by less experienced managers. I had difficulty with their inability to take risks when working within the confines of organisations, and I was irritated by my inability to really change things. I was filled with a sadness at receiving limited recognition for the expertise, passion, and knowledge of community I brought to my work. I was ready for a change. Clearly. Further, my work experience in South Australia had revealed a skillset that was my niche. My skills were also possibly in need (as our permanent residency visa was granted because my occupation of community worker was on the Occupations in Demand list for that State).

That sunny morning in the beachside courtyard, I remember pouring a coffee and saying to Dan, 'I think I'm going to be a community engagement consultant'. He replied, 'Are you sure there's a market for it?'. I launched into a confident speech that there was. Or at least, there would be.

In those days, governments had generally undertaken the bare minimum of public consultation, doing only what was mandated by legislative requirements, and they hadn't been doing it particularly well. Those projects or organisations that exceeded the bare minimum requirements were few and far between. Hardly any Councils or state government departments in South Australia had policies, frameworks or procedures in relation to authentic community engagement. There were signs of a movement forming across the country, through various public participation training programs and the new *Brisbane Declaration on Community Engagement*. Some forces were creating a catalyst for shared understanding, visions and goals for engagement in other parts of the world. Yet I could see few signs of adoption of any fresh approaches in South Australia.

On reflection, from a business perspective I was incredibly smart (or lucky?) to pick up on this gap in the market, given I hadn't been in the country for long. I noted the gaping hole in expertise in community engagement in general, which my skills, knowledge and experience could fill. Equally, I noticed how the immediate future was likely to need my expertise more than ever.

In addition to this, I was canny to establish that government would make a good target market for my business. They were the ones who would need to embrace the wave of best practice community engagement that was about to hit. And they were also the ones with budget to pay for it. This is where the fundamental difference in my community engagement practice occurs. My passion isn't government. They are simply the ones footing the bill. My passion is community.

In an ideal world (wherever that is), I'd earn a salary developing time-sharing projects across communities, editing community newsletters, or directly helping to empower people in their communities through up-skilling them in community leadership, community governance, and/or activism. I'm sure this would be possible if I set my mind to it, but up until now I've focused my efforts on the low-hanging fruit to generate a decent income that pays my mortgage: a need, a captive market and a service offering that will help that market address that need.

And this was a lucrative approach to take. Using the word lucrative almost feels vulgar when my practice is about the edgy, grass-root community engagement that I've become known for. However, let's be honest, the community engagement industry *is* a multi-million-dollar industry and there are a lot of people making good money in it. I'm speaking here about sole consultants such as myself, before I even think about the large multi-billion-dollar consultancies around the world offering community and stakeholder engagement services for huge profit and shareholders.

For years I have weighed up my worth and one of my biggest fears used to be the angry community member who shouts at my clients about 'these useless overpaid consultants' but I have come to the conclusion that good community engagement practitioners are worth their weight in gold. When they are good operators, the community should ideally love the consultants who are acting with their best interests at heart.

Vera, a participant in a workshop I was once facilitating for a local government client, is a prime example. At the start of the workshop that was going to be seeking community contribution into the planned future use of a local park, Vera had no shame in approaching me, the consultant, to blatantly say 'I don't like consultants. And I'm sick and tired of this Council wasting money on them.' and two-hours later, at the end of a highly participatory and very productive community discussion Vera turned to the Chief Executive Officer and said, 'You know I don't usually like consultants. But Becky is OK. Becky can stay. This was good.'

As a comparison, I think of other trained professionals who love their work with great passion but charge for it. Vets, I'm assuming, love animals. They would never want to see an animal suffer. However, they charge for their services because they are in an occupation that has taken multiple years of training and education, plus significant on the ground experience. They also have mortgage bills to pay, I imagine. Just as how a vet doesn't want to see an animal suffer, I would never want to see a community suffer. But my passion is also my business and so I have to charge for my expertise.

In saying this, being a consultant has some incredible perks that enable me to do a large amount of pro bono work for causes that I am personally passionate about.

In 2009 I was fortunate to be offered a scholarship to participate in Business SA's Young Entrepreneur Scheme which came with the bonus of a business mentor. The year that I spent meeting my mentor, Maurie Vast, over many coffees in his favourite local cafe overlooking the jetty at Henley Beach, changed my outlook on business forever.

Maurie was an active and very successful business consultant, with many similar clients to the ones I was after, and he taught me the ins and outs of being a good consultant. He was the one who reminded me that I'd never fully thrive in my business until I'd quit my part-time government job. He was the one who raised the bar and did the maths with me about income earning potential. He was the one who taught me that the power of relationships and doing a good job were the most critical methods for winning work, way over and above any number of social media posts. He was the one who helped me get my business plan on to one neat page, with some ridiculously clear goals of where I wanted to be, alongside a set of pragmatic steps I needed to take to get there. I write with no exaggeration, Maurie really was my guiding light and set me on the pathway to business success and I was honoured when he put me forward for the SA Young Entrepreneur of the Year 2010 award, which I won.

But more so, Maurie would turn up to almost *every* session with me looking super relaxed and like he'd just arrived back from a week at his holiday home on the south coast, or just stepped off his boat trip after sailing around Kangaroo Island. And this was generally because he had!

Maurie taught me about the concept of work life balance and demonstrated to me that he had found a sweet spot in both work and life that made him happy. As the famous parable of *The Businessman and The Fisherman* by Paulo Coelho goes, why work at break-neck-speed all of your life to enjoy a slower pace when you reach retirement, when there is a way that you can live a slower, more content existence for your entire life.

This sweet spot is something that I have strived for ever since. I operate as a sole practitioner by conscious choice, knowing that I can upsize through sub-consulting if I need a team for a particular job. I could aim to have a permanent team, a bustling city-based office and a plethora of high paying clients, but I choose not to for a number of reasons. The pressure of having to win enough work on enough of a constant basis to pay for a whole team of people's mortgages as well as my own, is way too stressful a concept for my desired sweet spot. As much as I love people too, the idea of managing the day-to-day work of people doesn't turn me on in the slightest and I'd much rather have only myself to answer to.

I share these insights about my journey into business as part of a very specific lesson. It is critical that we know and understand why we do what we do and the context in which we operate as individuals, organisations or businesses. For example, for me it's important to be nimble, able to pick and choose work that I want to do, and not to be bogged down by having to win only large contracts that will pay for my team's mortgages as well as my own. These criteria automatically filter in and out the type of projects I generally accept.

By contrast, a larger consultancy might have the motive that by being a bigger team, winning bigger work, they might thrive on working on larger scale projects because they want to make a bigger impact, whatever that might look like. For a public servant, they might have chosen to operate in a salaried position because they enjoy the security that the public service provides. Also, they might want to act as intrapreneurs, shaking the system from the inside. Whatever the context of our motives how we operate in the world of community engagement, this level of reflection can help us as we continue to move our sector forward in a positive and transparent way.

For me, the high point of my chosen sweet spot lifestyle (being one of an independent working life that involves being paid a premium hourly rate for the skill, expertise and convenience of my offerings, combined with very little wasted time on compulsory team meetings, gossip by the water cooler, or copious amounts of filling in of timesheets or other administration often associated with being in a job) is that I have plenty of spare time. And I choose to use this spare time to offer my skills to my own communities – whether they be communities of location, interest or something else.

When I was actively running an initiative called *Winey Kids* in my spare time, promoting my home of the McLaren Vale wine region as a great destination for families to visit, locals would often be puzzled at how Dan and I could be sipping wine in a cellar door on a Tuesday afternoon, to promote the experience to our social media followers. We made little money from this venture, but we did it because we knew it inspired our community of like-minded parents and being in a sweet spot with our consultancy businesses meant that we could clock out of the office and clock into a winery. I lost count of the number of times people assumed that I was a 'kept woman' and that Dan's business must be generating the big bucks to maintain our lifestyle. On a side note, to this day we both notice that as a couple at social events the questions about work and business are *always* asked in his direction first, and he's *always* brilliant in always making sure that he brings my successful business into the conversation.

The same would go for my involvement in other local community activities, or my ability to lead movements such as *Engage 2 Act:* a story I tell in Chapter 18. The generous income derived from the life of being a consultant enables you to pass on the fortune through involvement in the causes that don't necessarily have the financial availability.

I see these opportunities to use my spare non-consulting time to get involved with community initiatives pro bono, a bit like carbon offsetting on international flights. For every well-paid job I do as a consultant, I can give back through my own community involvement.

I call myself a consultant with conscience.

...

Conversation Starters

- **WHO** inspired you to work the way you currently work in community engagement?
- **WHAT** are your motives for why and how you undertake community engagement? How do these motives affect the way you engage or the work that you get involved in?
- **WHY** is it important that community engagement consultants operate as 'consultants with conscience'?
- **WHEN** have you given back to a community *pro bono*?
- **WHERE** is your 'sweet spot' for finding a balance between a love of community and generating an income? Where would you draw the line between people and profit?

15. Treat the community as your client

When you get these jobs that you have been so brilliantly trained for, just remember that your real job is that if you are free, you need to free somebody else. If you have some power, then your job is to empower somebody else. This is not just a grab-bag candy game.

— Toni Morrison[26]

A high point of the sweet spot lifestyle I have chosen by being a sole practitioner is my ability to pick and choose my work. I have reached a point in my career (some might call it luck, but I explain it as years of determination and calculated, focussed steps) where I generally have enough consulting opportunities presenting themselves in my inbox to pick and choose my work.

I enjoy remaining nimble, agile, and responsible only for my own actions. I decide what I'm going to work on next, or where I'm going to focus my energies. Recently, I've started declining work that is about conflict resolution in communities, knowing that this is not where my passion lies. I decline that work, explaining that I have chosen to apply my energy to situations where we can engage well and engage early, so we don't reach such points of tension. Just this week, I had a call from a local council inviting me to work with them on an 'issue' in their community. I declined, saying that I work only on 'opportunities' in communities!

Given my strong personal values and passion for community, my ability to pick and choose my work has meant that declining projects that don't meet my desire for authentic, high-quality, and genuine community engagement is a very real option. I take that option if I doubt the intent of work that comes across my desk.

Even more dramatically, from time to time, or for one reason or another, I'll end up actively working on a project that I suddenly realise doesn't align with my values. At that point, as a values-driven practitioner, I've had to make some hard decisions. In 2019, I was contacted by a state government department to undertake engagement on an organisational restructure to affect people on the receiving end of services that department delivered. I should have realised it was dodgy when it was exceptionally last-minute. All they really wanted was my group facilitation skills for a meeting with the affected people the following week.

In my briefing meeting with the client, after having said yes and my quote being accepted, I smelt a rat. I asked a few challenging questions about the purpose of the engagement process. I wasn't happy to hear indirectly that it was just a paper-shuffling process to get the new governance structure approved. There was little opportunity for participants to inform the decision-making process. My heart was pounding as I listened to the usual excuses: 'Things are moving too fast on this project for many changes now'. Or 'the Minister needs to get this through Parliament next month, so we really need to tick the box that we've held this meeting'. And I began to question my involvement.

I know that there are facilitators who will come onboard to help the meeting go smoothly for their client (in this instance, the client was the government). And there are facilitators who will come onboard with the interests of the people attending at heart. I consider myself the latter. I always introduce myself at these kinds of community meetings as a person who is there to help participants get the best out of the time they've contributed, but, equally, my role is to help my client get the best out of everyone's time together. I'm here to ensure that the decisions they make are well-informed.

But on this occasion, it was apparent that my client wasn't interested in hearing what the people had to say on the issue. They wanted the workshop run in a bog-standard format, with a PowerPoint presentation by the Suit-Wearing-Big-Boss-Guy to start and then the opportunity for Q&A from the 'audience'. Whenever I hear anyone propose such a drab, unengaging processes, I immediately suggest alternatives that would be more engaging and productive, and this occasion was no exception. I therefore prepared an interactive process that at least provided opportunities for comment on specific parts of the proposed restructure.

As the day drew closer, I was still questioning my involvement and began to hear murmurs that a large attendance at the meeting was likely. In my mind, I was weighing up the option of walking away. It wasn't a large piece of work so wouldn't be a financial disaster if I did, but I was concerned about letting a client down, no matter how little they apparently cared about genuine engagement. I'd heard that the participants were angry about both the proposed restructure *and* the so-called 'engagement' process. They, too, were smelling rats.

I decided it was too late to back out. And I also decided that I needed to manage this meeting with absolute precision. I empathised with the people attending and understood their frustration and anger.

The day arrived and everything I anticipated came true. The client was there to help set up the room, but then announced she was leaving to attend another meeting. She assured me everything would be fine in my hands. 'You can't even bring yourself to front up to them to listen to their concerns?' is what I shouted at her in my mind as she swiftly hopped into the taxi that pulled up outside. A couple of admin staff on the door, the Suit-Wearing-Big-Boss-Guy and I were left waiting for the angry people to arrive. I was livid.

The people started to arrive and take their seats. I could sense the tension in the air, but everyone was civil. None of us knew what to expect of the next couple of hours. I did my usual Becky-style meet and greets, particularly with the angriest-looking people, desperately attempting to build some rapport or trust with these passionate people. But of course, at that point in proceedings, I was the bad guy. They saw me as 'one of them' and if they'd worked out who I was, they then saw me simply as 'the consultant'.

The session began and the Suit-Wearing-Big-Boss-Guy began his presentation. It was dry, dull and severely lacking in lustre. People shuffled in their seats as he continued through his slides. I hovered with my run sheet on the sidelines, waiting for him to get to the end. As he did, I launched into the next part of the session where people could provide their feedback.

I'm never a fan of a theatre-style set up for this kind of meeting as it creates such a divide between 'us and them' with the experts at the front and people sitting neatly in rows in front listening. I had set up the room 'cabaret-style', with small tables with six or seven people, enabling a greater level of dialogue. I'd set up each table with a different topic for discussion and invited all participants to add their notes to the huge, pre-printed sheets of paper I'd placed on each table.

I announced that this session would be very much about *them* and their opinions. I wanted them to wander around to different tables in their own time, meeting others as they did, adding notes of the things they discussed on the paper at each location. It was like a hybrid World Café meets Open Space Technology methodology that placed the participants at the centre of the process, and allowed them to follow their own energy and interests.

We were about one-third into this session and the best thing happened. Perhaps not in my client's eyes, but I consider it the best thing because I'm all about supporting the needs of the *people*. Right? One participant wrote in large letters on one of my beautifully presented large pieces of paper in the centre of the table: 'This is not a consultation. This is a tick-box exercise. We have chosen not to engage because we don't feel listened to. Sign here if you agree'.

I was proud of this group for calling out bad practice. By this stage, I had decided that my role as the facilitator was not to hush their anger, but to support them and advocate for their voices to be heard, even if it wasn't what my client wanted. As my neatly planned workshop timeline and plan fell away, the participants became more and more animated, encouraging each other to sign the petition on the table, as well as other angered statements as shown in image 18. I used my position of privilege (as the person 'in control' of the workshop format and the one with the microphone) to announce that Kelly had started a petition on Table 6. Anyone was welcome to view it and sign if they agreed.

This one small move showed the participants that I was the 'real deal' and believed wholeheartedly in them, even if the organisation paying my bill didn't. As the momentum in the room gathered, they all started writing additional statements alongside the petition as shown in the image opposite. I couldn't leave my Suit-Wearing-Big-Boss-Guy looking so pale and bemused in the corner, so

I whispered to him reassuringly, 'I need to let them voice their opinions. They must be heard. I've got this'. He nodded, knowing there was no way out.

The workshop was rounded off with the planned Q&A session with the Suit-Wearing-Big-Boss-Guy. But everything was now different. I had let it roll. The voices that were to be silenced were heard. As the workshop came to a close, many people thanked me for being so flexible and adaptable, as well as giving them the opportunity to voice their concerns. My report expressed and supported their honest, angry perspectives. I owed it to *them* to offer authentic the opportunities to be heard. *They* were my client.

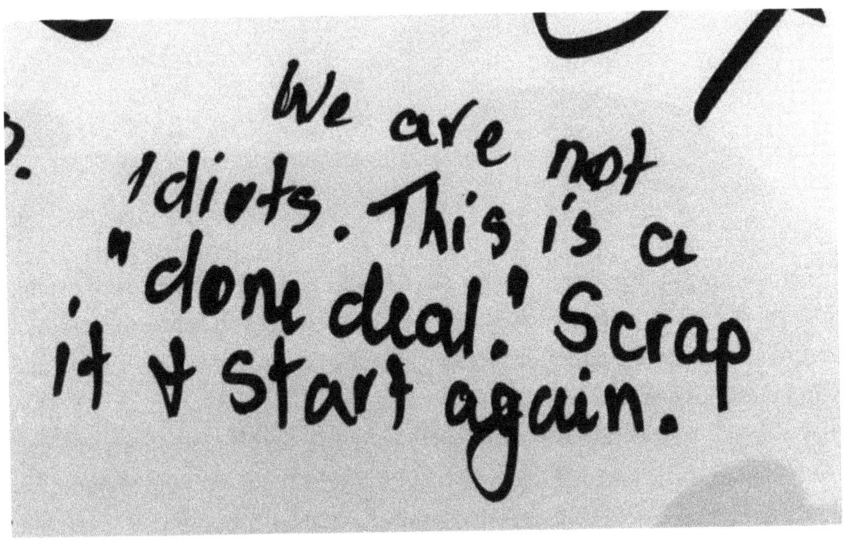

Image 18 - The participants of a disingenuous engagement process took pen to paper to start a petition in the workshop I was facilitating for my client. And I encouraged it.

On the way home from the meeting, I recorded an episode of *Thought Bubbles – Sparkling Insights into Community Engagement*, having a big rant about the client. I posted it to my YouTube channel. *Thought Bubbles* has always been a positioning tool for me and my business, with me providing thought leadership to interested viewers on a range of community engagement topics. But it has equally provided me a cathartic process of debriefing on processes that frustrate me, perhaps because of my lonely existence as a sole practitioner, with no water cooler in the office kitchen around which I could debrief with colleagues.

In this episode of *Thought Bubbles*, I'd kept the client anonymous and spoken only generally about the meeting's topic, and how I was so angry at my client's lack of interest in genuine engagement. Word soon spread, with people knowing the exact meeting I'd been talking about. When the local ABC radio called me requesting an interview about the client and their lack of genuine intent to engage, I declined on the grounds that they were still my client. I needed to draw the line somewhere on how far I took my disgruntled experience. That would be it for me as a consultant if every client feared I'd go to the media if they put a foot wrong!

...

I'm not always able to shift a client's focus. In 2015, I was involved with a state-wide project led by a prominent Minister with a business and economics focused portfolio. I prepared a community engagement strategy and his advisors ripped pages out of in front of my eyes. They knew best, of course, at least with what they wanted, and were more than happy to delete my suggested engagement methodology. I stuck with it and flew on a chartered flight with the Minister, his staff and film crews to some regional South Australian communities where the locals were pretty fired up about his proposals. As you'd imagine, I'd had some great processes planned for getting the conversation going about the options up for discussion.

However, when hundreds of angry people turned up, refusing to participate, and yelled at me, 'You bureaucrat!' the Minister whispered in my ear: 'Just go with it'.

So I sat back and let it roll. There was no point in trying to build any trust on this occasion. Quite bizarrely, our pilot was with us at the meeting and I remember the moment it was over, we all dashed to the plane saying, 'Let's get out of here!'. This event did not go down in history as best practice engagement and I cried when I got home. There is no bigger insult to me than being called a bureaucrat!

When I write a report of an engagement process, I write it with the agreement to myself that I owe it to the people who participated to get it right. In 2018, I worked on a huge community engagement project across South Australia the entire state on behalf of another Minister, regarding a significant reform of natural resource management. I upsized my team for this project. We were three facilitators and one administrator, and together we facilitated over sixty meetings across the State, over three months, with a diverse group of interested people.

After several months of the engagement process and several weeks preparing the final report, I reflected on the people I had met along the way. I asked myself whether Shane, an outback pastoralist would be happy that I've captured his opinion on the need for less red tape. How would Lucy, the environmental volunteer in metropolitan Adelaide, feel about what I'd written regarding revegetation projects? How would Abi, the eco-tourism operator on Kangaroo Island, feel as she read our report regarding grant funding for business. And so on. We wanted to please every single person my team met during the process. *They* were our clients.

It might feel strange at times. I know that. But putting the community first is so critically important. In 2012, one of my local government clients decided to host a panel event on the June long weekend. There residents would hear from a range of pro-nuclear speakers about whether their Council area would be an appropriate location for a new nuclear reactor. This event was totally 'tongue-in-cheek', as the Council's marketing manager was trying to stir up interest in World Environment Day. A risky project, I thought. As you can imagine, the topic attracted a great deal of interest. The hall was packed, and given the contentiousness of the topic, we had undercover police in the audience, as well as an armed security guard. We'd been warned to expect protestors outside the building. During my planning, I was eager to know their likely effect on our event.

After doing some research on the lead organisers, I'd discovered that their plan was to *levitate* the building in which we were meeting. I can honestly say that Googling 'How to levitate a building' is the strangest thing I've ever had to research. However, as the facilitator, I needed to know just how much disruption they were likely to cause. It turns out that to levitate a building you join hands around it and chant (or something along those lines). Actually, the meeting ended up quite undisruptive. Funnily enough, I didn't feel a thing!

When I'm facilitating a difficult meeting, I always observe people as they arrive to determine their objectives for being there and their level of enthusiasm (or otherwise). It's easy to spot people who are going to be dominant or outspoken. I believe that, as a community engagement practitioner, it is not my job to silence them, no matter how outspoken they are. It is, however, my job to help them be a part of the conversation. And to allow everyone else to participate too. If they're showing signs of frustration or anger (with folded arms or a generally standoffish stance), I take it as a challenge to 'flip' them. I want them to leave the meeting smiling, full of compliments for the process. That commitment makes me work extra hard. And nine times out of ten it works.

Take David, for example, who recently attended a meeting I facilitated as part of a strategic planning process for a Council in Adelaide's northern suburbs. Because of physical distancing restrictions (as a result of Covid-19), we'd opted for a series of short meetings we called *Mini-Meets*. David arrived looking like he was hatching a plan to be disruptive. He was rolling his eyes as he entered the room. So, in characteristic fashion, I decided to flip his experience process. I made a beeline for him, and via some chit chat, found out his history with the Council and that he loved poetry. So, in an almost flirtatious invitation, I challenged David to write me a poem for the end of the meeting to summarise what we'd discussed. David had a role. And it was going to put him centre stage. Plus, David felt special because the facilitator had taken an eager interest in his involvement. I'd established enough rapport with David that throughout that hour I was able to give him space to say what was on his mind without excluding others, and keep things on track. When the hour was up, David enthusiastically waved a scrap of paper at me. It was his moment to share his poetic summary. And he did, taking only one minute of our time and leaving everyone with big smiles on their faces. David left the meeting full of praise and compliments for our process.

I'm not suggesting that community engagement is a game, or that it's about winning over awkward or difficult people. Quite the opposite. It's about putting people at the centre of any process and respecting their opinions, whether we agree with them or not.

...

The stories I've shared about witnessing a lack of genuine intent and putting the needs of the community at the forefront of my work raise a question.

We need to ask ourselves: *who exactly we are working for*? And we all need to ask this question, repeatedly: from consultants, project teams, senior leaders, and elected officials.

Chinese philosopher Confucius in 450 BC wisely said, 'Tell me, and I will forget. Show me, and I may remember. Involve me, and I will understand'[8] In 1863, Abraham Lincoln spoke about 'a government of the people, by the people, for the people.'[27] More recently, Barack Obama suggested that 'we don't ask you to believe in our ability to bring change, rather, we ask you to believe in yours.'[28]

Honestly, putting people at the centre of decision-making that affects them is hardly a new concept. Yet, here we are in 2021, still preaching a citizen-centric approach. To be fair to all of us, whilst the concept has been around for thousands of years, from my recent observations of the Western world, we are coming out of decades where the focus has been incredibly government-centric or organisation-centric. Our engagement has developed many similar characteristics: shaped around what government or organisational decision-makers want to focus on, and not necessarily community priorities.

I would prefer to see traditional decision-making entities, such as governments and corporations, shift their operations to place their community people and citizens at the centre of everything they do. Those people and their specific needs would shape everything that needs to be delivered by that organisation. For too long our programs, services, policies, procedures and legislation have been the focal point for conversations. Sadly, the citizens (and local people generally) are considered last: at the tail end of any engagement process.

Instead, I want citizens' needs to be the starting point. Such an approach would need a radical shift in how we engage with communities.

Nowadays, I meet many public servants who favour a more citizen-centric approach. However, this shift in focus demands more than the goodwill of individual employees of organisations. It needs significant direction from the top – elected officials or board members. And it needs significant buy-in and drive from the bottom: the people.

There *is* hope on the horizon. Increasingly, local people and citizens demand that they be at the centre of government processes. In my experience, the majority of everyday people have turned off from politics. And we want to plan decisive roles in determining our social networks, living and working conditions, and the broader environmental and cultural conditions of environments where we live, work and play. People are demanding a role – and an authentic and effective role.

My proposed *Citizen-Centric Approach*, shown in image 19, aims to demonstrate the features and advantages of the old organisation-centric way of working, versus the new citizen-centric approach. Of course, the question isn't whether to apply this model in our work or not. I believe it is coming whether we like it or not! We are in the people business and we need to start applying a people-focussed lens to everything we do. We need to start by stopping our inappropriate behaviour: stopping being so government-centric.

I believe that for everyone working in the realm of public service, *the people* are our client and therefore, they should be at the centre of everything we do. And I mean *everything:* decision-making in the Council chamber, project planning by a consultant, service delivery, or community engagement. *Always.* No matter how much of the underdog they might appear to be.

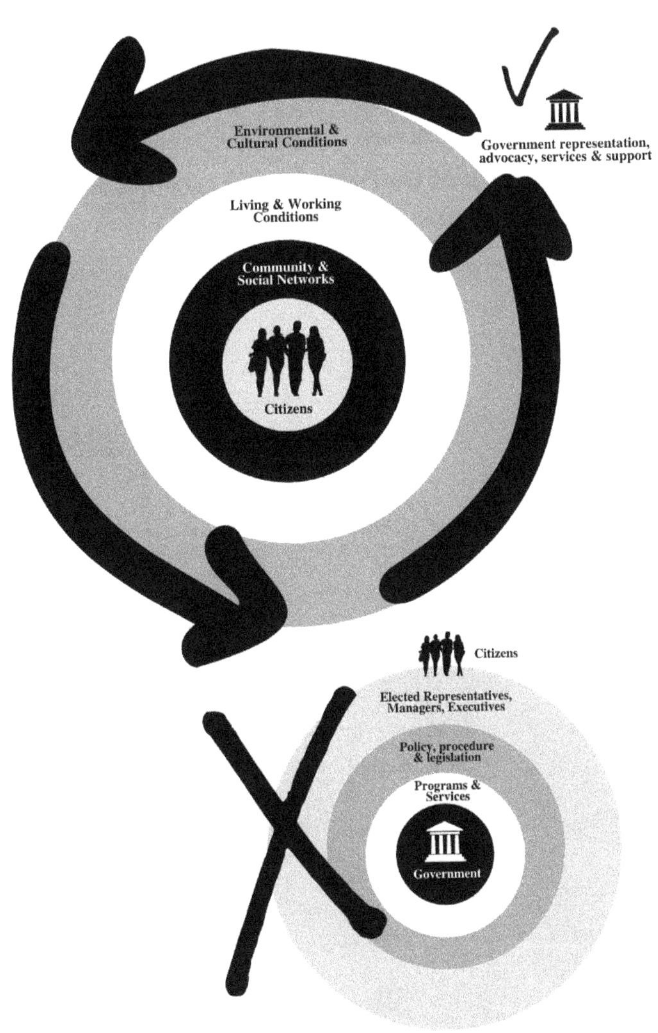

Image 19 - A Citizen-Centric Approach to Government. Hirst, B. 2021.

Conversation Starters

- **WHO** has a vested interest in what you're doing? Who's paying the bill? Whose needs are the most important? Who is most worthy of your consideration: Your client? Your boss? The communities?
- **WHAT** needs to change for people's needs to be at the centre of government or corporate activity?
- **WHY** should a community trust *you*?
- **WHEN** have you had to work hard to build someone's trust in you? How did you honour the trust that they put in you?
- **WHERE** will we end up if we don't begin to rebuild trust between communities and government?

16. Immerse yourself in your own community

You never have to ask anyone permission to lead.
I want you to remember that, OK. When you want to lead, you lead.

—*Kamala Harris*[29]

My childhood was heavily focussed on communities of interest. Whether it was through my Mum's involvement in the school fêtes, or her enjoyment of singing in church, we were always involved with something, somewhere, with groups of people with similar interests to ours. My claim to fame is that I'd watch the now-mega-Hollywood-superstar Simon Pegg wait for his bus to school at the stop across the road from my bedroom window at my parents' house in Gloucester. I'd also spend many an evening hanging out with his most lovely grandparents, John and Pam Pegg, at my Mum's amateur dramatics group, the Abbeydale Players.

In addition to my involvement in my Mum's interests, that I'd always tag along to with great enthusiasm, I had my own communities of interest. My favourite story book as a child was *Battle of the Bunheads,* with its depiction of the friendships that form at ballet class. I had a lovely group of friends with whom I'd dance as a child on a nightly basis and hang out with backstage at our annual summer and winter performances. So many of my communities were based around the theatre, from my Mum's involvement, my dance school, my high school dance clubs and school choirs, and my own involvement in my late teens and early twenties with the Gloucestershire Operatic & Dramatic Society. Even during my further education study for a National Diploma in Performing Arts, I had a huge sense of community beyond simply being a student in lectures. I remember when our 17-year-old minds and bodies burst into an impromptu performance of *One Singular Sensation* in a huge amphitheatre ruin whilst we were on a college trip to the ancient Greek city of Ephesus in Turkey.

My childhood communities of interest were accompanied by a strong sense of belonging. I learned at an early age that there is no greater sense of being a part of something than the experience of the performance arts. Dance was my equivalent of a team sport. The feeling of togetherness that we found as we waited in the wings with fellow performers moments before walking onto stage is unforgettable. As well, with the sense of belonging nurtured by a childhood in the arts also came my confidence. I believe that the piano exams, speech and drama lessons and festival performances, combined with my passion for dance, built the confidence that enables me to work with communities boldly and confidently. But there is more. Having experienced so much 'belonging', I truly know what it feels like to work together.

Much as I valued my Mum's hobbies, I have very fond memories of her work. By the time I was a teenager, my Mum had enrolled at university as a mature student to study for a Bachelor of the Arts degree followed by a Diploma in Social Work. However, when I was a young child, she had a job collecting life insurance premiums, which she used the earnings from to buy a caravan for us to holiday in. These days, our life insurance payment goes out once a month by the magic of automated direct debit. But back in the 1980s, it was someone's job to drive around to collect their cash payments. And for the London & Manchester Insurance company's Gloucester office, that job fell to my Mum. My Dad would help with counting cash at the end of the insurance round. I loved how his precision would always ensure the Queen faced up on the notes, and the coins were neatly piled in matching columns. Sometimes, he'd even let me clean the coins! But more exciting than the coin cleaning were the times where, as a six or seven-year-old, I'd accompany my Mum to people's houses to collect the money. It was rarely just about collecting the money and leaving. Instead, because of her genuine friendly and inquisitive nature, my Mum built rapport with the people, and we'd get a glimpse of their lives.

Those early opportunities to befriend people like Mrs De Gama, an elderly Indian woman (who'd always have the most delicious exotic smelling lunch on the stovetop), or to meet the family who were so in love with their Yorkshire terrier that they had photos of it smiling on every wall, were chances for me to open my eyes and ears to our community's stories. I was young and impressionable. And My Mum's interest, acceptance and embracing of all of the stories, no matter how quirky, demonstrated that people are diverse, interesting, and that everyone has a unique take on the world.

So we had a high level of involvement in communities of interests and we had a strong sense of both belonging and accepting of differences. However, my family didn't have much involvement or interest in activism. My parents are both active and passionate voters, we'd get involved in city events, and I'd always know who the Mayor of Gloucester or the local Member of Parliament was. But I cannot say that we went out of our way to be involved with politics or local decision making. My Dad undertook public consultation at work and has stories of his own about drop-in sessions and community meetings. However, as his speciality was nuclear energy, he often had somewhat fraught experiences!

In 1987, when I was nine, I wrote to the BBC's *Jim'll Fix It* television show, asking Jimmy Saville to organise for me to meet Michael Jackson (in hindsight, I'm glad that he didn't). By comparison, in 2021, my nine-year-old daughter has marched through Adelaide campaigning for marriage equality; she's marched with her sister on Invasion Day, proudly chanting *Always was, always will be, Aboriginal Land* (clap, clap); on her own initiative, she emailed our local MP to question why the women's cricket games at Adelaide Oval don't have pyrotechnic displays and celebration like the men's cricket games do (calling out gender inequity); and she has set up a Recycling Club at school as her contribution toward tackling climate change. She regularly writes motivational 'never give up'-themed songs as part of school 'passion projects'. Her bedtime reading includes *Good Night Stories for Rebel Girls*. Whilst I am conscious that both of my daughters are, not surprisingly, their mother's daughters, I believe that social activism is much higher on everyone's agenda these days. Children and young people are much more switched on and empowered to demand change than we were at their age.

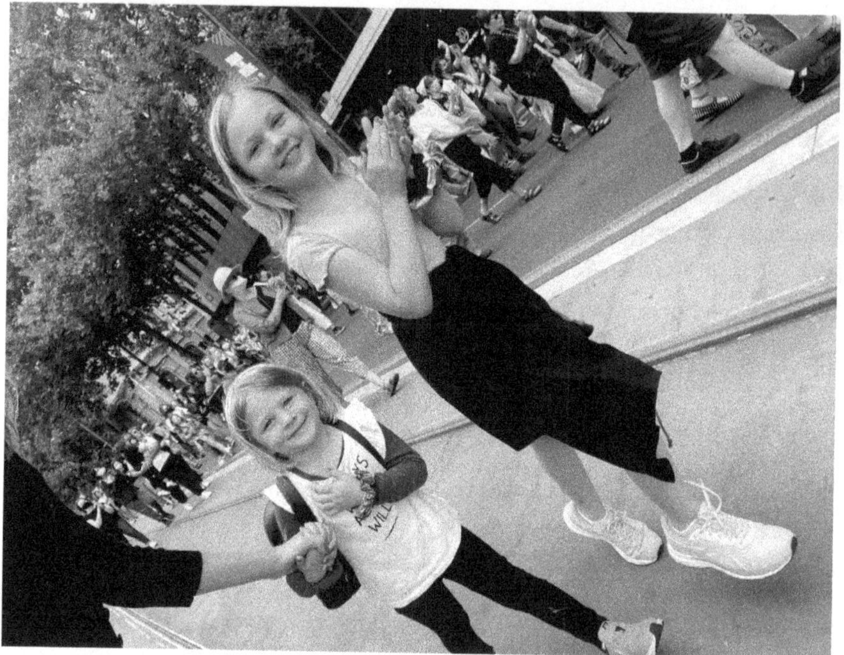

Image 20 – With my daughters Florence (4) and Elsie (9) at the Invasion Day march in Adelaide on 26 January 2021.

In my mid-twenties, my community of circumstance became the backpacking community. We'd socialise together, live together, often work together, and, of course, travel together because our circumstances often interwove with our interests.

When Dan and I moved to London in 2005, we adopted a much more private lifestyle, knowing very few people in the City other than work colleagues. We were no longer backpackers. Now we were a childless professional couple in a city of eight million people. We absolutely loved living in the leafy suburb of Chiswick in West London, our community of place, but our movements were very much about the two of us enjoying local cafés, bars, and long weekend walks along the banks of the River Thames. I'm not sure whether our limited community involvement or connection during those two-years in London was about being in the often-unengaged-transient-mid-twenty age bracket. Or that we just didn't come across opportunities to get involved in community life. Or that we just enjoyed each other's company enough not to be searching for any other form of escapism or belonging.

One significant (yet accidental) piece of activism we got involved with during our time in London was after the landlord of the beautiful high-ceilinged, large-windowed Victorian era flat where we lived during our first year failed to return our rental deposit at the end of our tenancy. We were distraught to learn that our rental agent had handed our £1,100 bond to the landlord upon him reporting that he'd needed to redecorate and recarpet after we moved out. This was totally and utterly untrue and we subsequently dragged him through the small claims court, suing him for the inconvenience. After this horrid experience, I contacted Shelter, a prominent UK housing and homelessness charity, to let them know about the situation and to offer our help in spreading the word about how tenants can protect themselves from ending up in financial hardship because of the duplicity of landlords like this. They were thrilled to hear from me, as the timing worked perfectly with a new Tenancy Deposit Protection Scheme that was soon to be launched.

A couple of weeks later, Shelter called me to ask whether Dan and I would like to attend a meeting at 10 Downing Street to meet the Prime Minister on this matter. I joke not. Um… let me just check my diary… of course we're available! By the end of the week, we were going through the security gate of Downing Street, nervously wandering along the street, through the famous Number 10 door, and up the beautiful and famous carpeted staircase lined with portraits of all the former British Prime Ministers. It was a magical moment!

Sadly, for us, just moments before we were due to meet Tony Blair, whilst we were sipping on our cups of tea served in the finest china, the Iranian President unexpectedly held a press conference in Tehran to announce that he was releasing a group of British hostages. At the last moment, the Prime Minister sent his apologies and instead in walked his Secretary of State for Communities and Local Government, Ruth Kelly, as the understudy. We had a productive meeting, but the afternoon ended with us being quietly ushered out through the underground corridors at the back of Downing Street, as the world's media descended at the front of the building for the Prime Minister's own press conference on the Iran hostage situation.

After we moved to Australia, and more specifically after finding our 'forever home' in McLaren Vale, we have thrown ourselves quite dramatically into our communities. It wasn't always that way though, as back in 2012 we were feeling despondent with where we lived. Whilst we loved the beautiful scenery, the beaches, the wineries, and the proximity to Adelaide, we didn't know many people. We lacked a sense of belonging or connection. By now we'd had our first daughter, who was still a baby, which gave us opportunity to meet some other parents through a local baby group. But living on the other side of the world from all our family, the days were long and lonely and, with Dan working long hours in Adelaide, sometimes the only interaction Elsie and I would have with another being would be a walk to see a donkey down the road. This was the first time I'd ever felt homesick for the UK since moving to Australia. We wanted more buzz, more connection, and to feel that sense of belonging that is so important. Confident that Australia was where we wanted to be, we researched the whole country, looking for the ideal location. In the end, we decided that where we lived *was* our ideal location, and that if it lacked the buzz that we craved then we simply needed to create that buzz!

And boy, did we create a buzz! Not long after this realisation, I started a blog about places in the McLaren Vale wine region that you could visit with children in tow. Ever since we'd had Elsie, we'd continued our love of good food and wine. So we continued to visit our favourite wineries and restaurants. Friends noticed this and began asking for recommendations of wineries they could go to with their children in tow and survive! The list grew so long that I started a blog, and after some brainstorming with friends on Facebook, I named the blog *Winey Kids*. I kept the blog quiet for quite a while because I felt awkward about the promotion of alcohol and the connection to children, but one day I mentioned it to a local winemaker in passing and his enthusiasm spurred me on to go public with it. By that evening, I had set up a Facebook page and had 30 followers.

Momentum for Winey Kids grew exponentially. Before I knew it, I had 3,000 local, wine-loving parents following my page. Then it grew to 4,000. Then 6,000. Then 10,000. We undertook no marketing or promotion, just simply word of mouth and a strong social media presence, with regular twice-a-day posts all about the latest wineries our little family had visited. Winey Kids went on to become a respected, well-known, and trustworthy online information source for people wanting to explore and enjoy wine regions. It was rated by many local cellar doors as one of their top three referrers for visitors. Most of my followers were parents, but many weren't. Many just enjoyed the positive coverage and 'winey' adventures shared via the various channels.

We won numerous awards for business, destination marketing and tourism at a local and state level. I ran over 35 packed-out Mummy's Wine Club events and dinners at the two local restaurants, featuring dozens of winemakers. Among our events were: a crazy Mummy's Gin Night; 3 Daddy's Beer and Meat Club events; a sell-out Teddy Bears' Picnic on the lawns at a cellar door; a pre-vintage walkabout through the vines evening with a winemaker and grape grower; and a kid's vintage winery tour at a working winery. We produced a *Guide to Cellar Door Etiquette*, still displayed in many cellar doors; sold a 25-page *Little Explorer Guide to McLaren Vale* via the local Visitor Centre and cellar doors; created personalised wine for Father's Day; and we even dabbled in branded clothing.

At times Winey Kids felt cult-like, with fellow parents coming up to me in the supermarket telling me I'd literally changed their life, as they now had the confidence to explore where they lived with their children in tow. I became a character known as the *Winey Mum* and people looked to me for inspiration. At times it was horrific, however, receiving photos of people with slit wrists because of alcohol abuse with the reminder that alcohol is not always fun. I did not appreciate being called *boozy bogans* in the local newspapers comment sections. However, as the positive comments far outweighed the negatives, I persevered.

In June 2018, I used my broadcasting platform to make one of my first negative posts about the region, complaining about an annual event called *Sea & Vines*, which had taken place for 27 years on the long weekend in June. In recent years, this event had turned into an alcohol and drug-fuelled festival, full of urinating men along roadsides and ambulance call-outs to wineries to pick up their unconscious patrons. My post, along with some coverage from another popular social media profile, generated a tsunami of reactions from fellow locals about their dislike of the festival. And, when the mainstream media got involved, my phone was ringing off the hook for interviews. The social media outrage led to the decision by the organisers to cancel the 27-year-long festival, which I'm told had been on the cards for a while. Nevertheless, I was still in shock that my single Facebook post had created such a snowball effect.

Interestingly, hardly anyone from the wine community spoke up alongside me when things escalated. Any sense of belonging I had had within the industry fell away rapidly and I resented all the years of time and energy I had given to this community.

In those Winey Kids days, we created the buzz we were looking for in our local community and felt phenomenally well connected. Ironically, at the same time, I had never felt lonelier. We moved on from Winey Kids because all our achievements were done in our spare time. It became too exhausting, especially with both of us having full time businesses, community commitments, a second baby, a bout of post-partum depression, and more. But more critically, we were giving and giving and giving to our community, and it felt like we weren't receiving much in return.

Tall Poppy Syndrome, the uniquely Australian concept of cutting down people who are achieving success, is rife in Australia. I continue to be amazed at the things I hear people say about me because of those Winey days. I'd been a member of an active wine industry Facebook group that included local people who worked in cellar doors. I found the knowledge they shared invaluable to pass on in promoting local business and events to my followers. But one day, I received a message that I'd been removed from the group, as I wasn't from the wine industry. Despite everything I was achieving for local wineries, local parents and local tourism, for some reason I didn't belong. I felt terribly hurt, particularly given I am *all* about working together!

Where I live, the wine industry is a community in itself, but a very cliquey one with some huge egos involved. In my experience, such a community doesn't easily tend to embrace much difference of opinion or ways of thinking, especially from 'incomers'. The egos (including the official industry organisations) didn't know how to cope with the whirlwind I created. So they either blocked my involvement, or completely ignored my efforts, no matter how much they achieved for the region. I was most definitely the underdog! This was the first time I had ever felt unwelcome in a community. I felt the opposite of the sense of belonging that I so rely on. I felt isolated, alone, depressed. My esteem was certainly depleted, and I was exhausted.

Living in an area where grape growing and winemaking are the primary industries (albeit with a high number of residents not working within the industry nowadays), you find layers and layers of communities of interest, all within one community of place. It makes for an interesting dynamic when you start to get involved! A great, but very complex game of Sim City!

As well as working with Winey Kids, I also threw myself into some more wholesome community activities, such as the Board of Management at the McLaren Vale & Districts War Memorial Hospital, where my efforts were welcomed. This wonderful local hospital was planned and built by local people back in 1945. Decades later saw a trend toward centralising services. So, not surprisingly, during my time on the Board, I became pretty passionate about the opposite: decentralised services that are relevant and responsive to the needs of local communities. The health sector is a prime example. At the same time that 40 kilometres north of McLaren Vale in Adelaide, the government was investing billions of dollars into the brand-new state-of-the-art Royal Adelaide Hospital, I continually advocated for smaller scale, community-run health services such as the McLaren Vale Hospital.

One of my highlights as Chairperson was leading the Board's development of the hospital's first-ever Strategic Plan, *Choose McLaren Vale* and sharing it with guests to our meetings, such as the now-Premier of South Australia, Steven Marshall, who was the Leader of the Opposition at the time. However, pushing against the tide, in a voluntary capacity, on top of the rest of life's commitments, is a hard slog.

In January 2016, I was 20 weeks pregnant when my parents flew from the UK to stay with us to help. I'd been so exhausted from the pregnancy, plus my consultancy work was in full flow, along with all the distractions of Winey Kids. I'd recently taken over as Chair of the Board of Management and was overseeing a massive organisational restructure, which had involved a redundancy of the existing Chief Executive, a position held by a local person. I found it horrible to go through the process of making someone redundant, especially a person from within your own community. And I was doing this work in my spare time as a volunteer. But we'd proceeded with the restructure, and I was in the middle of recruiting for a new leadership position, as well as trying to keep staff informed of the significant changes being implemented in the organisation. At the same time, Dan was heavily involved on the organising committee for a local event called the Harvest Festival, which was raising money for the hospital.

On Mum and Dad's first evening with us, whilst they were driving home from dinner, about one kilometre from home, my Dad momentarily lost consciousness at the wheel and they ended up both with multiple broken vertebrae and sternums, as well as a hire car that looked like a can crushed for recycling. They spent the night at Flinders Medical Centre, the largest hospital in the south of Adelaide, before being discharged the next day.

I couldn't believe that they were being sent home – to stay with us – with all these broken bones, as well as still being in shock. Not to mention their severely dented pride. A few calls later, I had them admitted to the McLaren Vale Hospital, where they were cared for, for a couple of weeks and given a more appropriate period to rest and recuperate within the small, friendly, community hospital (shown in image 21). The care they received over those weeks, alongside the convenience of them being close by for visits by us and our friends, convinced me of the need for localised, (and ideally) community-governed, healthcare. Large, impersonal hospitals serve many purposes, I'm sure, but the intimacy and personal care that can be provided by smaller, more boutique country hospitals can't be beaten for the overall health and wellbeing of a community. I believe the world needs more of that.

I share these stories about involvement in and connection to my own communities to demonstrate the importance of several things in relation to community engagement practitioners.

Image 21 – Dan, Elsie and I visiting my parents in the small, local community hospital in McLaren Vale (of which I was the Chair of the Board of Management at the time) after their car accident in January 2016. Photo by author, 2016.

We need to understand how our interactions with our communities have shaped us because this affects how we plan and deliver our own initiatives and projects. It can be incredibly useful to think deeply about what attracted us to become a part of a particular community and what kept us engaged in that community. Or, on the other hand, what turned us off from a community. Was it that you were looking for a sense of belonging or connection? Was it that you were at an age when community involvement was on your radar, for one reason or another? Was it that somebody pitched something to you as important and asked for your support? Whatever the reason for your immersion in community, understanding *why* can help you plan and implement your own initiatives and processes because you begin to think as a community member, rather than as a professional.

Doing this provides a stark reminder that we are human beings, just like the 'communities' we refer to in our work. So often I remind my clients that they too are local citizens, local people from somewhere. They belong to their own communities, of some sort. I ask them to think about whether they would get involved in whatever it is they are wanting others to get involved with. More often than not, their answer is 'no, I probably wouldn't'. That gives me an entry to ask: 'Why?'

It is important that we reflect on times in our own lives when a decision was made that affected us, either positively or negatively, and the role we played as community members within that process. Whenever I see my local Council encouraging involvement in something, I do exactly this: pondering on my reaction to the opportunity and delving deep into what encourages or prevents me from getting involved. Sometimes it's as simple as the topic doesn't interest me, or I don't feel motivated by a particular tool or technique they are using to try to get me involved. Sometimes it's because I have a sinking feeling in my stomach that it would all just be too depressing when I've given my all to their process, and they don't listen, or I don't understand why they made the decision they did. These are the moments of gold when we shape our community engagement practice, based on our own experiences in our own communities.

I recently attended a protest meeting in my community, organised by my local Member of Parliament, who happens to be part of the Opposition of our State Government. The meeting was well attended by over 300 passionate locals. My eight-year-old daughter and I were among them. The meeting was about an application lodged for a local landfill site to become a storage site for some pretty nasty, toxic chemicals. I attended the meeting because I told myself that we can't always rely on everyone else to fight the cause. It was important to speak up on an issue of concern in our community. As the meeting progressed, members of the audience were invited to a microphone next to the stage where the local politicians and experts sat.

As I sat there, my heart pounding at the prospect of speaking, I couldn't let my daughter think that it is only old, white men who have an opinion, as they were the only ones lining up at the microphone, confident in their own voices and not needing any time to mull over whether their opinion was worthy of sharing (as women more generally do). So, I forced myself to line up at the microphone and say my piece, with Elsie watching me. I observed how incredibly nervous I felt at the prospect of speaking in front of such a large crowd on something I felt passionate about. It was in stark contrast to how I usually feel when I facilitate a large public meeting as an engagement 'expert'. My legs were shaking. Immersion like this in my own community activism helps me to understand what it is like to walk in another's shoes. It makes me compassionate and eager to understand the needs of every individual who turns up to a meeting because they are passionate (and sometimes angry) about it. It reminds me that we need to plan for the different ways that people express their opinions.

I also regularly ponder the question of whether it is possible to be a good community engagement practitioner without being involved in (or at least passionate about) your community.

How can we expect people, groups, or communities to get involved if we have no understanding of what it is like to be a part of a community?

...

Conversation Starters

- **WHO** is your favourite activist? Why is that?
- **WHAT** role does a sense of belonging play in community engagement practice?
- **WHY** is it so important to be actively involved in your own community, even if community engagement is your day job?
- **WHEN** have you immersed yourself in your own community? What did you learn from this experience? How has this affected how you engage with other communities?
- **WHERE** do you fit in the ecosystem of the community in which you live or work?

17. Be led by the people

If you really care about starting a movement, have the courage to follow and show others how to follow. And when you find a lone nut doing something great, have the guts to be the first one to stand up and join in.

— *Derek Sivers*[30]

During late 2017, I was approached by a large infrastructure company, seeking my interest in joining their global communication and engagement team. It's incredibly flattering to receive a call from a person who is telling you how much they admire your work, and they want you on their team. I felt honoured to have had my work considered relevant enough to be part of a large international firm.

In my usual 'imposter syndrome' style, I found myself asking the person why on earth they wanted little old Becky Hirst on their global engagement team. The answer showed that the caller had been paying attention to a specific set of skills I had in the community engagement sector and other projects. My ability to create a *movement*. I remember her exact words. 'Becky, I've noticed you have a real skill in being able to create a movement. You know how to bring people along on journeys. This is a unique skill set, and I want that skill set on my global engagement team'.

These were powerful words, yet I still found enough internal self-doubt to tell myself that, whilst I appeared to create movements, I didn't really. Much like in the music industry these days, where there's a perception that you need to win the X Factor to become famous, I was seeing people who are defined as having created movements to be the likes of Greta Thunberg, leading the young people from all corners of earth to strike from school to sit outside their local parliament buildings to demand greater action on addressing climate change. Or how about Tarana Burke, who started the *Me Too* movement, empowering millions of women to share stories of how they, too, had been sexually abused.

My list has examples of incredible creators of movements that changed the way the world views or acts on a particular issue.

However, I was hearing these words from someone I respected and regarded as having a high level of intelligence. I chose not to ignore her but to consider her offer. At her invitation, I did join the corporate world for a few months. I absolutely loved getting to spend time in the Sydney, Brisbane, Melbourne, Adelaide and Perth offices, and video conferencing with the New Zealand and South African offices. Sadly (or perhaps not), I quickly learned that no amount of incredible salary or frequent flyer points would replace my love of being my own boss, the grit of being at the coalface of community engagement, and the ability (created through my business and lifestyle choices) to go where the energy is, as and when I choose.

'Go where the energy is' was a motto that I repeated to myself frequently during the establishment of Engage 2 Act, a global collective of people who are passionate about progressing the practice of high-quality community engagement. It's a motto I continue to follow today. Energy and movements go hand-in-hand. Energy is everything in my work. We need to consider how governments and corporations engage with communities from an energy standpoint. We need to be drawn where the energy already is within communities. And then we need to nurture and build on that energy as we collaborate to make considered decisions.

I use the analogy of a tiny little pilot light on a stovetop. We can find a match, strike that match, create a small flame, put it to the existing flame of the small pilot light, and boom – now you've got a bigger ring of heat to work with! For this particular analogy, as long as that bigger flame has enough fuel source to keep burning, you can do all sorts of handy things with it, such as boiling a pan of water or gathering around it to keep warm.

We can't create a movement without there being energy, even if it's just a tiny pilot light – not just from you as a leader. You need the people about to join your movement - to ignite that pilot light. As we know from Derek Sivers' famous 2010 Ted Talk, *How to Start a Movement,*[30] those first followers are absolutely critical to ensure you aren't acting as a lone nut. Part of our work as community engagement practitioners is to find that pilot light, and to nurture any potential ignition.

...

My *Engage 2 Act* journey, a story I recount in the next chapter, started with a pre-movement (an inspiring story in itself) and resulted in confirming my desire to move towards (or should I say, return to) a more community-led style of local decision making. A *pre-movement* is a concept I've arrived at purely to tell this story. I will define a pre-movement as a movement before a movement. You might call it the pilot light.

It was 2013, and I had been operating as a community engagement consultant in South Australia for four years. Things were going well, but I was still a relative newcomer to the State. So I needed to keep working hard at building my networks. The joy of doing business in a small city like Adelaide is that word travels super-fast. It's pretty easy to build a good reputation and have strong networks with a well-executed plan. Equally it's just as easy for a bad word to spread about you. So, my motto has always been: *always do a good job*. I had an ambitious plan: fast-growing client work, face-to-face and online networking in the government and community sectors, running half-day workshops on the basics of community engagement, and attending relevant events in Adelaide when I could.

During this era of what I'd call 'extreme networking', I was fortunate to cross paths with John Baxter, who had picked up on my passion for community and was in the midst of working on various ideas and initiatives. He wanted to pick my brain. We'd meet in the co-working space where he rented a desk, the Majoran Distillery on Grenfell Street, and talk for hours on community-led activism and our shared desire to see more collaboration happening at both community and government levels in South Australia. The timing of crossing paths with John, in his down-to-earth grey t-shirt and jeans, was perfect for me in my career. I'd left the grit of community work in the UK and was starting to feel like a bunny in the headlights of the heavily bureaucratic, top-down, suit-wearing way of engaging communities that tempted my South Australian clients. I certainly hadn't lost my way, as I was leading the way with creativity, innovation, and a genuine intent to engage. However, I needed a wake-up call. John provided that by reminding me of where my love of community was.

Those conversations with John would go pretty deep and philosophical. After one of our brainstorming sessions, I'd l drive back from the City down the expressway home to McLaren Vale wondering what exactly we'd just achieved. Of course, we always enjoyed a good dose of putting the world to rights. But when I look back, I see that my work with John completely altered the course of community engagement for me, for South Australia, and beyond.

John was passionate about unearthing collaborative opportunities. At the time he was observing initiatives such as 5000+, the integrated design strategy partnership; grassroots environment projects; and rapid growth in the business start-up space were creating a form of energy in Adelaide. Yet he'd observed that very few people got the chance to apply our energy to the things we cared about. Therefore, he led a group of passionate people to organise and host a one-day event called *CoCreate Adelaide*. The event took place at Plant 4 in Bowden, on the outer edge of the Adelaide Parklands. Our unprepossessing venue was a large, disused, empty and very dusty warehouse. The event was pitched to the public as an opportunity for people and community groups to come together to cocreate visions they were passionate about.

CoCreate Adelaide was the ultimate model for bottom-up, grassroots engagement. Sixty people paid ten dollars to attend this unique event, and to my amazement they weren't even offered a free lunch. Instead, we asked them to pay for lunch from the food truck located beside the shed. We donated our time so that the tiny grant from the local Council and income from the ticket sales could be spent on the event's basic operational needs.

My main involvement was assisting with the agenda-setting process, shown in image 22. We chose to use *Open Space Technology*, a technique developed by Harrison Owen in the 1980s. In this model, participants create the agenda for themselves. Owen observed that, as a general rule, the most useful and relevant conversations at a conference usually occur during the coffee breaks or at the post-conference networking drinks. Much like how fun at a party always happens in the kitchen!

I love the Open Space Technology technique a lot. However, I don't recommend it for the faint-hearted. In my experience, control-freak facilitators generally hate the idea of starting with a blank canvas. I am not one of those folks. I absolutely love seeing a blank agenda wall at the start of the day rapidly fill with participant-led topics as the day unfolds. The joy in this technique comes from an equal share of power, as the participants put what *they* want to see on the agenda, at that exact moment in time. Then (and this is a great feature of Owen's model), they lead the discussions with people who choose to come to their session. It is the most magical process to facilitate!

I use the concept of self-organising communities in my work a lot. As adults, and even as children, we thrive on being given responsibility. When I'm facilitating a group of almost any size, you will often hear me telling people to organise themselves into smaller groups, or to work out together how they will capture and record what's been discussed. I am far from prescriptive or dictatorial in how I do this. You will never find me tapping people on the head, giving them numbers, or prescriptively sorting them into order. I love observing the chaos of letting people sort themselves out, followed by the satisfaction of them successfully self-organising. I have found that this is not only a great way to build belonging and ownership in a group process, but it is also a great way to build high levels of trust and respect. While I might be relaxed in this regard, I'm a strict timekeeper. I'm known to be a stern headmistress in this department!

During our CoCreate Adelaide day, we eagerly discussed a wealth of topics. Some discussions were in small groups of two or three, while others involved a huge crowd gathered around. The topics were vast and varied, from environmental projects to how we might better support the business start-up community.

Image 22 - A crowd gathers in a disused warehouse during April 2013 to CoCreate Adelaide. Michael Kubler, 2013.

I distinctly remember a man in a high-vis vest offering a short presentation to a group of eager listeners about his vision for a Solar Thermal Power Plant in Port Augusta. This seemed so relevant, given the imminent closure of the town's coal-fired power station. To his inquisitive audience, he explained the science, the environment, the employment opportunities, and the high level of interest and support within his community. I remember thinking that this was a very progressive topic. I felt uneasy about my lack of knowledge. However, I was to observe that this project gained significant momentum with South Australia's Government in 2017. It was subsequently cancelled by the incoming government in 2019. I often wonder who that man was and what the trajectory of his journey must have been since that day.

CoCreate Adelaide was comprised of self-selected people willing to chip in to make real changes. I could hear the energy and the collaborative responses as I moved from session to session: 'I need a space to set up a hub' was quickly followed by 'I've got a space you can use'. I was reminded of the potential for change led by the community. It happens at a pace that is completely unfamiliar to our bureaucrat-led society. And, of course, it happens on a shoestring budget, if there is any budget at all.

Amid the buzz of energy that day, I found myself in some deep conversations with community engagement colleagues who worked in local government. One was fellow engagement enthusiast, Dan Popping, who worked in a local government job at the time. Dan and I were wearing our personal hats, but we couldn't help put our professional hats on to discuss the process that we were witnessing.

We were witnessing a genuine community-led initiative. For starters, CoCreate Adelaide was led by members of the Adelaide community, donating our time because it was something we truly believed. Other than a small grant from the local Council, there was no government involvement or funding. There was no agenda, either physically or metaphorically. We simply provided a space where people could bring topics of interest, along with their passion to make the world a better place. These 'everyday people' came together, created a ridiculously robust and rich agenda which they then worked through. Collectively! And they paid for their own lunches! It's always nice to offer a free lunch as an incentive to attend something, or as a polite thank you for people's time and energy. But CoCreate Adelaide taught me that if people are passionate enough about something, they'll come, even without the free lunch.

This experience had a galvanizing effect on us community engagement enthusiasts. We began mulling over how what we were witnessing was the total opposite of the accepted public participation (or community engagement) wisdom sweeping the country. This approach totally flipped the concept so popular with those at the top of the political game. You know what that looks like: shiny consultant project teams or bureaucratic policy makers, setting the agenda, and deciding how much or how little involvement they would grant any hapless community on any particular project. What we witnessed on that remarkable day in Adelaide in 2013 was the community deciding what was important, and then deciding what level of involvement they wanted or needed from government to enable their ideas to come alive.

I felt so inspired and invigorated by what I'd witnessed that as soon as I returned home, I pulled out my file full of popular models of community engagement – ladders, wheels, triangles, continua... And, of course, I realised that none of what was in my file reflected what I had just witnessed. I promptly doodled a continuum of my own that totally reversed the idea that the decision-makers would be the government agency or the large business. Instead, I asked myself, *what if the community were the decision makers?*

The scribbles on my notepad put the community as the decision-makers and the government entities as the enablers and facilitators. I created a vision where decisions could be made based on the specific community needs, as determined by community. Further, community-led initiatives would harness people's energy, even if that energy was nothing more than a tiny pilot light. I knew I was onto something and I felt really excited. In one fell swoop I had 'got' it. Yes, there *was* an alternative method to top-down, government-heavy community engagement processes that dominated the community engagement landscape. I really never turned back from that moment of insight.

Now my imagination was in full flight. I imagined communities where people would come together to generate ideas. Then they'd approach government to let *them* know the role they were to play in the decision-making process. In some cases, communities would make all the decisions, simply notifying the government that decisions would be made. At other times, community members might seek feedback from the government on ideas, or possibly even involve them in deeper conversations to explore alternative ideas. Occasionally, communities might invite government to work together with them on an issue, as joint decision makers at the table. There might even be times where communities decided to put all their trust in government to make all of the decisions.

Put simply, *the communities* would decide the level of influence that the government would have on decisions to be made in their communities. Not the other way around.

Several years later, I was fortunate to be working with a very progressive Chief Executive of a Council. This Council wanted to develop an approach to community engagement – a framework, a tool kit, or something else. I pitched that he should bring me on board for a period of three to six months so we could take our time in exploring ideas and options, working together with the staff, the Mayor, elected members, and the communities to decide on the best way forward. He accepted my proposal (an absolute joy for once not to rush an outcome), and my process began by meeting one-to-one with several key stakeholders – or as I prefer to call them: the *Very Important People.*

One of these *Very Important People* was Rachel, a relatively new elected member with a strong reputation as a local activist and community campaigner. Rachel's campaigning had paid off and she was now one of the team of decision-makers in the Council chamber. After feeling unheard for many years, she was passionate about genuine connection and engagement with the local community. Our chats would be lengthy and intense at times. I remember telling her that the things we were discussing involved breaking down hundreds of years of institutionalised decision-making. Nevertheless, I listened deeply and with genuine intent to find an approach that would work for this Council.

I showed Rachel some existing popular models of community engagement used by governments around the world. Not surprisingly, like me, she felt something was missing. For her, genuine engagement with communities wasn't just about the Council deciding when and where this would happen, and what the topic would be. She used her own examples of *Sidewalk Chats* that she'd host a couple of times a month in her township. She passionately explained to me that these chats weren't about her going to the community with issues that she wanted to discuss. Not at all! They were about her being available to listen to matters of importance to the people who attended. Then she would work with them to help them find a way forward. We also talked about those times where community members would attend Council meetings to present deputations: a formal way for them to bring matters of importance to Council's attention.

Her fellow elected members agreed that these community-led interactions were an important aspect of connecting with their community. So we dutifully wrote this into their framework which was officially adopted by the Council. We called it 'Public-Initiated Participation', with a nickname of 'PIP' for short. I've since drawn up this concept in greater detail, as shown in image 23, showing where the various levels of connection between communities and government range from. One thing remains certain though – all processes become community-led.

A Circle of Public-Initiated Participation:
What if the community became the decision makers?

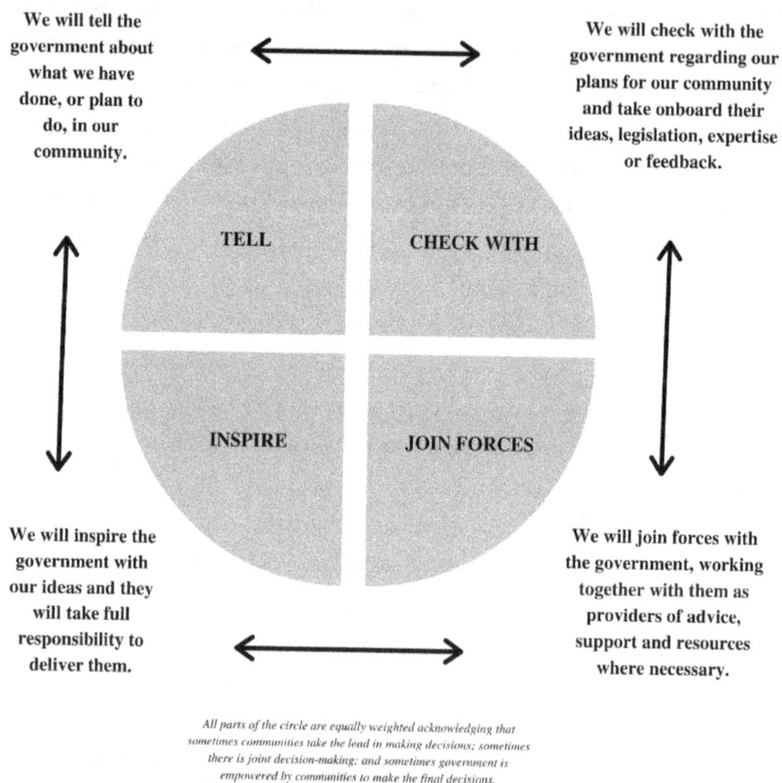

We will tell the government about what we have done, or plan to do, in our community.
We will check with the government regarding our plans for our community and take onboard their ideas, legislation, expertise or feedback.
TELL
CHECK WITH
INSPIRE
JOIN FORCES
We will inspire the government with our ideas and they will take full responsibility to deliver them.
We will join forces with the government, working together with them as providers of advice, support and resources where necessary.
All parts of the circle are equally weighted acknowledging that sometimes communities take the lead in making decisions; sometimes there is joint decision-making; and sometimes government is empowered by communities to make the final decisions.

Image 23 – A Circle of Public-Initiated Participation: What if the community became the decision makers? Hirst, B. 2021.

Reading my suggestions for Public-Initiated Participation might make some people feel a bit uncomfortable. And quite rightly so. What I am proposing is a far cry from the way things currently operate in the world of community engagement. I anticipate the discomfort from those who have been elected to represent their communities. These readers are likely to already have a taste of power and influence – perhaps even a love of it. Simply put, this matter needs readdressing. The role of elected officials must change from being about *their* agenda (whether a personal agenda or the agenda of a political party or party donors). It must be about ensuring the community they represent is enabled, activated and empowered to the highest level possible.

This flip of influence to a more community-led and citizen-centric approach is no easy feat for any organisation. But it is achievable if we have the right mindset, intention, and governance systems. To implement such a change might seem seismic in scale. However, the results are worth the effort: a significant growth in trust between communities and governments, and, in turn, stronger, healthier, and more thriving communities.

Let's imagine that some enthusiastic environmentalists form a group that meets monthly to plant trees together or tidy up weeds in a local park. If they are planting on private farmland and have organised their own funding via grants or sponsorship, they might simply *tell* the local Council about the exciting work they are doing. Or they might *check with* their Council about where they can and can't plant. Or they might *join forces* with experts from within the environment department within government for funding support or expert guidance. Their ideas could *inspire* government to employ a team of seasonal tree planters to deliver what the community have identified as important!

On a much bigger scale, imagine a group of informed and supported people who are part of a local Residents' Association with strong representation from their local area, including a wide range of people and interests. The Association is high-functioning, partly because of the local Council's investment in growing and nurturing it as part of their citizen-centric mode of operation. While their members are hearing stories about local people struggling to enter the rental market, the Association identifies a shortage of affordable housing and decides that more is needed. Their findings might inspire the government to put into action an Affordable Housing Scheme in their area. Or they might decide to join forces with the local Council to work together with landlords about rent affordability issues. Or what's to stop the community taking the lead on the development of an affordable housing project, with private developer investment and some kind of co-operative ownership arrangement? Admittedly, they'd need to check with their Council for planning permission. But they would be demonstrating that a community is capable of anything, given nurturing and support.

Community Engagement Officers in local Councils would see their roles change from being coordinators of intensive, short-lived projects where they desperately seek contributions from what they see as an apathetic and distrusting public, to roles about strengthening and enabling local people, groups, and communities of interest to thrive, and take true ownership. Government would become an enabler, an ally, and a supporter of community-led activity… And dare I say it, they would become a friend.

I drew the Public-Initiated Participation model as a circle purposefully to avoid anything linear. No piece of the pie is more desirable than any other. Sometimes the community make the final decisions. At other times, the communities inspire government to make the final decisions. Rachel advised me and the Chief Executive that things always seemed too *linear.* Well, authentic community engagement is most certainly *not* linear.

I'm not suggesting that this model works for all engagement across all topics. But it works. And people love it. I certainly encourage us to consider how we might shift our focus back so that our engagement processes are driven by the people who matter.

…

Conversation Starters

- **WHO** has inspired you to the point that you became one of their followers? What effects did your involvement in their cause have on their movement?
- **WHAT** can we learn from the creation of movements to apply to our community engagement practice? Do we currently place enough emphasis on leaders and their first followers? Do we go where the energy is? How can we do that more often – and more effectively?

- **WHY** are some people able to create a movement, and others cannot? What can they teach us?
- **WHEN** might a community come up with an idea and tell the government that they will keep them informed on its progress as it is being implemented? When might they need to check with the government about something? When might a community inspire the government to take full responsibility for implementing their idea?!
- **WHERE** would you draw the line between decisions that could be led by communities, and decisions needing to be led by governments?

18. Be bold and brave in pushing new frontiers in community engagement

We cannot become what we want to be by remaining what we are.

— Max DePree[31]

After the success of CoCreate Adelaide, along with the rest of the team, John and I were buzzing. CoCreate Adelaide gave us both the confirmation that we were on the same page. Now, how to proceed on our mission to make the world a better place through conversation, collaboration and connection?

One day, John asked me whether we should consider inviting community engagement practitioners with an interest in community-led engagement to meet for a coffee. South Australia was lacking any kind of network like this and we saw this as a natural next step from the magic of CoCreate Adelaide. We had a working title for the gathering: *Engage & Activate*. In addition to the working title, some words we threw around to inspire the right like-minded souls to join us were *engage, activate, empower, participate, development, together, co, forum, community, led,* and *centred.*

Our first gathering in May 2013 was relatively low-key. About eight of us gathered in an Adelaide café, and had some casual conversation about the industry in general, concepts around citizen-led engagement, our current projects, and where we saw the sector heading. As a few had known each other for a few years, we had a relaxed conversation, free-flowing and as frank as it needed to be.

I could not attend the second gathering that happened a month later no doubt because of a client diary clash, or parenting responsibilities, being a Mum of a two-year old at the time. That gathering was pretty productive and the group decided on our name: *Engage 2 Act*. By that evening, Valli Morphett had mocked up a great logo, sporting a stand-out V sign hand gesture, well known to have been adopted by anti-war activists as a symbol of peace after the Vietnam War. Part serious, and part mocking, reflecting our engagement geek dorkiness, *Engage 2 Act*, with its new whizz-bang logo, was born.

The group was really relaxed, and I loved our monthly coffee catch ups. However, before long we realised that the topics we were discussing, and the things we were learning from each other were so valuable that we really should be sharing them with a broader audience. After all, we are committed to progressing high-quality community engagement more widely.

By August that year we'd organised our first event, introducing a practitioner who spoke about her inspiring work with an innovative civic engagement organisation based in the Netherlands. MC'd by John, the event included an interactive discussion and a chance for participants to think about opportunities to enhance relationships between communities and government.

Now we were launched. We ran some amazing events, all with a super creative twist to them. We wanted to practice what we preached about being engaging, relevant and creative – as well as always being affordable and accessible. Soon after that first event, some members organised a debate for and against social media being defined as community engagement, inviting a similar professional network that specialised in social media to be on the 'pro' team; versus Engage 2 Act on the 'con' team.

Another debate we held was on the topic of 'Incentivised Democracy'. It was managed by fellow Engage 2 Act founder, Andrew Coulson, and I in the Adelaide City Council library on Rundle Mall. Andrew and I hatched plans on so many initiatives over the years that I lose count. Andrew has had a similar background to mine, as he also moved from a very person-centred approach of engagement in the UK, to the world of community engagement in Australia. He is an absolute shining light in the industry for ideas around innovation and pushing boundaries. When I first met Andrew, I nicknamed him *Mr Pinterest*, as he has the best Pinterest board, I've ever seen that shares ideas for innovation in community engagement.

The debate event in the library attracted everyday people from between the bookshelves to debate against professionals in the engagement space about whether we should offer prize draws or other incentives to encourage people to get involved in public consultation by government. We also broadcasted it live via both Facebook and Twitter. One of the strengths of the Engage 2 Act movement was its eagerness and willingness to involve *anyone* who had an interest in progressing high-quality community engagement. And not just those paid to do it. We could learn a lot from Bill, who'd wandered in off the street to see what it was all about, just as Bill could learn a lot from the professionals in the room who'd prepared their speeches days in advance. We were practicing what we preached: being inclusive and accepting is fundamental to the creation of any kind of movement.

Towards the end of 2013, we were trying to think of affordable venues we could hire to host a conference, and after a small amount of weighing up the pros and cons, I put forward that my big open-plan newly built house in McLaren Flat, just 45 minutes south of Adelaide, could work just perfectly! We called it a *Kitchen Table Conference*, booked some caterers, invited some people to run some mini-workshops and off we went! The conference was a resounding success, including the after-party at a local winery, and I still chuckle at the memories of all those people attending workshops in my lounge room, on my back deck, and in the spare room set up as my daughter's playroom!

Years later, my family and I had moved to a larger property and I couldn't help but daydream of ways to make use of a large, empty shed in my large paddock to progress the practice of high-quality community engagement. Of course, I had eager co-conspirators for this project. And so, we held an Engage 2 Act *Escape to the Country* away day, with 50 enthusiasts sitting in my shed, hearing speakers on a range of interesting and diverse community engagement topics. A Minister who had been my client earlier that year was one of the speakers. As I probed him on his views on community engagement, including the approach of former governments, little did I know that a previous Premier's partner was sitting in my shed listening to us engage in this frank and dynamic discussion, and was quite offended at what had been said. I was devastated that someone would have been upset and so I apologised as much as I could.

On later reflection, I have formed the opinion that if you come to an event I've organised, on *my* property, in *my* shed, to listen to *me* talk with the guests that *I've* invited, you can damn well listen to *my* opinion! This was an immensely powerful career moment. I realised that I always felt like the bridesmaid and never the bride. It was a personal lesson about a huge transition in my professional life: from the *independent-fence-sitting-facilitator-type* (the bridesmaid) to the *let-me-tell-you-what-I-actually-believe-type* (bride). And even more, it was a confirmation that our sector needs to grow and change. And to do that – with integrity – we need the strength and quality of frank and dynamic reflective discussions. And grow and change we must!

One of my favourite events was held very early in the Engage 2 Act journey, in September 2013. We threw an Engagement Party in an underground bar, on the night of another organisation's national community engagement conference in Adelaide. We respectfully made sure our event didn't clash with anything on their program, but operated with total independence, self-labelling ourselves as an unofficial fringe event. Word spread across conference delegates and engagement enthusiasts from across the country swarmed into the dark, crowded bar where we undertook a hybrid of Open Space Technology meets World Café processes with our glasses of wine in one hand and sticky notes in the other. You can imagine that this event, like all our other ones, was a huge success.

The Engage 2 Act movement was well and truly in full flow in South Australia. We were having a lot of fun with it, but more so, we were facilitating really meaningful ways for people to progress the practice of high-quality community engagement, whether or not they were professionals. None of us was in it for money, or profile raising. We were simply seeking a genuine connection with likeminded souls. Much like with CoCreate Adelaide, we were going where the energy was. And it was working.

...

At the same conference at which we'd held our unofficial fringe event, were some of our community engagement colleagues from across the border in Melbourne. They were curious about what we were up to. (We were, too!) So they asked to meet with some of the Engage 2 Act group over a beer. We met, and we were amazed and flattered that they had been watching what we'd been up to in South Australia, that they found our approach very fresh and inspiring, and they wanted to do something similar in Victoria. Enter stage left: Engage 2 Act Victoria!

A group quickly formed in Victoria and events began to emerge. They launched with a fabulous drinks event, in the centre of Melbourne. I'd flown over to listen from the back of the dark room to Wendy Sarkissian, as our guest keynote speaker, make her opening remarks about the polite young women in the large engineering firms who wore pencil skirts and stilettos (when she recommended 'sensible shoes' for those of us who were more down-to-earth about our engagement approaches). Their events were similarly creative and interesting, ranging from peer learning on arts and engagement, through to hearing from local practitioners on their recent experiences of delivering engagement training in partnership with Oxfam in Palestine, and what they'd learned about the relevance of community engagement in conflict zones. The team in Victoria also held a large *unconference* event, which I was invited to MC and facilitate it (whilst heavily pregnant with my second daughter) using Open Space Technology. It was a huge success, was very well attended and enabled participants to explore topics of interest to them with each other.

With Engage 2 Act collectives now up and running in both South Australia and Victoria, a group of us decided that it was time to formalise our collective by forming an official not-for-profit organisation. To do this, we did all the necessary paperwork and formed a Board. This was an exciting time, all still totally voluntary, and we had some amazing people apply and be selected to join the organisation in a governance capacity. I was more than happy to put my hand up for the role of President to guide this exciting ride.

Most of our meetings took place via video conferencing, given our geographic distance, and we had some work in figuring out what the role of the Board should be, communicating these changes to our members, and planning for the future.

We got together face-to-face one weekend in Melbourne and had an amazing day sharing lots of ideas, as well as setting a few goals. From this day, we launched a very clear and accessible membership model, with membership to Engage 2 Act being totally free and just requiring a sign up to our mailing list. Within a year, largely to the credit of Andrew Coulson and his social media dedication, we had over 800 members worldwide signed up to our collective.

Further, from that in-person meeting, we'd walked away having agreed that we would organise the conference of all conferences. It still gives me goosebumps to recall Board member Amy Hubbard sharing a suggestion that we should hold a conference like no other, that would inject passion and grit and excitement into the world of community engagement. And that we should use the tagline, *For the Love of Community Engagement* – because that's why the likes of us do this work – because we love it!

The hands-on commitment of the Board, particularly those on the ground in Melbourne, created the conference of all conferences. Actually, it was called an *unconference*, based both on the concept of including an element of Open Space Technology (where participants would create the agenda then and there), but also, I think to indicate that this conference was different from business as usual.

The stunning St Kilda Town Hall was draped in rainbow flags in support of the current campaign for marriage equality, and we'd decided that the unconference team would wear *Love is Love* t-shirts to get behind the cause, given our focus was so love- and passion-orientated. We'd debated whether as usually independent community engagement practitioners, often not sharing our own opinions but facilitating two sides to reach agreement, should have such a strong opinion on marriage equality, but decided to go ahead, as we deemed it a basic human right for equality.

If you've ever suffered any kind of anxiety or depression, you might be familiar with the concept of visualisation. The process usually involves you visualising yourself at a point in your life where you feel great, happy, calm, in control, content, or something else positive. Watching the hall fill up with excited, smiling engagement practitioners, with an upbeat playlist blaring out around the hall, with the team in *Love is Love* t-shirts, knowing that we had a kick-ass two days ahead of us is the exact moment I visualise these days if I need to undertake a bit of self-care. It was, without a doubt, one of the absolute high points of my career to see hundreds of people on board with the Engage 2 Act movement, embracing it with open arms.

At this unconference we also announced the winner of the inaugural *Wendy Sarkissian Award for Courage in Community Engagement.* A story in itself, the award had been born out of a conversation between Board member Desley Renton and Wendy Sarkissian over dinner one night. The Engage 2 Act Board members were eager to launch an award process, and some had been facing challenges where they'd needed to call on their own bravery and courage in their community engagement practice. I understood this deeply, as I often talk about how we can have our souls destroyed in community engagement, where we've put our personal energy and hearts on the line to work with a group of people or a community, and when decision-makers end up not listening or making decisions that deeply affect and concern that community, it can be incredibly emotional.

In talking with Desley, Wendy, unaware that we'd been having this conversation, announced that she felt strongly that Engage 2 Act should have a bravery citation of some sort. Desley stared at her and then explained that, coincidently, we had been discussing this exact idea, and that if Engage 2 Act were to do this, then we'd very much like it to be named in Wendy's honour.

In an interview with Wendy after the award process, she said to me '…the professionalised, corporatised business of community engagement is often gutless. If we don't put courage on the agenda, and talk about it, then we're never really going to confront it. The amount of corporate, gutless engagement that you and I encounter these days is almost demonic'.

I agree more than ever with Wendy's words. I recently attended an online awards ceremony for the community engagement sector. I was blown away that all the winners just happened to have a perfectly polished, professional video reel of their engagement process up their sleeve for this award-winning moment. One of the organisations I had worked with in regional South Australia was up for an award as a finalist, but as soon as I saw the slickness of the promo flicks announcing the winners, I knew that the little video snapshots I'd just remembered to capture on location, in deepest regional South Australia, via my iPhone just weren't going to cut it.

We ended up with a Highly Commended award, which we were thrilled with, but the corporatisation, and almost vulgar budgets, that the award-winning engagement of the 21st century is displaying does not excite me for one moment. In my opinion, that approach is pushing community engagement even further from the 'real people' of the world. Our sector is becoming elitist, and we're the ones making it happen.

We set up the award process and put a call out around the world for nominations for the inaugural *Wendy Sarkissian Award for Courage in Community Engagement*. We received nominations from three continents which we were so grateful for, as this was our first attempt at an awards process.

Wendy described one nomination as 'absolutely stellar' and 'knocked our socks off'. Members of the judging panel were spread out across the world and each noticed the story about the Pang Jai Fabric Market in Hong Kong as a standout. Wendy noted that she couldn't begin to imagine how courageous it was for the hawkers from this market to even be an entrant for a community engagement awards process, given that Hong Kong is not particularly well known for its democracy, even more so in recent times. In my interview, Wendy went on to say:

'Here was this group of ordinary folk, who had gathered around them all manner of support from every possible realm, not just to save their market… but to come up with an alternative to a government plan to demolish their fabric market. It was so innovative, so courageous, so gutsy. The very fact that they even applied was courageous.'

The judging panel was unanimous that these people, who'd been fighting the hard fight, going above and beyond what was being thrust at them by their government, and showing incredible initiative and vision whilst they were at it, were the winners. We were so excited at this and even more excited that we managed to find enough money in the conference budget to fly the group to Melbourne to collect their award.

I still have goosebumps recalling that day at the unconference when they accepted the award. They didn't all speak English, but those who did braved the 200+ crowd of Australian community engagement professionals, amongst all kinds of rainbow colours and *Love is Love* merchandise (undoubtedly making this like no other conference they had probably ever attended in their home country), and expressed their passion and determination to fight for what they believed in. I was MC'ing the event, standing on the stage alongside them with tears streaming down my face.

In fact, I invented my concept of the *Goosebump Measure of Significance* at that very moment. At this single event, and through my entire Engage 2 Act journey, I kept getting goosebumps. Not because I was in Melbourne and feeling chilly, but because I was feeling intense emotions of excitement, awe, pride, and happiness. As the MC, my *Goosebump Measure of Significance* would be announced over the microphone as necessary, generally meaning that something significant had just occurred (like the Australian Broadcasting Association's Q&A program following us on Twitter after Andrew had tweeted something that I'd said about having enough members to form a political party!). I still use this random measuring success tool today. What better indicator of something being 'right' could there be than your own body's uncontrollable, physical, and emotional reaction? As Wendy often reminds me, we're animals, after all!

Witnessing the level of passion and gutsy determination from the Pang Jai Hawkers at a community engagement conference was ridiculously refreshing. We had not only welcomed 'real people' from a 'real community' to the event to share their story, but we had also awarded them for their courage and persistence. This was without a doubt one of the most significant moments of my career. I just got goosebumps again!

We said at the time that we'd be best friends forever (they loved our peace sign logo and adopted the correct Engage 2 Act pose in all photo opportunities, as shown in the photo overleaf). Wendy has since visited Pang Jai to present them (again) with their award at a press conference, receiving the warmest of warm welcomes, even with her name on a massive yellow banner hanging above the market.

Image 24 - Wendy Sarkissian and I with the winners of the inaugural Wendy Sarkissian Award for Courage in Community Engagement from the Pang Jai Fabric Market in Hong Kong, at St Kilda Town Hall. From left to right: Ms Tang Oi Foon, Miss Arabii So Man Wa, Mr Ho Ying Hoi, Becky Hirst, Ms Na Na, Dr. Wendy Sarkissian and Ms Margaret Lee.
Photo owned by author, 2017.

She brought me back a gift from them of some beautiful fabric, stitched together in a patchwork pattern which hangs proudly on my office wall. Andrew has also visited Pang Jai, and I've recorded a couple of interviews for documentaries about their plight, and the significance of how winning our award helped boost their confidence and help them feel supported by others who understand what such a campaign means for democracy.

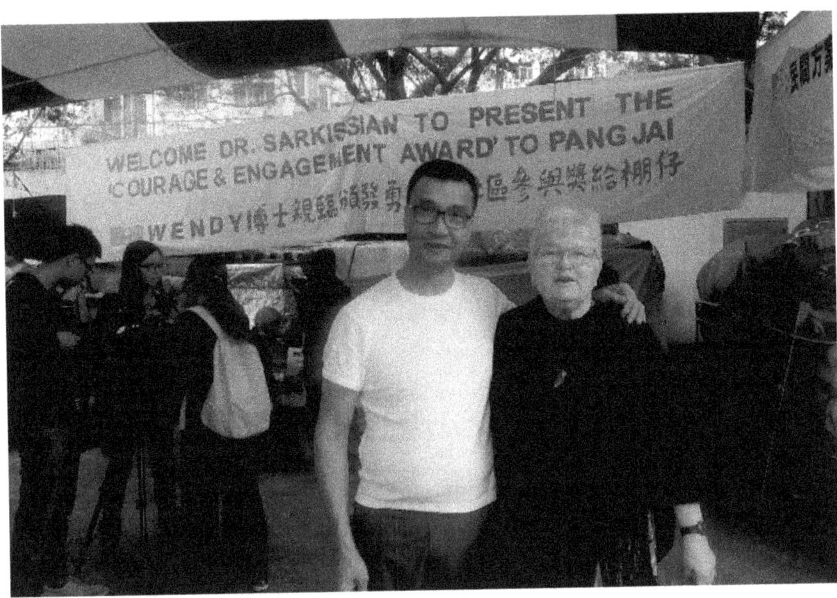

Image 25 - Dr. Wendy Sarkissian with Mr Ho Ying Hoi during a visit to Pang Jai, Hong Kong in November 2017 to present the hawkers (again) with their award.
Photo owned by Wendy Sarkissian, 2017.

I recently attended an online launch of a documentary about the main hawker who'd been driving their plight, with the entire film in Cantonese, with Mandarin subtitles. For the Q&A section after the launch, they kindly typed what was being discussed into the Zoom chat feature so that I could use Google Translate to work out what was being said.

Questions came in from viewers about fear of reprisal and had they worried about being identified and beaten up for having opinions about government decision making. Seeing those words pop up on my Google Translate tab reminded me why this award made so much sense. Theirs was true courage. A far cry from our shiny Australian community engagement promo videos!

This experience also demonstrated the powerful tools we have at our fingertips for connecting and engaging across cultures – where these days even language doesn't need to be a barrier!

Another wheel set in motion at this single event was *Engage 2 Act Youth*. Ever since Paul Kooperman told me he used to be a writer for *Home and Away*, I've loved him. I grew up watching *Summer Bay* and reckon I happened to be home from school on a sick day for the first-ever episode. All that aside, Paul is a fantastic practitioner, who does some brilliant work with children and young people through an initiative called *The Field Trip*.

Paul submitted a proposal to run a session about how to engage with children and young people at the 2017 unconference. What he didn't tell us, however, that he was going to be bringing ten children and young people to run the session. It didn't really even register with me until I was on stage, welcoming everyone, and then I saw Paul's cheeky smile beaming up at me. He was surrounded by a group of children. Goosebumps!

Their session was one of the most popular parts of the unconference and I spotted this as another pilot light opportunity: an energy in the room that needed to be explored. So I suggested to Paul that we think about what more we could do to involve these children and young people in progressing the practice of high-quality community engagement.

Paul is one of those people where you just know this is going to lead to brilliant things. When two doers' cross paths and share an idea, it's going to happen and it's going to be big. Building on the analogy, perhaps this is where an additional energy source comes in to contact with the pilot light, the match, and the pan of boiling water. Perhaps it's the tea-towel that catches on fire, or the pasta cooking in the boiling pan of water. Either way, the momentum was there, and we developed a plan.

Just a month later, in October 2017, we held an Engage 2 Act Youth gathering in Melbourne, facilitated by me, Clare Murrell from the Engage 2 Act Board, and Paul and the children and young people from *The Field Trip*. Clare and I felt it only right that we should include our own children in the meeting, so Elsie (who was about to turn seven), joined me on the interstate flight and absolutely loved the hotel with room service dinner! We made them little Engage 2 Act t-shirts to feel the part. And both Clare and I enjoyed the opportunity to include our mini-mes this exciting work.

Image 26 - Clare Murrell & I with Elsie and Bea, at the Engage 2 Act Youth event, October 2017. Photo owned by author, 2017.

The group of fifteen children and young people gathered around a large boardroom-style table and the discussions began. The first challenge when working with children and young people on the topic of community engagement is explaining what exactly it is. I used a whiteboard to draw people, and communities, and then spoke to them about democracy and how we vote people into government to represent us. Then I spoke about the need for those people, and the people who support those elected people's work, to connect with us about decisions that they make about things that interest or affect us. Explaining community engagement to a room of children is a challenge that I set to any practitioner who is serious about this career. It makes you really think through the concept at the most basic level, and in turn, it will help you explain it to your friends and family who still struggle to understand exactly what you do for a living!

The scene was set, and our conversations moved on issues of importance for the children and young people at the table. More goosebumps ensued, as they read out prepared speeches on marriage equality, poverty, climate change, and more. I was blown away by the level of intellect and consciousness these young people displayed regarding many of the big issues affecting our world. This moment opened my eyes: I could now see that children and young people have many of the answers we're looking for – they speak a lot of uncomplicated sense – and sometimes all we need to do is ask them what's important to them, and the floodgates open.

This work led on to Paul inviting me to attend a *Kidference* that the children and young people were organising in Sunbury, 39 kilometres north-west of Melbourne. The brilliant concept of a kidference was something he'd devised as a conference for children and young people, organised by children and young people. And when I say organised, I mean fully organised, with the children even catering for their own event – homemade lemonade and jam sandwiches all round!

When Paul invited me to attend, we both felt it was important that I was seen as someone of significance. The children and young people would present their findings to me at the end of the weekend. But it was critical that I was not seen as an 'expert' there to teach or preach! We came up with the title of *Keynote Listener* to address this issue, and other local people of significance attended under the same premise. I've since been involved with other engagement-related events that used the role of *Keynote Listeners*, and find it sends a very clear message to those *Very Important People* in attendance about their proper role during proceedings.

Engaging with children and young people isn't hard. It's just a matter of finding them, and once you've found them, providing them with an opportunity to speak about what's important to them, without your predetermined guidance. Let's nickname it *Helicopter Engagement*, where you're hovering over them nudging them to say what you want to hear.

The final magical moment from the Engage 2 Act movement was our decision to found *Global Community Engagement Day*. The story goes that in true Andrew Coulson style, he had a great idea. He had been thinking about how every day now seems to have a celebration attached to it, and that days celebrated locally, nationally and globally were not just for religion, countries or famous people's anniversaries, but celebrations for really random things like International Fun at Work Day, or Doughnut Day, or Chocolate Day. These fun days, and tales of popular movements that had taken off with various hashtags and followings, got Andrew thinking about how Engage 2 Act was on a mission to build a community of people interested in advancing community engagement practice, by putting engagement on the map and in the minds of all. And so, at one of our virtual Board meetings he said, 'Why don't we start a Global Community Engagement Day?'

He was met with 'oohs' and 'aahs' from the other Board members and we really couldn't find a reason not to agree. I think we all loved the idea of a day where we could celebrate our profession, especially being that so many people generally don't understand our profession. We felt the need to put a match to that pilot light.

We needed a date for this new annual celebration. Andrew took the initiative to take to the Engage 2 Act social media channels to ask our members, 'Who is it that has really inspired you in what you do? Which pioneer of community engagement stands out for you? Who do you love to quote, or simply can't live without when engaging the community?' It was agreed that whoever came out as the top choice, we would find out the date of their birthday and this would be the date for our sector to celebrate what we love.

Several popular names were thrown into the hat. It really is a good question to ponder over as our sector grows: *Who inspires us*?

It will come as no surprise, that Wendy Sarkissian was the top of our polls and so we approached Wendy to ask her whether she would be happy for us to use her birthday to launch the first-ever Global Community Engagement Day. This was so fitting, given Wendy's involvement with Engage 2 Act to date. She was in the midst of grief following a tragic car crash where she had recently lost her beloved, Karl. It was just the tonic she needed.

With a big, bold YES from Wendy, 28 January was officially declared Global Community Engagement Day. I think it was also at this moment that Aunty Wendy officially declared herself to be our mascot!

For the first year, we chose a theme and invited people to get creative by submitting videos, or poems, or drawings, or whatever they felt inclined to do. This got the ball rolling with content and since then, we haven't looked back. Because Andrew ensured that the Day was officially registered on daysoftheyear.com, it appears that the majority of promotion about the day happens automatically around the world!

Just Google it – it's everywhere! So now, every 28th January, not only do we sing 'Happy Birthday' to Aunty Wendy, but we watch the world celebrate our profession!

...

We had had some great successes with Engage 2 Act and the snowball effect continued long after the infamous unconference of 2017. Our flame was well and truly burning and we felt energised by the momentum we were feeling, and ongoing positive feedback from members that this was the change the community engagement sector needed.

Some people even noted how Engage 2 Act caused factions within the community engagement sector, probably best described as a divide between a grassroots, bottom-up loving, and edgy network and a more traditional model, where people came from more of a communications or marketing background within the government or corporate sector. These statements are hugely generalised, and we had many tense moments within the sector during those active Engage 2 Act years defining our purpose and explaining how we'd only tried to fill a gap that was missing, never intending in any way to compete or rival existing networks.

On occasions, voices were raised, and tears occasionally flowed as I undertook this rationalising of our existence. I found myself repeatedly justifying Engage 2 Act by telling the story you've just read – how we'd evolved out of a group of practitioners who started having coffee together monthly in Adelaide. All we did was follow the energy we were feeling and buckled in for the ride! I was sad that it ruffled some feathers within our sector, but now when I look back, I think it wasn't a bad thing to shake up the community engagement world a little.

For the community engagement sector to have these so-call factions within it means we're growing, emerging, learning, and evolving. Whether we realise it or not, these are significant years for our industry, with high-quality community engagement needed now more than ever, and the way Engage 2 Act shook up the sector, particularly in Australia, happened because it needed to.

Engage 2 Act finally came full circle during 2019, returning to being a grassroots network of practitioners. The Board achieved some great things but, in the end, it was demanding too much time from us as volunteers (with no paid staff to help) and we'd been sensing that the moment we added the layer of governance via a Board, the magic was lessened. This was a big lesson for me in building momentum and movements. I found myself saying to myself that the moment we formalised the organisation, it became something else – and what it became wasn't necessarily what the movement was about.

In my local community, every year at Christmas, residents make life-sized Santas and place them out the front of their houses. With Christmas being in summer here in Australia, this is much more fun to drive around and look at these displays with the kids, rather than waiting until late in the evening for light displays to come on. The initiative started in a small township called Kangarilla, just five kilometres from our place, and its popularity has spread to now include hundreds of Santas across a vast area throughout the region. I like to use this as an example of a movement that started from an idea in one small community and organically evolved to be a huge deal! As we drive around looking and laughing (hysterically for my four-year-old at some of the antics the life-sized Santas get up to), I really hope that no smart Alec comes along and tries to formalise the initiative. There'd be nothing worse than them suddenly running it as a competition or setting a theme – it just needs to keep rolling with the people-led momentum – otherwise I worry we'd all end up not bothering. Heaven forbid, what would happen if the bureaucrats at the Council got their hands on it!

...

Conversation Starters

- **WHOSE** responsibility is it to grow the professionality of the community engagement sector?
- **WHAT** do you think about incentivising people to become involved in something? Do you think offering a free lunch helps motivate them to attend? Or is it more a gesture of thanks? Would people get involved without an incentive?
- **WHY** is it important to involve 'real people' and not just professionals in advancing community engagement practice?
- **WHEN** did something in your community, or in your community engagement work, last give you goosebumps?
- **WHERE** (and how) are you celebrating next year's Global Community Engagement Day?

19. Consider digital first

Technology is nothing.
What's important is that you have a faith in people, that they're basically good and smart, and if you give them tools, they'll do wonderful things with them. It's not the tools that you have faith in — tools are just tools.
They work, or they don't work. It's people you have faith in or not.

— Steve Jobs[32]

I was feeling flush in 2009, still working part-time for the Children, Youth and Women's Health Service and in the early days of consulting with my own practice. So, I treated myself to a ticket to attend the annual International Association of Public Participation's (IAP2) conference in Fremantle, Western Australia.

I was excited to return to Fremantle, as a few years earlier in our final few months as backpackers, Dan and I spent three months working for the Rottnest Island Authority, taking accommodation bookings for the popular island a short ferry ride from Fremantle. We'd had many great times in the Fremantle call centre and had been fortunate to work on the island learning about everything from the most in-demand villas on the island to identifying the tiny little quirky scrub wallaby inhabitants, quokkas.

I was also excited to be making my IAP2 speaking debut, delivering a workshop on engaging with culturally and linguistically diverse communities, using examples from projects I'd worked on in London. I shared footage from a news report from Channel S about the Bengali Quit & Get Fit program. I remember feeling proud that I was now in Australia sharing these successes.

The most significant moment of this conference was bumping into Crispin Butteriss during a break. We had been following each other's work via social media and recognised each other instantly. Each of us was eager to know more about the other. I respect people who don't use social media, but I have no clue how they ever connect with people without it! I am a huge fan of face-to-face networking, but nine times out of ten, my connections arise from having seen someone's work online first!

Crispin is the co-founder of Bang the Table, and, along with Matt Crozier, was pioneering a new venture providing an online community engagement platform. We did the chit-chat thing over our morning tea, and before we headed off, Crispin suggested that we should really chat about how we might work together. What a thrilling opportunity. By February 2010, I was onboard as their South Australian Associate and they flew me to Melbourne for a few days to get the ball rolling.

These were such exciting days – both for me and for them. I was branching out in forming affiliations with like-minded, progressive, community engagement businesses. For them, they were growing – fast. That gathering in Melbourne in early 2010 was the first time their team had grown beyond Crispin, Matt, and their technical co-founder, Karthik Reddy. Now it included Associates. All of us were entering the unchartered territory of enabling high-quality community engagement online. Image 27 shows me with Crispin and Matt, after our meeting in Melbourne, cementing our association with corporate headshots!

I have the utmost amount of respect and admiration for Crispin, Matt and Karthik. I grew up with adoration for my older sister's first husband, Simon, who came into my life when I was just five and showed me his entrepreneurial spirit. So I have had a soft spot for anyone who can take an idea and turn it into a business. Plus, anyone who knows how to party gets a big tick in my book too – Crispin, Matt and Karthik know how to do this in leaps and bounds – although those stories will not creep into my book!

Image 27 - Working together with Crispin Butteriss and Matt Crozier of Bang the Table as one of their first Associates in February 2010. Photo owned by Bang the Table, 2010.

Our good times notwithstanding, my respect for the founders of Bang the Table comes from their commitment to high-quality community engagement. I learned so much from them in the early days, and I still do. They aren't just about building an online platform; their mission is about building stronger communities through meaningful engagement. They aren't jumping on the bandwagon of the world of digital engagement – they *lead* the world of digital engagement – and have done so for well over a decade. We definitely sing from the same hymn sheet.

By April 2010, Crispin and Matt had delivered training in Online Community Engagement in Adelaide. I'd managed to rustle up a small group of interested bureaucrats who were willing to test-drive this new-fangled concept of engaging people *online* in government decision making. The training went well but there were absolutely no nibbles from anyone taking the next step to sign up to use the tools. As it turns out, it took several years to get South Australia onto the online community engagement bandwagon, However, before long, it became part of normal engagement practice in that State. That's not to say that the tools being provided were being used particularly well – if at all!

In 2020, however, when Covid-19 struck and Australia was sent into lockdown with most of the rest of the world, we found a sudden interest in online community engagement. For my part, I found that after ten years of trying to get clients to use online tools and techniques, suddenly they were open to it! During 2020, I undertook some of the most comprehensive community engagement ever, purely because my clients gave me the freedom to use a combination of paper-based, face-to-face (working around the limitations that 2020 gave us) and online engagement. Never before had there been such an easy sell of online engagement tools!

I continued to work with Bang the Table in delivering training for a few years. I loved delivering the new ground-breaking content, often alongside Crispin, in Sydney, Melbourne, and Perth. Working with Crispin, I learned so much. At the same time, I delivered some capacity building-work on behalf of Bang the Table for the Mackay Regional Council in Queensland and for the Kimberley Performing Arts Centre in Broome, Western Australia. Having lived in Australia for only a few years, I would regularly pinch myself that I was having opportunities to travel to such beautiful places!

During these years, I learned some fundamental lessons about community engagement that I still carry with me. You might think that these lessons would be highly technical, given the online element of the work, but they're quite humble.

The first lesson was that when government is trying to engage with the community about a particular topic, the topics that attract the largest amount of contribution are generally emotive AND concrete. Crispin used to have these words on a PowerPoint slide in training sessions.

EMOTIVE AND CONCRETE.

He would explain that topics that aroused emotion in people – those that got their heartbeat going – would, generally, generate high levels of interest. He would explain that topics that were not abstract, but tangible to the everyday person would also generate interest. So, for example, if you undertake online community engagement about a dog park (*tangible, concrete*) next to a children's playground (*Oh, that gets me worried*) you'd be more likely to gain participation than if you try to involve people in a conversation about a new government Park Management Plan. It doesn't get your heartbeat going, and definitely doesn't mean much to the everyday person.

Second, I learned that the joy of online community engagement is the ability to measure the success of any given process. You'll note I say *process* here. By that, I mean clicks on links, document downloads, video views, and participation in discussion forums. We must differentiate these processes from measuring outcomes, which will inevitably be more about the participants' influence on the final decision. Whilst impacts and outcomes are the most important variables to measure in any community engagement process, online engagement provides us with a whole new world of measuring process. In printed or face-to-face engagement, we could measure that we'd placed one advertisement in a local newspaper or put three posters up in a local café. However, we wouldn't know how many people had seen them and were now aware of our project. In face-to-face engagement, we cannot necessarily measure how many people read more about our project and maybe even come to the venue but decide not to participate. The online world offers a whole new suite of measurements for our processes.

As a result of data being available in 21st century community engagement, concepts such as the *90-9-1 Rule for Participation Inequality*[33] have been developed. According to Jakob Nielsen, and shown in image 28 overleaf, in most online communities, 90% of users are 'lurkers' who never contribute (in other words, read or observe, but don't contribute), 9% of users contribute a little, and 1% of users account for almost all the action.

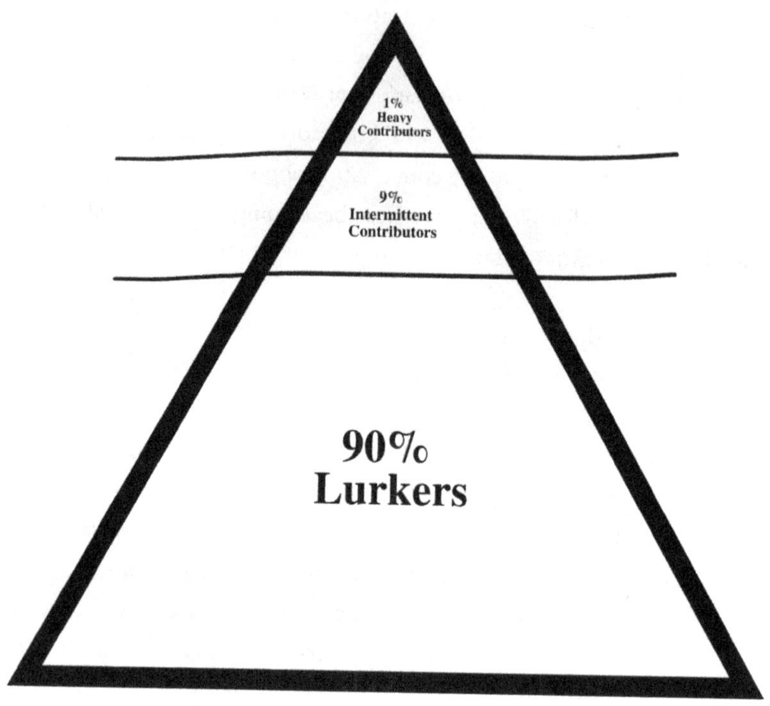

Image 28 - The 90-9-1 rule for Participation Inequality. Reproduced from Nielsen, J. 2006.

I use this rule a lot with my clients, finding it helpful to explain to often disappointed elected members. They may read reports that say that, whilst 1000 people visited their online engagement hub, only 10 people contributed to the conversation. Of course, the ratio changes, depending on how emotive or concrete a topic is. But the 90-9-1 rule serves as a good benchmark for estimating this. I also often remind clients that whilst I don't have statistics, I have observed that the 90-9-1 rule is applicable to the offline world as well.

If I take my own neighbourhood as an example, we are a country community with only 300 residents spread over a large area. If we tried, we could probably rustle up a crowd of 27 active-ish people for a community BBQ: the 'intermittent contributors' that Nielson identified. However, having just signed up as the sixth member of the Community Hall and Progress Association, I am not surprised that there's such a low number of 'heavy contributors' in our community! In fact, we're punching above our weight in having 3% of our population involved! I jest, but it's worth considering (when planning community engagement processes), that the majority of the population 'lurk', rather than 'contribute'. We mustn't become disheartened but instead continually examine our processes, outcomes, and try to understand the reasons why people don't get involved. We need information if we are to maximise their participation.

Thirdly, I've learned that you can build the most 'all-singing-all-dancing' online community engagement experience, but just because it's online it doesn't mean that people will come. Again, we don't want this to dishearten us. It's just how things work in this space. As with any engagement process, we need to put some serious thought into how you're going to promote opportunities to become involved. In my most recent work with local government in South Australia, I've been fortunate to work with dedicated social media teams who have created highly engaging content that drives people to the engagement hub. I've fallen in love with the use of video to present information, teasers, questions, or updates that signpost people to the online conversations.

During 2020, I worked on a consultant team on strategic planning as part of a Council's vision for residential and economic growth. I discovered that a video interview (via Zoom) with the subject matter expert received very positive feedback from community members, who thanked us for taking the time to explain the project. We also used the same technique to provide updates during the engagement period, enabling real-time feedback on what we'd heard to date. I loved the idea that by sharing our insights during the engagement period, we would build trust with the communities involved.

I feel I must sound a note of warning here, however. Please don't be fooled in thinking that social media is community engagement. I have had lots of experience in this space, so I say this with some confidence. If you are seeking the best online tool for gathering quality contributions as part of a problem-solving or decision-making process, do not rely on social media. I've worked on many projects where I've been able to assess the balance of contributions received via different communication modes, when we've included the social media commentary as well as contributions via face-to-face or purpose-built community engagement platforms. And I believe that social media is not as effective as some might claim – for this sort of work. I observe that when people respond to a question via a government Facebook page, for example, it seems that their comments are made without much thought. The comments are short, often feel uninformed, and generally appear to be just 'front-of-mind' opinions.

Most of the time we are seeking deeper and more thoughtful reflection on important community issues. This kind of contribution is not generally useful to decision makers for making considered decisions. In contrast, I have noticed that the quality of the contribution is much higher from people who take the time to click through to a purpose-built space, to log in or sign up, and add their thoughts and opinions. On balance, I have found that in most cases, their answers are longer and much more considered, and therefore more useful to decision makers.

The results from research undertaken by Global Research on behalf of the City of Melbourne support my observations.[34] Their key findings included that comments made directly to their dedicated online engagement platform, *Participate Melbourne*, were substantially more valuable than Facebook comments in directly informing decision-making. They observed that comments made directly were double the length of Facebook comments, contained two and a half times more points than Facebook comments, were twice as relevant to the topic being discussed, were slightly more understandable than Facebook comments, and contained one-third more unique ideas than Facebook comments. Other findings did however note, however, that Facebook has a role in increasing reach for engagement processes, through stimulated thought and reaction, which although not always informative, can widen the reach of the public engagement.

As an added difficulty for anyone who's collated community contributions, social media has no simple download features for the contributions received. I find myself in a laborious process of copying and pasting. Ain't got no time for that!

In recent years, I have noticed the advent of social media has led to mass opinion pouring freely all around the world. Never before in history have the communication channels been so open for every person to speak out about every conceivable topic! Henry DeVries defines this 'White Noise' as meaningless chatter, hubbub, or constant background sounds that drowns out all other sounds.[35] I believe that, as professional community engagement practitioners, we must be careful to tailor processes to avoid amplifying White Noise. Instead, we must search for mechanisms that support high-quality, insightful, and informed contributions and conversations.

Finally, as I reflect on my experiences delivering multiple large community engagement projects, I've developed an approach whereby most of my work takes a three-fold, integrated approach to the three main techniques: print, face-to-face, and online engagement.

I believe that it is critical to offer 'something for everyone' when planning our tools and techniques, acknowledging that some people prefer to attend a meeting, some prefer to participate online at their own convenience, and others don't want to do anything beyond a good old written submission. And that is fine. We just need to offer lots of different opportunities to engage.

It's imperative that we cater for the range of needs within any 21st century community, including digital first. What I mean by that is that online community engagement must be front-of-mind, carefully planned from the outset, and not treated as an afterthought. And I beg my colleagues to remember that a poorly designed paper-based survey questionnaire is still going to be inadequate if you put it online. It won't magically improve simply because it's being delivered in a digital format. We must be pragmatic about ensuring our engagement tools and techniques are methodologically sound, whether they are written, face-to-face, or online. I am becoming a broken record on this topic. In my Facilitating Online Conversations workshops, I repeat and repeat: *We mustn't forget our values just because we're online!*

The local councils I have worked with recently on long-term strategic planning processes have had great success with this approach, using three-pronged tools and techniques. I found it helps to use the same overarching text and questions across all the methodologies and tools – whether they are mail-out surveys, online discussion forums, or community meetings. Not only does this create equity for people participating (they can be confident they will have the same opportunities to contribute no matter what tool they choose), but it also makes writing up (and in turn making considered decisions) much easier!

I am also a fan of integrating written, face-to-face, and online engagement where possible. In January 2014, I was working with the City of Adelaide to involve users of the City Skatepark in plans for the relocation of the facility. The skatepark, in a prominent location on North Terrace in Adelaide, was being relocated to make way for a new University building that had long been earmarked for the site. My team undertook a significant amount of face-to-face engagement, talking with users about their most important considerations for a new location. We went to listen to them at busy times during the peak summer school holiday period. We absolutely loved being on-site, listening to and getting to know this community of interest, and gathering many rich contributions to report back to our client. We used iPads to gather their ideas, adding this straight to the Council's online engagement hub (yay for saving on admin!).

However, in an added twist we also wore skater t-shirts with QR Codes printed on the back, for skaters to scan and add their own contributions to the hub. We used the hashtag *#sk8relocate* to generate interest and encourage them to share opportunities to contribute. With the help of a partnership with some key skate bodies, as shown in image 29, we managed to initiate and sustain great momentum with this fascinating project.

I used QR Codes more recently in 2020 with a client who was upgrading a streetscape in an inner metropolitan suburb. We recorded video messages from the Mayor talking about the various aspects that needed consideration – car parking, greening, active transport, access, and inclusion – and attached the QR Codes to lampposts along the street for people to scan at their convenience, linking them to the video messages and online engagement hub. Whilst we didn't get a massive response, tracking of the codes revealed that people did scan them. I was heartened to discover that we had reached some people we might not have reached via our other more 'conventional' approaches, such as questionnaires delivered to each household.

Image 29 - Skaters gather at the Adelaide City Skatepark on North Terrace to share their ideas for its relocation. Photo owned by author, January 2014

I have recently witnessed my two young daughters, more than likely as a result of Covid-19 global tracking systems, become big fans of QR codes. At any moment, if they spot a QR code on something, they grab the nearest device to scan it and see where it takes them. Our Easter Bunny even used QR codes to lead them on a treasure hunt to find their eggs! Last weekend we went for a walk at a nearby beach. They spotted a code to scan on an information board about the beach environment. They were greatly disappointed when the code led to a 'Page Not Found' message on the local Council's website.

All this is said before I even mention how I see them beginning to use social media platforms such as TikTok. Tracy Francis and Fernanda Hoefel note that Generation Z are true digital natives, and that the way that they are being exposed to the internet, social networks and mobile systems, is producing a hypercognitive generation very comfortable with collecting and cross-referencing many sources of information and with integrating virtual and offline experiences.[36] This generation of children are using technology as naturally as we pick up a pen. I consider our generation of professionals as a stepping-stone towards a future where digital technology is used more consistently. We need to up our game – and up our game fast!

As we enter a hugely diverse future, the range of appropriate online tools and techniques will only increase and become more commonplace in community engagement. I cannot imagine what some of them will be, but I hope to be part of the conversation! I know that they won't replace the richness of face-to-face engagement, but I believe that if we use new approaches artfully and ethically, they will only enhance the chances of building and sustaining thriving, connected communities whose members know that their voices are being heard.

...

Conversation Starters

- **WHO** do you know who would be likely to become involved in a local issue if it was online, but wouldn't get involved if it involved attendance at a face-to-face event? And vice versa?
- **WHAT** are your favourite online tools for engaging in deep and meaningful dialogue about your communities of interest?
- **WHY** is it important to offer a hybrid of written, face-to-face, and online tools and techniques to engage with communities?
- **WHEN** have you successfully measured the process, impacts, and outcomes of a community engagement process? How did that go?
- **WHERE** do you see online community engagement heading in the next few years... next few decades?

20. Go back to the future

World peace can be achieved when the power of love replaces the love of power.

— Sri Chinmoy[37]

When we turn our thoughts to the future of community engagement, I often find myself in discussions about how our tools and techniques might evolve. You might be expecting that a chapter on the future of community engagement is going to be exploring the role of augmented reality, or whether robots can replace practitioners. You might be expecting me to share my thoughts on the future of town hall meetings versus online discussion forums.

Whilst these are interesting topics, I don't believe they are the most important thing to be discussing right now. We need to be looking to the future through a strategic lens. We need to be doing that as mature adults. And, as the title of this chapter suggests, we need to be looking back to help us look forward. The lessons I present in this book are my mandate for community engagement practice moving forward. I believe my lessons are a strong foundation for building, growing, and developing our practice.

There is no shortage of tools and techniques for engaging with communities in decision-making and problem solving. Numerous international case studies show leading practice examples to enable people to 'have their say' in an upcoming decision on just about every topic imaginable. Further, there appears to be no end to the governments introducing community engagement policies, frameworks, and procedures. Practitioners have toolkits overflowing with creative, eye-catching, and accessible techniques. As a sector, we have come a long way in recent years. We are in a strong position.

And now is the time to apply the emergency brake.

I need to sound a word of warning here. I have grave concerns for the future.

I believe we are close to breaking point of over engaging with our wealth of sophisticated tools, techniques, frameworks, and procedures. Some fundamental things are missing in the world of community engagement. And, right now, we need to focus our energies on them. As a matter of urgency.

I was recently invited to interview a Minister at a state government event about some community engagement that he and his department had undertaken. We sat on the stage at the Adelaide Convention Centre in front of a crowd of almost five hundred public servants. We reflected on how, less than a decade ago, community engagement was very much on the sidelines of government. We compared that situation to the current situation, where an invitation to hear a Minister speak about community engagement fills a convention centre to the brim with interested bureaucrats. The ways in which government involves communities in decision making and problem solving is a hot topic.

However, as we sat there, surrounded by the huge sound systems and screens, with an echoey backdrop noise of clinking teaspoons against coffee mugs, reality dawned on me. Yes, we can pack a room with professionals interested in community engagement. But could we pack a room out with community members who could say they believed that they truly had influence over government decision making? Could we find the same number of people who felt heard and respected by government? Could we fill a room with people who say they trust their government?

And the same goes for our professional awards processes. As I suggested earlier, nowadays awards for community engagement are nothing but glossy show reels and shiny trophies (destined to collect dust on our bookshelves). In my view, in our sector, they represent almost incestual pats on each other's backs. Don't get me wrong here. I love awards and have quite a few myself. And I wholeheartedly agree that it's important to celebrate and recognise our good work. But a much bigger question needs to be answered here.

I challenge all of us to consider when we last heard a community member saying that they were thrilled with an engagement process undertaken by the government that represented them. How they felt truly heard. That they had genuine influence in their local community. These people do exist. My colleagues tell me they do. But they are few and far between.

As we demonstrated with the Wendy Sarkissian Award for Courage in Community Engagement in 2017, we need to find something other than 'business as usual'. We need to explore what courage really looks like in our sector. *And* we need to look more critically at the issue of *influence*. We tried a few years ago to get Engage 2 Act members to explore that issue and the submissions were so woeful we did not award a prize that year. Again, we saw nothing but showreels of corporate and bureaucratic Australia, reeling off textbook like statements about how critical engaging communities in decision making is. But very little 'grit' and true passion came through. It was incredibly disheartening.

How about an awards process where communities nominate government projects for recognition? Now that gets me interested!

Over the years, in my work with government I've witnessed a huge growth in community, government and practitioners understanding of community engagement – from both communities and government. Time and time again, I've witnessed communities demanding to be involved through genuine consultation or deeper engagement. Our sector has risen to the challenge with a multitude of amazing resources. To my astonishment and delight, the layers of bureaucracy have even embraced it in their own unique ways.

Community engagement positions have been created in local councils and state government departments. I've seen managers begin to grasp the concept, senior leaders who recognise its importance (even if they have an occasional tantrum about it). As I write in 2021, I know I can walk into any Chief Executive's office and engage in a dialogue about the topic, anticipating reciprocity of interest. Everybody is getting with the program.

So what's the problem, I hear you ask? Well, we've spread the message far and wide. To be sure. But I believe that we have failed to nail the basics. There are three, only three, that worry me right now: trust, influence, and courage.

What we need to do now is to get back to basics. Rather than looking to more complex solutions or more sophisticated community engagement tools and techniques, we need to strip back community engagement to its core. As Andrew Coulson says, *we need to put* the community *back in community engagement.*[38]

To do this honestly and effectively, we need to rebuild trust between government and our communities. Trust overrides any fancy tools and techniques we might use. We can have all the bells and whistles you like as part of your engagement process. However, if ultimately what the community says gets completely ignored, it's all been a waste of time. A big waste of time for everybody!

We need to ensure that the decision-making power isn't held tightly in one pair (or 12 elected pairs) of hands, but that broader communities have influence. And we need to be bolder and have the authentic, visceral courage to genuinely listen to each other. Listen fully, openly, and persistently.

As a community-minded person, if I can see the worth in getting involved in something in my local community, I will jump at the opportunity. But the moment I hear that my Council is involved, or even leading it, in all honesty, I often reconsider... They can show me a splendid array of bells and whistles for a brilliant process. Truth be told, I simply don't trust them. I don't trust them to listen to me. Until recently, where a new Mayor has taken the time to get to know me, I'd never even met the people elected to represent me. I use my own council as an example, but I am sure that I would feel the same about any council.

When I say 'them' or 'they', I'm not necessarily referring to the staff who implement a process. These days, staff working in community engagement are often committed to it and have a good sense of why and how involvement leads to better decision making. Wide experience teaches me that those higher up the chain are neither knowledgeable nor committed.

Elected officials and their advisors lack knowledge and understanding. Repeatedly, I ask myself this question: 'Why is it that the moment someone gains a glimpse of power, their being is drained of every skerrick of empathy they might ever have had?' Are they overwhelmed? Is it fear? Terror? Are their egos so fragile that they cannot function? Is it as crass as the priorities of political donors? Or having to toe the party-political line? I can't decide. What I *do* know is that the higher up the decision-making tree you climb, and the more 'power' you have, the further removed you become from the people you serve.

I'd like to see the powers-that-be actually be present in community engagement processes, valuing those processes. I have lost count of the number of times I have worked on significant and politically sensitive issues, where the responsible Minister turns up to make an awkward welcome speech (generally from notes written by someone else), gets a photo in front of the banner and scarpers onto his or her next meeting. This rushed dropping-in style of 'engagement', showing zero interest in participating in conversations with the people who have given up their time to be part of a process irritates me no end. What irritates me more is that nobody challenges this terrible practice. 'Oh, Ministers are very busy people.' is the usual gutless response from my bureaucrat colleagues.

I also think it's not always the politicians' fault that they become so disconnected from the communities they serve. It's just as much the fault of the government departments working on behalf of them. I call this engrained culture a process of putting 'Politicians on Pedestals'. As a society we seem to forget that Mayors, Elected members, Ministers, Members of Parliament, Senators are just everyday folk who've been voted into the system by people in a particular place. Of course, this certainly buys them *some* kudos, but let's not forget they are just people, like you and me. One of my biggest frustrations is the pomp and ceremony protocol of not even being able to call a Minister by their first name! It's British sitcom *Yes Minister*, at its finest!

I am now about half-way through my career – 22 years under my belt, and hopefully at least another 22 years to go. As the media article in image 30 reveals, I am now asking myself this question: *Am I making a difference?* I believe

I am because my work offers people a space to be heard and to have critically important conversations.

Helping communities tackle the big issues

MICHELLE ETHERIDGE

COMMUNITY STRENGTH: Becky Hirst runs Becky Hirst Consulting – a business focused on community consultation – from her Blewitt Springs home. Picture: TOM HUNTLEY

TIME zone shifts, climate change and natural resources management reform – Becky Hirst has tackled some controversial topics in her consultancy role.

The Blewitt Springs woman set up Becky Hirst Consulting a decade ago in a bid to help organisations and government agencies better engage with the public.

At times, that has involved facing rooms packed with angry people, dealing with those disillusioned with bureaucracy, or facilitating 60 meetings on a topic in just four months.

But despite its challenges, she loves ensuring people get an opportunity to have their say.

"I literally don't switch on the news or radio without hearing about public consultation gone wrong or communities that don't feel heard," Ms Hirst says.

"There's an overarching distrust of governments in general. People feel like the bureaucracy is very disconnected with their everyday life, and I totally agree with that."

> There's a real power to the people movement

Among the most hotly debated topics she had managed was a question over whether SA's time zone should be changed to align more closely with Western Australia, or the eastern states.

During the debate in 2015, Ms Hirst says communities in the state's west, such as Ceduna and Port Lincoln, were outraged.

"They were going to have to drive their children to school in the dark," Ms Hirst says. "What I really loved was going to Mount Gambier – I assumed they'd say, 'We'd love to join Victoria', but they said, 'No, we're sticking with our regional friends in Ceduna and Port Lincoln'."

Ms Hirst hails from Gloucester, in the UK, moving here about 11 years ago and finding a vastly different environment to what she was used to there.

"I saw this gaping hole here for community engagement experts," she says.

"In the UK, there's more of a bottom-up approach."

She says consultation had been done badly for years, and many people feel there is little point in taking part as their input will have little impact.

The best way for organisations to involve the public in decision-making processes, she says, is to give people a good amount of time to respond to ideas and allow them multiple ways to provide feedback. Decision makers must also be open to changing their plans, she says, and should also communicate with the public about how they came to their decisions. Social media is also giving the public more power to be heard and drastically changing the landscape for businesses and organisations.

"You can organise a rally in hours," Ms Hirst says.

"That's a sign of our times, how communities can connect with each other – people can mobilise themselves and I love seeing that happen.

"There's a real power to the people movement. It just means that ultimate decision makers have to be more accountable and better at engaging, as does business."

It could be disheartening when people's views did not seem to change plans, Ms Hirst said. "I ask myself, 'Am I making a difference?' but I think I am because I'm providing people with a space to be heard."

Image 30 - Helping communities tackle the big issues, The Advertiser, South Australia. 9 April 2019.

But my current reality is a far cry from my dream. My dream. I dream of a gigantic shift. I dream that decision makers will shift from simply consulting with communities (because they are required to), to embodying a new ethic and, in their strong voices, saying, *I want to make really good, considered decisions, and for that to occur I know that I need to have the right people involved.*

Or even better, I dream of them saying, *before we proceed any further on this idea, have we discussed it with the relevant local communities? What do they think needs to happen? Let's take our time to find out.*

And if we're going for my absolute wildest fantasy, in my heartfelt dream, future community engagement scenarios will resonate with words like this: *We, members of various communities, know there's an issue with X. We want to discuss it to decide the best way forward. That includes having the government at our table to support us as we develop our vision and our plan to tackle it.*

Hearing words like that would rock my world. And it would take us right back to those days in 1945 where in *my* community, local people decided that they wanted a local hospital. So what did they do? They began building one.

I dream of more robust conversations not just at the local level, but at national and global levels. I dream of meeting politicians and leaders who aren't afraid to start the difficult conversations that face our generation. I dream of clear evidence of courage and guts demonstrated through greater connection and collaboration. I dream of honest acknowledgement that the 'soft skills' are the hard skills.

I dream of community engagement become something more all-encompassing: a combination of community engagement with concepts of community development, community leadership, and community resilience building, rather than the project-by-project, simplistic and bureaucratic 'have your say' cookie cutter approaches that currently dominate the engagement landscapes I travel through.

My dream is one of thriving communities. We can't get to my dream via Helicopter Engagement. My dream emerges from deeply rich and respectful connections with and amongst people, groups, and communities. And government.

My dream is of loud and proud community engagement practices across the world. I dream of the day when the concept of community engagement is as mainstream as bricklaying, where I can make small talk with people at parties about my work, without them looking blankly at me in return.

I dream of people being treated as people, communities being treated with the respect and recognition they deserve, and our leaders being open, transparent and empathic.

I long for more conversation, collaboration, and connectedness.

For the love of community engagement.

...

Conversation Starters

- **WHO** else needs to read this book?
- **WHAT** do you dream about the future of community engagement? What is your wildest fantasy for community engagement's future?
- **WHY** do you think it is difficult for elected officials to listen to the people who they represent in genuine and open ways? Is it a lack of skills or knowledge of how to? Or something else?
- **WHEN** have you felt listened to in a decision-making process or by a decision-maker? Or when did you feel that you had genuine influence over a decision t that affected you?
- **WHERE** could you start a conversation with someone about something that inspired you in this book? And where might that lead?

100 At-a-Glance Conversation Starters

At the end of each chapter, I posed some Conversation Starters to be used as a prompt for discussion about the lessons and stories I shared. The questions were based on the five Ws – who, what, why, when, and where – to provide a range of opportunities for contemplation about people, purpose, places, and timing of community engagement.

The questions aim to challenge the bureaucrat to reconnect with their inner citizen; and aim to challenge the citizen to consider their connection to the powers that be.

These Conversation Starters are a combination of different calls to action for the reader to both reflect *and* act.

Here are all 100 Conversation Starters for quick and easy prompting! I encourage you to have these on standby for team meeting stimulation, event ice breakers, or even dinner party game time with your community minded friends!

- **WHO** were the political leaders during your childhood? What impacts did they make on society? How did they affect your outlook on your life or your career?
- **WHAT** does community engagement mean to you? How do you define it?
- **WHY** does community engagement interest you? What sparked that interest?
- **WHEN** we look to the future, what effects do you think the current political and/or societal climate, either locally or globally, is likely to have on children and young people as they embark on their career paths? Will what they are experiencing now affect how they interact with their communities? If yes, how?

- **WHERE** do you see signs of distrust within your own communities, or communities where you work? As a society, how can we work towards building more trust and sustainable trust?
- **WHO** is the underdog in your work or in your life? What's your relationship like with them? How do you react to them, physically and emotionally?
- **WHAT** kind of community engagement could you achieve with a budget of just $50? You don't always need big budgets to engage a community. The next time you find yourself saying, 'There's no budget', consider how you might reframe the situation. What can we do with what we have? What resources can we draw on?
- **WHY** is it so important to genuinely involve people in activities in their neighbourhoods? And why is it so important that we avoid doing everything for them?
- **WHEN** did you last wander around the community in which you live or work, with no purpose other than to become immersed in observing its happenings?
- **WHERE** do you come from? How does this affect your perspective of community engagement?
- **WHO** could you be having a conversation with about something important: a person you haven't yet had a conversation with?
- **WHAT** fascinates you about communities? Is it the people? The infrastructure? The environment? Health needs? Housing? Or the whole ecosystem?
- **WHY** is it important to put communities at the centre of everything we do? How can we do this better?
- **WHEN** have you witnessed a community or communities demanding to be heard?
- **WHERE** do you sit on the political spectrum? How does this affect your perception of communities and/or community engagement?
- **WHO** would you like to see proactively working together in your workplace or communities?
- **WHAT** partnerships have you been involved with? This can be personal or professional! What did you learn from the experience? How can you use

what you learned during this experience to form strong partnerships in the future?

- **WHY** collaborate? What benefits might collaboration bring?
- **WHEN** have you witnessed great things being achieved by people, groups or organisations working together?
- **WHERE** have you seen significant financial investment in infrastructure happen in your communities? Were you interested or involved in it? If yes, did you have much influence over the process? If no, what stopped you being interested or getting involved?
- **WHO** is the most creative person in your team or your community? How could they be involved to enhance your community engagement practice?
- **WHAT** could you do to make reporting processes more creative?
- **WHY** don't we apply creativity and innovation to all of our community engagement practice? What stops us?
- **WHEN** have you worked creatively? Or witnessed creativity in your own community?
- **WHERE** have you been that is *on* the beaten track, and where have you been that is *off* the beaten track? What did you see that is different between places that are seen, and places that aren't seen?
- **WHO** represents you in your communities? When did you last have the opportunity to tell your story to them? When did you last feel heard by them?
- **WHAT** do you think about small, local government versus bigger, centralised government? What are the pros and cons of each in relation to building thriving communities?
- **WHY** is conversation important? Think about this in relation to your personal relationships, at work, in your communities, as well as with governments.
- **WHEN** did you last have a rich conversation with someone about something important in your local community?
- **WHERE** could you provide opportunity for people to share their stories? At the dinner table? In your next team meeting? At the local market?
- **WHO** is missing from your decision-making table? Who would add value, insight and perspective that isn't currently there?

- **WHAT** is your experience of the 'third sector'? What role does it play in your work or community life?
- **WHY** is community engagement so often delivered on a project-by-project basis and not seen as a more ongoing philosophy?
- **WHEN** did you last bring together a group of people who share different perspectives to work towards one common goal?
- **WHERE** fascinates you? Why?
- **WHO** are you specifically trying to work with in the community? Be specific.
- **WHAT** steps can you take to find out more about the people within a particular community?
- **WHY** is empathy so important in community engagement?
- **WHEN** have you put your own beliefs aside to work neutrally with a group of people on something that is important to them?
- **WHERE** do the people you are trying to work with already go? Where do they feel safe?
- **WHO** has significant influence in your communities? Who is well networked? Who holds critical knowledge that you could tap into? Who can introduce you to the right people?
- **WHAT** is different about the community or communities you work with to the community you live in?
- **WHY** do we so often assume that leaders in our communities are simply the people who have been voted to make decisions via the political system?
- **WHEN** have you been a leader in your own community?
- **WHERE** do the people in your communities get their news and information from? Is there a specific website, local newsletter, social media or TV channel that they tune into?
- **WHOSE** responsibility is it to build strong, connected communities?
- **WHAT** can you add to your community engagement practice to enhance community connectivity that could build resilience?
- **WHY** is it important for communities to be resilient?
- **WHEN** have you experienced a community working together in the face of difficulty or disaster? What was already in place to help them work together?
- **WHERE** do you turn for information in your communities when something bad happens?

- **WHO** stands between you and relevant decision-makers in your communities? How many layers of people or processes are there?
- **WHAT** can we do to raise the profile of the much-needed skills, knowledge, and expertise that community engagement practitioners have?
- **WHY** is community engagement not a skill required to be understood by all leaders within the public service?
- **WHEN** have you been challenged on your beliefs regarding community engagement? How did this make you feel?
- **WHERE** does the expertise of community engagement sit within your local Council? Where do you think it should sit?
- **WHO** would benefit from witnessing your community engagement processes in action?
- **WHAT** could you do to make your community engagement activity more visible to those who need to witness it?
- **WHY** is it important for community engagement to be visible?
- **WHEN** have you felt uninspired by an inappropriate or uncomfortable venue?
- **WHERE** has your community engagement typically taken place? Where else could it take place?
- **WHO** has inspired you to listen deeply to others? Who do you know who is a really good listener?
- **WHAT** is your knowledge and understanding of the traditional owners of the land on which you live? How could you learn more?
- **WHY** is the Western culture so obsessed with taking notes? When did we lose the art of conversation? Did we ever actually have it?! How can we create more invitations to authentic conversations?
- **WHEN** did you last listen deeply to what was being said, without feeling the need to respond or find a solution?
- **WHERE** do your favourite conversations take place? How could you apply the essence of these conversations to your community engagement practice?
- **WHO** inspired you to work the way you currently work in community engagement?

- **WHAT** are your motives for why and how you undertake community engagement? How do these motives affect the way you engage or the work that you get involved in?
- **WHY** is it important that community engagement consultants operate as 'consultants with conscience'?
- **WHEN** have you given back to a community *pro bono*?
- **WHERE** is your 'sweet spot' for finding a balance between a love of community and generating an income? Where would you draw the line between people and profit?
- **WHO** has a vested interest in what you're doing? Who's paying the bill? Whose needs are the most important? Who is most worthy of your consideration: Your client? Your boss? The communities?
- **WHAT** needs to change for people's needs to be at the centre of government or corporate activity?
- **WHY** should a community trust *you*?
- **WHEN** have you had to work hard to build someone's trust in you? How did you honour the trust that they put in you?
- **WHERE** will we end up if we don't begin to rebuild trust between communities and government?
- **WHO** is your favourite activist? Why is that?
- **WHAT** role does a sense of belonging play in community engagement practice?
- **WHY** is it so important to be actively involved in your own community, even if community engagement is your day job?
- **WHEN** have you immersed yourself in your own community? What did you learn from this experience? How has this affected how you engage with other communities?
- **WHERE** do you fit in the ecosystem of the community in which you live or work?
- **WHO** has inspired you to the point that you became one of their followers? What effects did your involvement in their cause have on their movement?
- **WHAT** can we learn from the creation of movements to apply to our community engagement practice? Do we currently place enough emphasis

on leaders and their first followers? Do we go where the energy is? How can we do that more often – and more effectively?

- **WHY** are some people able to create a movement, and others cannot? What can they teach us?
- **WHEN** might a community come up with an idea and tell the government that they will keep them informed on its progress as it is being implemented? When might they need to check with the government about something? When might a community inspire the government to take full responsibility for implementing their idea?!
- **WHERE** would you draw the line between decisions that could be led by communities, and decisions needing to be led by governments?
- **WHOSE** responsibility is it to grow the professionality of the community engagement sector?
- **WHAT** do you think about incentivising people to become involved in something? Do you think offering a free lunch helps motivate them to attend? Or is it more a gesture of thanks? Would people get involved without an incentive?
- **WHY** is it important to involve 'real people' and not just professionals in advancing community engagement practice?
- **WHEN** did something in your community, or in your community engagement work, last give you goosebumps?
- **WHERE** (and how) are you celebrating next year's Global Community Engagement Day?
- **WHO** do you know who would be likely to become involved in a local issue if it was online, but wouldn't get involved if it involved attendance at a face-to-face event? And vice versa?
- **WHAT** are your favourite online tools for engaging in deep and meaningful dialogue about your communities of interest?
- **WHY** is it important to offer a hybrid of written, face-to-face, and online tools and techniques to engage with communities?
- **WHEN** have you successfully measured the process, impacts, and outcomes of a community engagement process? How did that go?
- **WHERE** do you see online community engagement heading in the next few years... next few decades?

- **WHO** else needs to read this book?
- **WHAT** do you dream about the future of community engagement? What is your wildest fantasy for community engagement's future?
- **WHY** do you think it is difficult for elected officials to listen to the people who they represent in genuine and open ways? Is it a lack of skills or knowledge of how to? Or something else?
- **WHEN** have you felt listened to in a decision-making process or by a decision-maker? Or when did you feel that you had genuine influence over a decision t that affected you?
- **WHERE** could you start a conversation with someone about something that inspired you in this book? And where might that lead?

Glossary of terms

A handy reference guide for some terms used in this book. Some are broadly used in the context of community engagement, others are Becky-isms.

Community Engagement

Widely used term, particularly in Australia, to mean the process of involving communities in government decision making or problem solving. Elsewhere in the world terms such as Public Consultation, Civic Engagement, and Public Participation are used in similar contexts.

Community Immersion Process

A process I undertake on any project with a new community. It's my critical exercise in learning about the people who live there and understanding how they live. It general involves spending time in a place, simply observing every little detail.

Very Important People

Whilst this is a widely used expression, Becky uses it as a term as an alternative to 'key stakeholders' which she feels brings an impersonal element to community engagement.

The Goosebump Measure of Significance

A Becky-ism, defining the moment that something gives you goosebumps being a tool to measure significance or success. What better indicator of something being 'right' could there be than your own body's uncontrollable, physical and emotional reaction?

Helicopter Engagement

Another Becky-ism, meaning processes of so-called community engagement put in place by institutions that are so tightly controlled with their questions or opportunities for real influence to occur, that the organisation is almost hovering over the community, telling them what to say. Think Helicopter Parenting, but with institutions rather than parents!

The Black Hole of Bureaucracy

A Becky-ism used to describe the sense of saying, sending or submitting something to a government department and never hearing anything about it – ever again!

Public-Initiated Participation (PIP)

A term devised whilst working with a local Council to explain processes where community members lead interactions or initiatives with government. Under this approach, communities are enabled, activated and empowered by government.

Citizen-Centric Organisations

Organisations that place people (and their needs) at the centre of everything they do, rather than programs, services, policies, procedures or legislation.

Keynote Listener

A term used as an alternative to Keynote Speakers at conferences or events. The title supports the concept of a guest or influential person in attendance who is there to listen instead of talk.

Politicians on Pedestals

A Becky-ism that defines the engrained culture of the pomp and ceremony that often surrounds politicians, often forgetting that they are just everyday people, like you or me.

Chronology of Landmark Moments

1996-1999

Studied Bachelor of Arts (with Honours) in Contemporary Dance, University of Leeds.

1997

New Labour campaign video arrives in the mail, followed New Labour winning the election. Tony Blair serves as Prime Minister of the United Kingdom until 2007.

1999

Graduate from University of Leeds and start work as the Community Involvement Officer at
Matson Neighbourhood Project

2001

Whilst working as the Food & Health Projects Officer at the West Gloucestershire Primary Care Trust, study for Graduate Diploma in Health Promotion Education at the University of Gloucestershire.

2002

Begin working as the Living & Learning Centre Manager located at the brand new GL1 Gloucester Leisure Centre.

2004

Becky & Dan meet whilst backpacking in Sydney. Undertake a wealth of backpacker jobs, including working in the Community Development Team at Parramatta City Council.

2005-2007

London life. Worked at the Kensington & Chelsea Social Council and Camden Primary Care Trust on Community Stop Smoking initiatives.

2007

Becky and Dan migrate from London to Adelaide, Australia.
Arrive in Adelaide with nothing but a couple of backpacks and a thirst for adventure. First job is as Community Engagement Officer for a metropolitan Council.

13 February 2008

Kevin Rudd, Prime Minister of Australia gives apology to the Stolen Generations.

2009

Becky Hirst Consulting is born, whilst still working part time at the Children, Youth & Women's Health Service.

2010

Whilst at Women's Health Statewide, learned valuable lessons in deep listening from the Aboriginal Health Team. Co-facilitated Reconciliation: Let's See It Through event.

2009-2021

Becky Hirst Consulting goes full time in 2010 and works with over 100 local Councils and state government clients, engaging with over 50,000 people in conversations about things that matter.
Winner of Business SA's Young Entrepreneur of the Year 2010.

2011

First daughter born: Elsie.

2013-2015

Appointed by the Premier of South Australia to the Community Engagement Board; CoCreate Adelaide & the formation of Engage 2 Act in South Australia; Chair/Deputy Chair/Board Member of the McLaren Vale & Districts War Memorial Hospital.

2016

Second daughter born: Florence.

2017

Engage 2 Act unconference in St Kilda, Victoria.
Wendy Sarkissian Award for Courage in Community Engagement.

2018

Andrew Coulson suggested we form a global day of celebration for community engagement. Global Community Engagement Day (January 28) is born!

2021

Published *For the love of community engagement*.

Acknowledgements

I'm a collaborator. The majority of things that I make happen, I make happen with others. I love that moment when I meet someone, a conversation happens, a spark flies and magic just seems to happen. To everyone who has ever felt sparks fly with me – thank you!

Thank you to my partner Dan, and our children Elsie and Florence, who are so accepting and supportive of my unstoppable nature. Even at home, communication and collaboration is essential in making our work, life and family balance work so well. My favourite conversations in the whole-wide-world are our dinner table conversations.

Thank you to my Mum for the socialism and Dad for the logic, though I know my Mum has this in spades too. Thank you for giving me so many great childhood experiences and a great sense of belonging on which to base a career that places value on conversations, connection and community. I love our weekly conversations on Skype, but they're even better in person, usually at a restaurant table overlooking the ocean, when you visit us in Australia.

Thank you to Dana, who since becoming my friend during an engagement process in 2017, has been at my side for daily debrief conversations on the crazy work-life-family balance that so many of us juggle these days. Our conversations, most often late at night via Facebook Messenger, include so many deep belly-laughs, straightening of crowns and a fair amount of making the world a better place together too.

Thank you to Gerry for the Jimi Hendrix quote (which as it turns out wasn't actually said by Jimi Hendrix[37]) which he threw into a telephone conversation whilst I was writing this book. I love our conversations over coffee or whilst eating curry that cover every topic known to woman - from amateur psychology and global politics to tacos, puppies, share prices and birds we've spotted.

Thanks to Amy Hubbard (and the rest of the Engage 2 Act board – Desley, Andrew, Sandra, Anthony, Clare, Eleanor, and Megan) for starting the conversations back in Melbourne in 2017 about how there needs to be more love in our community engagement practice. Amy's enthusiastic plea at the time, where she down-right demanded that for the love of community engagement we add some passion to the sector, went on to name the most fabulous unconference ever held and inspired the title of this book. The rest of the board were instrumental in raising the profile of community engagement at the 2017 Unconference in St Kilda, Victoria (Australia) – it really was a defining moment for me. Thank you too to the crew who got things started initially in Adelaide – John Baxter, Valli Morphett, Dan Popping and others – connecting up like minded souls for simple conversations over coffee. Thank you especially to Andrew Coulson for the conversations that usually pop up out of the blue but very quickly turn into world changing projects – like the time when he said, '*I think there should be a global day that celebrates community engagement!*' or the time I said, *I think we should host a community engagement conference in my shed.'*

Thanks to my clients and former employers who have funded this adventure so far (in other words paid my mortgage), particularly the ones who give me the freedom to be creative, innovative and try different approaches in connecting with communities. It's these opportunities that create stories worth sharing. The only way we will progress high quality community engagement is by putting what I preach into practice, so without you, I am nothing. Naming my favourite clients would be like picking a favourite child, so I won't do it, but you know who you are.

And last but by no means least, thank you to dear Aunty Wendy, who is arguably one of Australia's most experienced community planners. Being the recipient of over forty professional awards and having pioneered innovative community engagement processes in most Australian states and territories over several decades, there is no better wing to be under. As the author of four major books on planning, housing, and community engagement, her guidance and involvement in helping me to write this book has been invaluable. Our conversations inspire me no end and I truly value both your professional and ever-growing personal friendship.

About the Author

Becky Hirst

Becky Hirst is a multi-award-winning community engagement specialist, author, public speaker, mentor, and trainer. She lives in the beautiful McLaren Vale region, 45-minutes south of Adelaide in South Australia (Australia), with her partner Dan and two daughters Elsie and Florence.

Born and bred in Gloucester (UK), Becky began her community-focused career in 1999 in the early Blair years of UK politics – a time when social inclusion and community involvement were high on the agenda.

After migrating to Australia in 2007, and since founding her consultancy practice in 2009, Becky has worked with over 100 government agencies and local

Councils, helping them to successfully involve people, groups and communities in problem solving and decision-making processes. She estimates that this work has included connecting with over 50,000 people in conversations about things that matter!

Becky is proud to have been one of the founders of Engage 2 Act and a co-instigator of Global Community Engagement Day, which is now celebrated internationally every year on 28 January.

Becky is well known and respected for her innovative and creative approach to community engagement and has a genuine desire to build stronger communities through getting the right people involved in the right conversations.

Please contact becky@beckyhirstconsulting.com.au

About Wendy Sarkissian

Dr. Wendy Sarkissian

Having worked in the field of community engagement since 1966, Dr Wendy Sarkissian has done more banging on about community engagement than most people have had hot dinners.

But Wendy has not been involved exclusively in community engagement. She's been a community planner for decades, owner-built an eco-house in Nimbin, written books about planning history, housing design, healing grief (www.stay-close.com) and the healing power of wild Nature (forthcoming 2021) and done a midlife PhD in environmental ethics.

She is an expert social planner, social researcher, author, facilitator, trainer and speaker. Her consulting work has involved numerous clients across Australia and overseas, helping to solve complex problems about community engagement, housing planning and design, planning policies, and the design of open space. When she was elected to a Life Fellow of the Planning Institute of Australia (2011), she was absolutely amazed. How could that be!

Regardless of everything she's been involved with, her passion remains "listening to the softest voices."

For Wendy, who now lives in Vancouver, Canada, that includes listening to the voices of the greater-than-humans.

She's delighted to partner with a greater-than-human human, Becky Hirst, and to support her book by writing its Foreword and assisting with its editing.

Please contact Wendy at wendy@sarkissian.com.au

Image references and permissions

Cover image - *Trellick Tower.* Photographed in North Kensington, London, UK on 25 October 2006. Photographer Simon Stone. Science Photo Library/Alamy Stock Photo. Reproduced under License Agreement with Alamy.

Cover design by Manuel Adduci Spina.

Image 1 - Boys at Crofton High School rehearsing for The Road We Travel, my final assessment at University. Photo by author, 1999.

Image 2 - Myself, with leaders His Excellency the Honourable Hieu Van Le AC and Kate Simpson at one of our regular Community Engagement Board meeting. Photo by author, 2013.

Image 3 - Journalist not named. (1999) *'Kids' wall unveiled'*. Published 22 October 1999. Photograph by Paul Nicholls. Reproduced with permission.

Image 4 - Fawcett, A. (2000) *'I really like my link role'*. Gloucester Citizen. Photographer not named. Reproduced with permission.

Image 5 - Journalist not named. (2001) *'Help with cooking up healthier mealtimes'*. Gloucester Citizen. Published 25 October 2001. Photographer not named. Reproduced with permission.

Image 6 - Original work - Hirst, B. (2013), *'Healthy Communities Create Healthy People'*. Becky Hirst Consulting. Blog post. https://www.beckyhirstconsulting.com.au/2013/02/healthy-communities-create-healthy-people/ based on Dahlgren & Whitehead (1991) *Determinants of Health* as shown in Naidoo, K & Wills, J (2000) *Health Promotion - Foundations for Practice*. Second Edition. Harcourt Publishers Limited.

Image 7 - Reproduced image. Original image McLeod, S. (2020). *Maslow's*

Hierarchy of Needs'. Webpage. Simply Psychology. Accessed 18 January 2021. www.simplypsychology.org/maslow.html

Image 8 - *Living it Up at GL1's Family Learning Weekend* with Chris Catlin and Thinus Delport, who played for the Gloucester Rugby Club at the time. Photo by author. 2002.

Image 9 - *More car parking or more green space?* That was the question we posed at a SpeakOut, held in a popular beachside destination. Photo by author, 2020.

Image 10 - An audience gathered at the Speakers Corner, as part of the Open Ideas Marketplace to consider the future land use of the former Royal Adelaide Hospital. The then Premier of South Australia Jay Weatherill can be seen amongst the crowd, standing on the back row, actively listening to people share their stories and ideas. Photo by author, 2013.

Image 11 - Former Chair of the Kensington and Chelsea Social Council, Robin Tuck, participating in one of the arrival activities to keep tabs on postcode participation in the borough. Photo by author, 2006.

Image 12 - Hennessy, N. (2006). *'Irish community gets help to quit smoking'* . The Irish Post. Published 16 December 2006. Photographer not named. Reproduced with permission.

Image 13 - National No Smoking Day, working with members of the London Irish Rugby team on Kilburn High Road. Photo owned by author, 2007.

Image 14 - Making my debut on Channel S, reaching out to London's Bangladeshi community. Photo owned by author, 2007.

Image 15 - Facilitating dynamic group conversations about things that matter - at the Cultural Diversity Forum of the Children, Youth & Women's Health Service. Photo owned by author, 2008.

Image 16 - Staff from the Children, Youth & Women's Health Service developing a Cultural Diversity Framework, getting 'hands on' by sharing their place of birth with others to highlight the diversity in the room. Photo owned by author, 2008.

Image 17 - Working together, side-by-side, towards reconciliation. Ingrid and I co-facilitated the Reconciliation: Let's See it Through event at Women's Health Statewide as part of Reconciliation Week. Photo owned by author, 2010.

Image 18 - The participants of a disingenuous engagement process took pen to paper to start a petition in the workshop I was facilitating for my client. And I encouraged it. Image owned by author, 2019.

Image 19 - Original work - Hirst, B. (2013) *"A Citizen-Centric Approach to Government - Are we ready?"* Based on webpage. Accessed 18 January 2021. https://www.beckyhirstconsulting.com.au/2013/04/a-citizen-centric-approach-are-we-ready/

Image 20 - With my daughters Florence (4) and Elsie (9) at the Invasion Day march in Adelaide on 26 January 2021. Photo by author, 2021.

Image 21 - Dan, Elsie and I visiting my parents in the small, local community hospital in McLaren Vale (of which I was the Chair of the Board of Management at the time) after their car accident in January 2016. Photo by author, 2016.

Image 22 - A crowd gathers in a disused warehouse during April 2013 to CoCreate Adelaide. Michael Kubler, 2013. Reproduced with permission.

Image 23 –*A Circle of Public-Initiated Participation: What if the community became the decision makers?* Hirst, Becky. 2021.

Image 24 - Dr. Wendy Sarkissian and I with the winners of the inaugural Wendy Sarkissian Award for Courage in Community Engagement from the Pang Jai Fabric Market in Hong Kong, at St Kilda Town Hall, September 2020. Image owned by author.

Image 25 - Dr. Wendy Sarkissian with Mr Ho Ying Hoi during a visit to Pang Jai,

Hong Kong in November 2017 to present the hawkers (again) with their award. Photo owned by Wendy Sarkissian, 2017. Reproduced with permission.

Image 26 - Clare Murrell & I with our mini-me's (Elsie and Bea) at the Engage 2 Act Youth event, October 2017. Image owned by author, 2017.

Image 27 - Working together with Crispin Butteriss and Matt Crozier of Bang the Table as one of their first Associates. Photo owned by Bang the Table, 2010. Reproduced with permission.

Image 28 - Reproduced from Nielsen, J. 2006. *The 90-9-1 Rule for Participation Inequality in Social Media and Online Communities.* Nielsen Norman Group. Accessed 17 January 2021. www.nngroup.com/articles/participation-inequality/

Image 29 - Skaters gather at the Adelaide City Skatepark on North Terrace to share their ideas for its relocation. Photo owned by author, January 2014.

Image 30 - Etheridge, M. (18 April 2019). *'Helping communities tackle the big issues'*. The Advertiser. Photograph by Huntley, T. The use of this work has been licensed by Copyright Agency except as permitted by the Copyright Act, you must not re-use.

Photo of Becky Hirst. Image owned by author, 2020.

Photo of Wendy Sarkissian by Arek Rainczuk, Five Castles Photography, Melbourne, 2019. (www.fivecastles.com.au)

References

Abraham Lincoln Online. *The Gettysburg Address, 19 November 1863.* www.abrahamlincolnonline.org/lincoln/speeches/gettysburg.htm Accessed 15 January 2021.

Acocella, J. 2021. *Steve Paxton*. The New Yorker. www.newyorker.com/goings-on-about-town/dance/steve-paxton-3 Accessed 17 January 2021.

Cubis, J. *Good Neighbours* (2018). LinkedIn. https://www.linkedin.com/pulse/good-neighbours-jacinta-cubis-1d/ 24 September. Accessed 13 March 2021.

Cochrane, K. 2018. *How do we engage when there is no trust?* https://iap2.org.au/news/how-do-we-engage-when-there-is-no-trust-board-member-kylie-cochrane/ Accessed 16 January 2021.

Coulson, A. *5 Real Ways You Can Put Community Back into Community Engagement*. LinkedIn. 28 January 2020. https://andrewecoulson.medium.com/5-real-ways-you-can-put-community-back-in-to-community-engagement-67cfb126bcf9 Accessed 15 January 2021.

DePree, M. 1989. *Leadership is an Art.* New York: Bantam Doubleday Dell Publishing Group.

DeVries, H. 2019. *Breaking Through the Marketing White Noise.* Forbes. www.forbes.com/sites/henrydevries/2019/01/24/breaking-through-the-marketing-white-noise/Accessed 23 February 2021.

Fairchild, M. *What Hendrix Never Said.* https://rockprophecy.com/hendrix_quotes_hoax.html Accessed 18 January 2021.

Fisher, A.S. *Stay with the feminine leadership principles of collaboration, empathy, strategy, long-term planning, and people first.* Authority Magazine. 2 May 2019.

https://medium.com/authority-magazine/stay-with-the-feminine-leadership-principles-of-collaboration-empathy-strategy-long-term-fbbb3e93e9a6# Accessed 14 January 2021.

Francis, M. and F. Hoefel (2018). *'TrueGen': Generation Z and its implications for companies.* McKinsey & Company. https://www.mckinsey.com/industries/consumer-packaged-goods/our-insights/true-gen-generation-z-and-its-implications-for-companies 12 November. Accessed 13 March 2021.

George Eliot Quotes. https://www.quotes.net/quote/1044 Accessed 16 January 2021.

Gilbert, E. 2016. *The Kind Gesture that Helps Elizabeth Gilbert Find the Light on Her Worst Days.* Oprah.com. http://www.oprah.com/inspiration/elizabeth-gilbert-may-2016-o-magazine#ixzz6hrltPCRo Accessed 3 January 2021.

Global Research for the City of Melbourne (2018). *Assessment of Social Media as a Community Engagement Tool.* Christchurch, New Zealand: Global Research 18 December. www.globalresearch.nz Accessed 12 March 2021.

Goodell, J. *Steve Jobs in 1994: The Rolling Stone Interview.* 2011. Rolling Stone. www.rollingstone.com/culture/culture-news/steve-jobs-in-1994-the-rolling-stone-interview-231132/ Accessed 16 January 2021.

Houston, P. 2003. The Truest Eye. *O, The Oprah Magazine.* http://www.oprah.com/omagazine/toni-morrison-talks-love/Accessed 3 January 2021

Jacinda Ardern: It takes strength to be an empathetic leader. 2018. Video. BBC News on YouTube. https://youtu.be/ruDJp64prhc Accessed 2 January 2021.

Kamala Harris: You never have to ask anyone permission to lead. 2019. Video. DMRegister on YouTube. https://youtu.be/6j-KWb1J9T8 Accessed 5 January 2021.

Knoblock, J. 1990. *Xunzi: A Translation and Study of the Complete Work*. Volume 2: Books 7 to 16. Stanford: Stanford University Press.

Korff, J. 2019. *Deep listening (dadirri)*. Creative Spirits. https://www.creativespirits.info/aboriginalculture/education/deep-listening-dadirri Accessed 30 December 2020

Labour's 1997 Party Political Broadcast: Things Can Only Get Better. 1997. Video. Great British Politics YouTube channel. https://youtu.be/gi5j7jjhm4M Accessed 2 December 2020.

McCarthy, E. 2015. *Roosevelt's "The man in the arena"* Blog post on Mental Floss. https://www.mentalfloss.com/article/63389/roosevelts-man-arena. Accessed 4 January 2021.

McLeod, S. 2007. Maslow's Hierarchy of Needs. *Simply Psychology*. http://www.simplypsychology.org/maslow.html Accessed 4 January 2021.

Naidoo J. and Wills, J. 2000. *Health Promotion: Foundations for Practice*. Edinburgh: Baillière Tindall/RCN Harcourt Publishers.

Nelson Mandela Foundation. 2021. *Selected Quotes*. www.nelsonmandela.org/content/page/selected-quotes Accessed 18 January 2021.

Nielsen, J. 2006. *The 90-9-1 Rule for Participation Inequality in Social Media and Online Communities*. https://www.nngroup.com/articles/participation-inequality/ Accessed 17 January 2021.

Obama, B. *Barack Obama's Feb. 5 Speech. The New York Times*. 5 February 2008. www.nytimes.com/2008/02/05/us/politics/05text-obama.html Accessed 18 January 2021.

Parliament of Australia. 2008. *Apology to Australia's Indigenous Peoples*. https://www.aph.gov.au/ Accessed 18 December 2020.

Phillips, M. 2003. *The Body Shop Founder says Being Good is Good for Business. Albany Business Review.* www.bizjournals.com/albany/stories/2003/03/10/story8.html Accessed 24 February 2021.

Sarkissian, Wendy and Wiwik Bunjamin-Mau with Andrea Cook, Kelvin Walsh and Steph Vajda. 2009. *SpeakOut: The Step-by-Step Guide to SpeakOuts and Community Workshops.* London: Earthscan/Routledge.

Sarkissian, Wendy and Dianna Hurford with Christine Wenman. 2010. *Creative Community Engagement: Transformative Engagement Methods for Working at the Edge.* London: Earthscan/Routledge.

South Australia. Children Youth & Women's Health Service, Government of South Australia. 2008. *The Past, The Present & The Future: An Action Plan for Reconciliation.* Adelaide, South Australia: Children Youth & Women's Health Service.

TED. *Derek Sivers: How to Start a Movement.* 2010. Video. https://www.ted.com/talks/derek_sivers_how_to_start_a_movement Accessed 16 January 2021.

The Fuller Center for Housing (n.d). *Well-known quotes by Millard Fuller.* https://fullercenter.org/quotes Accessed 28 December 2020.

The Isadora Duncan Dance Company. https://isadoraduncan.org/foundation/isadora-duncan Accessed 17 January 2021.

The Obama White House. 2017. *President Obama's Farewell Address.* https://medium.com/obama-white-house/president-obamas-farewell-address-d6f45155d245 Accessed 14 January 2021.

Turner, M. 1998. *The Literary Mind: The Origins of Thought and Language.* Oxford, UK: Oxford University Press. Revised edition.

Turner, T. 2017. *Belonging: Remembering Ourselves Home.* Salt Spring Island, British Columbia: Her Own Room Press.

Wheatley, M. J. 2009. *Turning to One Another: Simple Conversations to Restore Hope to the Future.* Second edition. San Francisco: Berrett-Koehler Publishers.

Endnotes

[1] Obama, B. *Barack Obama's Feb. 5 Speech. The New York Times*. 5 February 2008. www.nytimes.com/2008/02/05/us/politics/05text-obama.html

[2] *Labour's 1997 Party Political Broadcast: Things Can Only Get Better.* 1997. Video. Great British Politics YouTube channel. https://youtu.be/gi5j7jjhm4M

[3] Cochrane, K. 2018. *How do we engage when there is no trust?* https://iap2.org.au/news/how-do-we-engage-when-there-is-no-trust-board-member-kylie-cochrane/

[4] Fisher, A.S. *Stay with the feminine leadership principles of collaboration, empathy, strategy, long-term planning, and people first. Authority Magazine, 2 May 2019.* https://medium.com/authority-magazine/stay-with-the-feminine-leadership-principles-of-collaboration-empathy-strategy-long-term-fbbb3e93e9a6#

[5] Wheatley, M. J. 2009. *Turning to One Another: Simple Conversations to Restore Hope to the Future.* Second edition. San Francisco: Berrett-Koehler Publishers.

[6] Acocella, J. 2021. *Steve Paxton*. The New Yorker. www.newyorker.com/goings-on-about-town/dance/steve-paxton-3

[7] *The Isadora Duncan Dance Company.* https://isadoraduncan.org/foundation/isadora-duncan

[8] Knoblock, J. 1990. *Xunzi: A Translation and Study of the Complete Work.* Volume 2: Books 7 to 16. Stanford: Stanford University Press.

[9] Naidoo J. and Wills, J. 2000. *Health Promotion: Foundations for Practice.* Edinburgh: Baillière Tindall/RCN Harcourt Publishers.

[10] McLeod, S. 2007. Maslow's Hierarchy of Needs. *Simply Psychology.* http://www.simplypsychology.org/maslow.html

[11] Turner, T. 2017. *Belonging: Remembering Ourselves Home*. Salt Spring Island, British Columbia: Her Own Room Press.

[12] Sarkissian, Wendy and Dianna Hurford with Christine Wenman. 2010. *Creative Community Engagement: Transformative Engagement Methods for Working at the Edge*. London: Earthscan/Routledge.

[13] Turner, M. 1998. *The Literary Mind: The Origins of Thought and Language*. Oxford, UK: Oxford University Press. Revised edition.

[14] Cubis, J. *Good Neighbours*. LinkedIn. 24 September 2018. https://www.linkedin.com/pulse/good-neighbours-jacinta-cubis-1d/

[15] *George Eliot Quotes*. https://www.quotes.net/quote/1044

[16] The Fuller Center for Housing. *Well-known quotes by Millard Fuller.* https://fullercenter.org/quotes

[17] Gilbert, E. 2016. *The Kind Gesture that Helps Elizabeth Gilbert Find the Light on Her Worst Days*. Oprah.com. http://www.oprah.com/inspiration/elizabeth-gilbert-may-2016-o-magazine#ixzz6hrltPCRo

[18] Nelson Mandela Foundation. 2021. *Selected Quotes*. https://www.nelsonmandela.org/content/page/selected-quotes

[19] *Jacinda Ardern: It takes strength to be an empathetic* leader. 2018. Video. BBC News on YouTube. https://youtu.be/ruDJp64prhc

[20] McCarthy, E. 2015. *Roosevelt's "The man in the arena"* Blog post on Mental Floss. www.mentalfloss.com/article/63389/roosevelts-man-arena

[21] Sarkissian, Wendy and Wiwik Bunjamin-Mau with Andrea Cook, Kelvin Walsh and Steph Vajda 2009. *SpeakOut: The Step-by-Step Guide to SpeakOuts and Community Workshops*. London: Earthscan/Routledge.

[22] Parliament of Australia. 2008. *Apology to Australia's Indigenous Peoples.* https://www.aph.gov.au/

[23] South Australia. Children Youth & Women's Health Service, Government of South Australia. 2008. *The Past, The Present & The Future: An Action Plan for Reconciliation.* Adelaide, South Australia: Children Youth & Women's Health Service.

[24] Korff, J. 2019. *Deep listening (dadirri).* Creative Spirits. www.creativespirits.info/aboriginalculture/education/deep-listening-dadirri

[25] Phillips, M. 2003. *The Body Shop Founder says Being Good is Good for Business. Albany Business Review.* www.bizjournals.com/albany/stories/2003/03/10/story8.html

[26] Houston, P. 2003. The Truest Eye. *O, The Oprah Magazine.* http://www.oprah.com/omagazine/toni-morrison-talks-love/

[27] Abraham Lincoln Online. *The Gettysburg Address, 19 November 1863.* www.abrahamlincolnonline.org/lincoln/speeches/gettysburg.htm

[28] The Obama White House. 2017. *President Obama's Farewell Address.* https://medium.com/obama-white-house/president-obamas-farewell-address-d6f45155d245

[29] *Kamala Harris: You never have to ask anyone permission to lead.* 2019. Video. DMRegister on YouTube. https://youtu.be/6j-KWb1J9T8

[30] TED. *Derek Sivers: How to Start a Movement.* 2010. Video. www.ted.com/talks/derek_sivers_how_to_start_a_movement

[31] DePree, M. 1989. *Leadership is an Art. New York:* Bantam Doubleday Dell Publishing Group.

[32] Goodell, J. *Steve Jobs in 1994: The Rolling Stone Interview.* 2011. Rolling Stone.

https://www.rollingstone.com/culture/culture-news/steve-jobs-in-1994-the-rolling-stone-interview-231132/

[33] Nielsen, J. 2006. *The 90-9-1 Rule for Participation Inequality in Social Media and Online Communities.* https://www.nngroup.com/articles/participation-inequality/

[34] Global Research Ltd for City of Melbourne. *Assessment of Social Media as a Community Engagement Tool.* 18 December 2018.

[35] DeVries, H. 2019. *Breaking Through the Marketing White Noise.* Forbes. www.forbes.com/sites/henrydevries/2019/01/24/breaking-through-the-marketing-white-noise/

[36] Francis, M. and Hoefel, F. 12 November 2018. *'TrueGen': Generation Z and its implications for companies.* McKinsey & Company. www.mckinsey.com/industries/consumer-packaged-goods/our-insights/true-gen-generation-z-and-its-implications-for-companies

[37] Fairchild, M. *What Hendrix Never Said.* https://rockprophecy.com/hendrix_quotes_hoax.html

[38] Coulson, A. *5 Real Ways You Can Put Community Back into Community Engagement.* Medium. 28 January 2020. https://andrewecoulson.medium.com/5-real-ways-you-can-put-community-back-in-to-community-engagement-67cfb126bcf9

Printed in the USA
CPSIA information can be obtained
at www.ICGtesting.com
LVHW091530220124
769340LV00003B/181